MUTT

Nancy Dolensek and Barbara Burn

DRAWINGS BY *Roy McKie*

 *Clarkson N. Potter, Inc./Publishers* **NEW YORK**
DISTRIBUTED BY CROWN PUBLISHERS, INC.

WE WOULD like to thank the New York Public Library for the use of the illustrations appearing on pages 18, 21, 82, 105, 186, and 272. We would also like to thank the Massachusetts Society for the Prevention of Cruelty to Animals and its educational affiliate the American Humane Education Society for the use of the chart of poisons and antidotes on pages 154–155.

Special thanks is also due the Museum of American Folk Art for mounting their extraordinary show The All-American Dog, and to the contributors to that show who so generously allowed us to reproduce their works of art.

Copyright © 1978 by Nancy Dolensek and Barbara Burn
Illustrations copyright © 1978 by Roy McKie

Published simultaneously in Canada by General Publishing Company Limited.
First edition
Printed in the United States of America

Designed by Joan Stoliar

Library of Congress Cataloging in Publication Data

Dolensek, Nancy.
  Mutt.

  Includes index.
  1. Dogs. I. Burn, Barbara, 1940— joint author. II. Title.
SF427.D57   636.7   77-17491
ISBN 0-517-53185-2
ISBN 0-517-53186-0 pbk.

Acknowledgments

During the course of our research for this book, we received help, inspiration, and support from many sources—mutts, mutt owners and enthusiasts, organizations, manufacturers, writers, and artists—far too many to list here. We have tried to give credit where credit is due throughout the book, but we would like to make a special note of thanks to the following, whose assistance was particularly valuable: Jenny Baum, Ted and Dorothe Brun, Bruce Buchenholz, Bill Cole, Emil Dolensek, Ian and Christian Dolensek, Paul Duckworth, Michael Fragnito, Doug Gruber, Bob Hendrickson, Andrea Kaliski, Earl King, Mal MacDougall, Jim Maeda, Nancy McNally, Bruce and Jimmy McWilliams, Hugh Mohr, Nancy Novogrod, Amy Pershing, Gail and Werner Rentsch, Bill Rogers, Hope Ryden, Linda Sanders of the MSPCA, Kristen Sternberg, Caroline Thompson, Arnie Webber, Jane West, and Rick Willett.

To merely say thank you to Roy McKie, Joan Stoliar, Carol Southern, and Mary Bloom is hardly enough; the enormous amounts of time, care, and patience that each contributed are exceeded only by their talents.

Contents

7 A Guide to Careers

8 Moving On

A really companionable and indispensable dog is an accident of nature. You can't get it by breeding for it, and you can't buy it with money. It just happens along.

E. B. White

WHY mutts? If that's really a question in your mind, you might as well be asking yourself why dogs at all, for every dog is a mutt if you look far enough up the family tree. In order to arrive at the very specialized breeds that exist today, men had to breed in certain characteristics and breed others out. Bull mastiffs, for instance, are the result of a cross between the bulldog and the Old English mastiff. And the mastiff had passed on his genes to many other breeds as well, including the boxer, Great Dane, and Doberman pinscher. And so we can go through the entire AKC registry, tracing the crisscrossing lines of breeds back to whatever wild dog (or dogs) it was that was first tamed and domesticated by men more than 10,000 years ago.

We, too, are mutts ourselves, the randomly bred offspring of many different types of people, rather than the planned progeny of a specific line of very similar individuals. Can you imagine what life would be like if people were bred the way dogs are? We'd have to marry people just like ourselves, have babies just like ourselves, and be judged solely on our appearance, which would have to match an arbitrarily designated standard to be acceptable.

So when we look at the mutt and admire his rich blend of traits, we are seeing a bit of ourselves in him. Sure, not all of those traits are good ones, and not all of those mutts are terrific, but how many people are really perfect all the way through? We all have our faults and we learn to live with them or correct them in some way. We are adaptable, and so are our mixed-breed dogs. For mutts don't have an easy life. In a world where many people insist on show specimens as house pets because they win prizes and the envy of neighbors, a mutt is an outcast, born by accident, living by his wits to make his way in the world. It's not surprising that the mutt who works his way into someone's home and heart has to be something special, a survivor, the crème de la litter.

In researching this book, we came across an enormous number of mutt enthusiasts, including people who had waited for years, with no forum, to spill out their great mutt stories. We read countless tales in which mutts were the heroes and heroines. We met mutts who had so much to recommend themselves that we asked them to be in the book. We found like-minded organizations, which had been working for a long time to remove the negative connotations from the words *mutt* and *mongrel*.

You may wonder as you turn the pages of this book why we are so set against breeding when it comes to the average house pet. It may seem contradictory of us to admire mutts on the one hand and to plead for the extinction of them on the other by recommending that all dogs be spayed or altered to prevent them from reproducing. But there is a good reason for this. There will never be a shortage of mutts. Accidents will always happen. Careless and ignorant people will always allow their animals to roam down the primrose path, in spite of all the good work being done by humane societies to educate the public about the excessive population of unwanted, un-claimed dogs. The primary function of humane societies and dog pounds is to round up stray dogs and to remove them from the ranks of the homeless, either by finding

Preface

good homes for them or by destroying them. Regrettably, the latter course is all too often the only one. We can only hope for the day to come when a shortage of mutts will actually exist. For that would mean that the shelters and the streets would be empty of unfortunate mongrels and that all dogs would once again be prized companions, treated with the same respect and affection that they are so willing to give to us in return.

Mutts are the quintessence of dog—the very personification of man's best friend. They come in all shapes and sizes, all coats and colorings, and all temperaments, but they all have something irresistible in common—each one is unique.

I like a bit of a mongrel myself, whether it's a man or a dog; they're the best for every day.

George Bernard Shaw

Get the best of everything. Adopt a mutt.

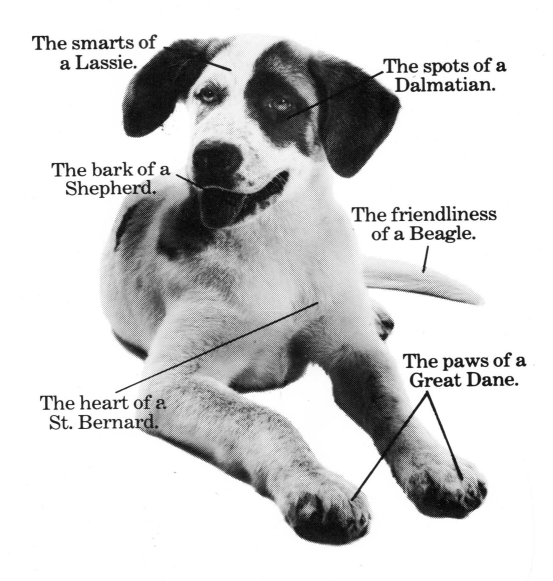

The smarts of a Lassie.

The spots of a Dalmatian.

The bark of a Shepherd.

The friendliness of a Beagle.

The heart of a St. Bernard.

The paws of a Great Dane.

1.
The
Right Mutt
for You

A bitch is more faithful than a dog, the intricacies of her mind are finer, richer and more complex than his, and her intelligence is generally greater. I have known very many dogs and can say with firm conviction that of all creatures the one nearest to man in the fineness of its perceptions and in its capacity to render true friendship is a bitch. Strange that in English her name has become a term of abuse.

Konrad Lorenz

NO matter how long a dog's pedigree may be, no matter how many Best of Breed championships his forebears have won, every dog on earth today has a mongrel in his past. Although scientists know that dogs are one of the oldest domestic animals— having been around for thousands of years—no one is certain exactly when or how the dog became man's best friend; in fact, it is not even known what sort of dog was the true ancestor of *Canis familiaris*, the species that we know today as the domestic dog. Most experts assume that the wolf was the original dog; but some say the jackal, while others believe that dogs came from several different types of wild dogs. When you look at a greyhound and then at a Pomeranian, it is difficult to imagine what that original dog must have looked like.

Anthropologists and geologists studying the remains of humans have found that dogs were living in human dwellings as long as 14,000 years ago, when man was still a hunting species. Because early man generally looked upon other animals as prey for food, it is assumed that the dog's special role as companion came about because dogs were helpful to man in hunting. With their greater speed and more proficient sense of smell—to say nothing of their teeth—dogs make excellent hunters, and when coupled with the more intelligent human, equipped with crude but effective weapons, the pair must have made a good hunting team. Dogs, like people, are social creatures (unlike cats, who tend to be solitary), and the early dogs may have thought of their human co-hunters as a kind of special super-dog. By hunting alongside man, the dog was always assured of plenty to eat and a warm, comfortable place in which to lie down after the meal, while his human companion was able to benefit from the dog's talents as a hunter and his companionship as well.

As man learned to cultivate the land and to domesticate other animals for food, dogs expanded their usefulness as beasts of burden (pulling sledges and carts) and as shepherds to keep other animals under control. Some dogs stayed at home to serve as guardians of the family or as pets around the house, while others made themselves useful as sources of amusement for sport and show. In some cultures, dogs were worshipped as gods (or despised as devils), eaten as food, or used as sacrifices.

Although the Bible says little about dogs, the Zoroastrian scriptures of ancient Persia included several chapters on the divine rights of dogs, laying down laws against dog abuse and specifying instructions on proper care, including feeding: "Bring ye unto him milk and fat with meat; this is the right food for the dog." There were four kinds of dogs described—the shepherd's dog, which guarded sheep; the house dog, which guarded the home and family; the trained hunting dog; and the Vohunazga, or stray, which was called the dog that was his own master. This dog, obviously a forefather of our beloved mongrel, was to be treated with the same respect accorded the Zoroastrian priests themselves.

Several hundred years later, in Roman times, dogs were again classified—this time in six categories: house dogs, shepherd dogs, sporting dogs, war dogs, dogs that hunted by scent, and those that hunted by sight. There were no specific breeds at this

The Origin of the Species

THE GARDEN OF EDEN
Howard Dietz
1956
Oil on canvas
45″ × 59″
Lucinda and Howard Dietz

Thomas Bewick
Engraving
Circa 1790

Illustration from
THE BELMAN OF LONDON
by Thomas Dekker
1616
London

time, but as man learned to regulate dog breeding, and as it was discovered that certain kinds of dogs bred true to type, breeds were established, classified, and revised as new characteristics were recognized as desirable.

The first "breed" classification in English (a forerunner of the American Kennel Club, if you like) was the *Boke of St. Albans,* a treatise on hunting attributed to Dame Juliana Berners of the Sopwell nunnery and published in 1486. Along with greyhounds and mastiffs, one can find a classification for "mengrell," which, if nothing else, shows that mongrels have always been recognized as different and special. Nevertheless, a century later, mongrels were getting a bad name. When Dr. Johannes Caius, the author of the first book on dogs in England, wrote a letter about English dogs to a Swiss naturalist, he placed mongrels at the bottom of the canine barrel, after "Highbred" and "Country" types. In a classification chart he called them "Degeneres," and in his letter he described them as follows:

> Of mongrels and their mixed varieties I have little to say, for they display no signal mark of race or breed; I dismiss them as useless. Still in daytime they announce visitors by barking and giving notice to their owners—hence their name *Admonitores.* Again in the kitchen when roasting is going on they help to turn the spits by a small wheel, walking round it, and making it turn evenly with their weight. No cook or servant could do it more cleverly. Hence the name *Versator*—or more commonly *Veru Versator;* these are also taught to dance to the drums and to the lyre and are the last of the classes at first mentioned. Our mongrels do perform in many other ways, standing or lying; they have learnt these tricks from their owners when they were in a state of vagrancy and want.

REUNION DE CHIENS DIVERSES
Annibale Carraci
Cabinet des Dessins
Louvre
Paris

Communal behavior [among wild dogs] is developed to such a degree that when a litter of nine pups . . . was orphaned at the age of five weeks, they were reared by the eight remaining members of the pack, all of which happened to be males.

Edward O. Wilson, Sociobiology

So, even if Dr. Caius was willing to dismiss mongrels, he couldn't help but say a few nice things, remarking on the usefulness of the creature. Versator, of course, means "turner," as in turnspit, but we can see a hint here of versatile, which is something that mongrels have always been and still are today. Another point worth noting is the "state of vagrancy" of the mongrel, something else that is also, sadly enough, true today.

Long before the white man came to America, Indians depended heavily on dogs for transportation, companionship, and food and developed some seventeen varieties to perform these various functions. The Eskimo dog is familiar to us today in the form of the Siberian husky or the Alaskan malamute, and the Mexican hairless and the Chihuahua are modern versions of what the Spanish writer Hernandez observed in the sixteenth century. But there were other Indian dogs, too, many of which would seem like mutts to us today, although they are considered actual breeds by Indian anthropologists. These dogs pulled a travois laden with children or house-hold items for the Plains Indians, were worked as hunters, and were raised for their meat and for their wool-like fur, which was made into clothing.

Following the lead of their predecessors on the American continent, early pioneers also developed a "breed" of dog to act as hunter, companion, shepherd, and friend on the way west. These dogs, said to have been crosses of hounds and herding dogs, were called curs and were known for their hardiness, intelligence, and adaptability to climate and difficult conditions. Daniel Boone, Lewis and Clark, and many less-well-known Americans who explored and settled the West were helped along by their loyal curs, whose very name was said to denote faithfulness and ability. Nowadays, of course, the breed no longer survives, and the word cur, which has acquired a bad connotation, is applied to any inferior or disputable dog, with or without papers.

When the great Carolus Linnaeus set about to classify all forms of animal and plant life in the eighteenth century, he pointed out that dogs will interbreed readily and that the dog is subject to more varieties than any other animal, yet he took little

Chien Domestique   Chien Barbet   Nicole

The Right Mutt for You

notice of mongrels. In his description of varieties, he does, however, include a "turnspit," which may well be our old friend the mutt, harnessed to the wheel. This dog was said to have short legs, a long body—mostly spotted—and came in three different styles: with straight legs, crooked legs, or long, shaggy hair.

Since that time, however, the mongrel has rarely if ever appeared in classifications, which have been made in many countries. Although 400 distinct breeds of dog are known throughout the world, only about 120 breeds are recognized by the American Kennel Club. As new breeds are imported and established here, they will eventually become recognized, but it is hardly likely that the AKC will ever allow a mongrel—whether or not he turns a spit—to come anywhere near this elite group, unless he proves himself to be a true breed, one that will reproduce its own kind for several generations.

LURCHER, Canis familiaris
". . . usually the companion of poachers
and disreputable characters."

PORTRAIT OF A DOG
U.S.
Late 19th century
Pastel
20″ × 24″
James M. Rickard

*I*t is believed by certain experts that the wild dingo dog of Australia is like the American mustang, a feral animal that escaped domestication and learned to fend for itself in nature. Stray mutts who have delusions of grandeur in thinking that they, too, can form a unique species simply by running wild in city parks, should reconsider, however. One of the reasons the dingo could make it without human help was that there were no competing placental mammals in Australia at that time, enabling the dogs to establish themselves successfully and, by isolation, to create a separate species.

The Origin of the Species   **21**

Hope Ryden

DOGS aren't the prized often pampered pets in other countries that they are in America. In the East they are often considered pariahs, scavengers of the streets, and the Chinese, Koreans and Japanese, among other Asians, commonly eat them. Englishmen of earlier times used dogs primarily for hunting and kept them outside or in a rude shelter, not generally as house pets. The dogs were fed table scraps there wasn't any further use for and these they had to fight over. It didn't seem much fun, a dog's life, and Englishmen of the sixteenth century began to compare anyone who had become impoverished, who was going to utter ruin naturally or morally, with their maltreated canines. To *lead a dog's life* was to be bothered every moment, never to be left in peace; to *go to the dogs* was to come to a miserable, shameful end. There were many other similar phrases that arose before the dogs had their day in England and America: *Throw it to the dogs*, to throw something away that's worthless; and of course *a dirty dog*, a morally reprehensible or filthy person.

     Robert Hendrickson

The Right Mutt for You

Wully

THE STORY OF A YALLER DOG

WULLY was a little yaller dog. A yaller dog, be it understood, is not necessarily the same as a yellow dog. He is not simply a canine whose capillary covering is highly charged with yellow pigment. He is the mongrelest mixture of all mongrels, the least common multiple of all dogs, the breedless union of all breeds, and though of no breed at all, he is yet of older, better breed than any of his aristocratic relations, for he is nature's attempt to restore the ancestral jackal, the parent stock of all dogs.

Indeed, the scientific name of the jackal (*Canis aureus*) means simply "yellow dog," and not a few of that animal's characteristics are seen in his domesticated representative. For the plebian cur is shrewd, active, and hardy, and far better equipped for the real struggle of life than any of his "thoroughbred" kinsmen.

If we were to abandon a yaller dog, a greyhound, and a bulldog on a desert island, which of them after six months would be alive and well? Unquestionably it would be the despised yellow cur. He has not the speed of the greyhound, but neither does he bear the seeds of lung and skin diseases. He has not the strength or reckless courage of the bulldog, but he has something a thousand times better, he has *common sense*. Health and wit are no mean equipment for the life struggle, and when the dog-world is not "managed" by men, they have never yet failed to bring out the yellow mongrel as the sole and triumphant survivor.

Once in a while the reversion to the jackal type is more complete, and the yaller dog has pricked and pointed ears. Beware of him then. He is cunning and plucky and can bite like a wolf. There is a strange, wild streak in his nature, too, that under cruelty or long adversity may develop into the deadliest treachery in spite of the better traits that are the foundation of man's love for the dog.

—Ernest Thompson Seton,
from *Wild Animals I Have Known*

The Right Mutt for You

THE DOG STORY OF THE BIBLE
Reverend Howard Finster
Georgia
1976
Bicycle paint on wood
18½″ × 24½″
Chuck and Jan Rosenak

MANY breeders and canine experts over the years have told us that purebreds are much better as pets, and for years they were right. But let's listen to them now. Mutts are coming into their own.

Dr. Michael Fox, author of *Understanding Your Dog* and an experienced canine psychologist, says:

> Ten years ago, I would have agreed with you that a person buying a particular type of purebred dog could predict its future temperament. Not so today, thanks to unethical breeders. . . . Many amateurs—and worse, many commercial wholesalers—mass-produce purebred pets that are often far inferior to any mongrel. Such irresponsible overbreeding is causing the sad demise of all popular breeds today. For the person who has difficulty locating a truly good breeder and who just wants a dog, I still unconditionally recommend the random-bred mutt over the inbred and overbred pedigree with papers. When breeders start licensing only the best registered animals of each breed for reproduction and thus indirectly control commercial "puppy mills" and unethical "professionals" I will be more confident about unconditionally recommending specific breeds.

The Natural Superiority of Mutts — How to Find Yours

In his book *Between Animal and Man*, Dr. Fox explains the reasons why overbreeding is a bad thing:

> A genetically overspecialized animal and a culturally overspecialized person share the same limitations. Similarly, an inbred strain of dogs and an inbred village of people or "aristocracy" may all reveal a higher incidence of genetic defects than more randomly bred populations of mongrels and people alike. The phenomenon of hybrid vigor, where crossbred offspring acquire the best qualities in both parents, is evident. There is an analogy between the purebred dog and the human "specialist," with the mongrel and the human jack-of-all-trades and "Renaissance man," the latter being more adaptable in many ways than the former.

Konrad Lorenz, the Nobel Prize-winning animal behaviorist, has been a mutt fancier for years. As he writes in his famous book *Man Meets Dog*, addressing himself to the owner of a purebred:

> Believe me in this: your pride that your dog conforms almost exactly to the ideal physical standards of his breed will dwindle with time but your annoyance at psychological defects, such as nervousness, viciousness, or excessive cowardice, will not. . . . In the long run you would certainly derive more pleasure from an intelligent, faithful, and plucky non-pedigree dog than from your champion which probably cost you a fortune.

An English naturalist named Phil Drabble, a longtime breeder of a marvelous hunting dog called the lurcher, a cross between a whippet and terrier, has nothing but disdain for the specialized breed, since he believes that it matters more that a dog has brains and health and a good temperament than a show-quality appearance. He believes "that many modern show dogs are but miserable caricatures of the original animals that made their breeds famous," but that people continue to breed and buy them for

Kristen Sternberg

all the wrong reasons. "If one has no background himself," he writes in his book *Of Pedigree Unknown*, "it has become almost a social necessity to own a dog, almost any dog, so long as his claims to nobility are documented by a pedigree with a champion in almost every line. So long as the price is obviously prodigious, it does not seem to matter if the dog is physically unsound or mentally insane."

There is little to add to these strong words from the experts, except to caution the inexperienced potential dog owner that not all purebreds are bad and that not all mutts are terrific. Though crossbreeding usually "strengthens the line," any dog can combine the worst as well as the best of his forebears. One must go about the process of selecting a dog on his individual merits and not on the presence or absence of a pedigree. Before examining the ways in which one can find and intelligently select a pet, however, the question of quantity must be considered along with that of quality.

It is estimated that there may be almost as many as 50 million dogs in the United States, only 15 to 20 percent of which are registered purebreds. This means, of course, that in terms of pure numbers, mutts are by far the most populous type of dog in the country. Although many mutts are allowed to reproduce with the blessing of their owners, most are not, and it is an alarming fact that the majority of these dogs end up as strays or as statistics in pounds and shelters. The conscientious dog owner, who wants to help improve the quality of life for the species as well as for himself, can effectively do so by learning to share his life with a mutt that might not otherwise have a chance to prove his great potential as a pet.

People in the market for a purebred dog have it pretty easy; once they decide which breed they want, they find a breeder (through the American Kennel Club, the newspaper, their local veterinarian, or friends) and try to pick the best of the litter, according to the published standards for that breed. But *how* does one go about finding a good dog of no particular breed? Many of the best dogs around are mongrels, but there is no AKC for them, and an advertisement for breeders specializing in purebred mutts has yet to be seen.

Where to Find a Good Mutt

Perhaps the best way to locate a good mutt is to search for a litter of "mistakes," who arrived because the local unspayed female somehow managed to get herself pregnant by the local unaltered male. Her litter may combine the glorious attributes of George the German shepherd from down the street with her own splendid cocker spaniel genes, but because there is no ready market for cocker shepherds or German spaniels, no matter how attractive they may be, it is likely that the owners of the female will be happy to give away the puppies or sell them for a small fee to anyone who promises a good home. The advantages of selecting a puppy in this way are many: You will be able to get a good look at the mother and assess her physical characteristics, her temperament, and her intelligence; it may be that the owners know who the father is, giving you even better insight into the future of the puppies; you will get to meet the people the puppies have lived with for the first weeks of their lives and gauge the quality of people-contact they've had; and, you can see for yourself under what physical conditions the puppies have been kept.

Bruce Buchenholz

Look for these litters in the newspaper, under the "Adoption" section of the pets column, or on signs in local stores. You can also call a veterinarian in your area (or in a suburban area if you are a city dweller, since "mistakes" are more common in the suburbs). Vets are often the first to hear about new and unwanted litters.

If you find the puppy you want, try to arrange with the owner to be allowed to return the dog within a period of time (a week, say) if all does not go well. This will give you a chance to have the vet give your new pet a clean bill of health and for you to see what living with the new puppy is going to be like. A week is much too short a time to tell about the dog's personality (some dogs take longer to adjust than others), but at least you will be able to determine if the animal is healthy and able to adapt himself to you and your home. If no money changes hands, draw up a document specifying a transfer of ownership; if you pay a small fee, a bill of sale.

If no "mistakes" are available, go to the local dog pound or humane shelter and look around for a dog that appeals to you. This is not easy for softhearted people, especially when you know that the dogs you don't pick are likely to end up on death row. But keep a strong sense of purpose and firm idea of what you want, and you may find a splendid dog. Community dog pounds often get their dogs by rounding up strays, but some pounds, along with privately operated shelters, are repositories for dogs that people can no longer keep. The choice, therefore, is usually a wide one—puppies, older dogs, purebreds, and mutts. The selection process is further complicated when one remembers that some of these dogs may have ended up in a shelter because of neglect, abuse, disease, and similarly unhappy circumstances. Well-run shelters always screen out physically disabled and diseased dogs and give the healthy ones inoculations, but they are usually so overloaded with unwanted animals that they cannot screen them for psychological health as well. It is important to pick the happiest, most congenial dog you can find—the one that responds to you with a wag of the tail rather than a meek or defensive expression. It goes without saying that the shelter kennel area should be clean and odor-free and that the dogs have access to water and are not packed into tiny cages. If the dogs up for adoption have been confined in unpleasant quarters for several days or weeks, their normal well-being may have been badly affected. Question the shelter operator about the dog's history and his behavior during his stay at the shelter—the more you know, the wiser your selection.

You will probably have to prove to the shelter management that you have an address or a suitable home, and you may also be asked to pay something for the dog—a nominal sum to cover the shelter's expenses, the cost of a dog license (if it is a public shelter), a part or full payment for an eventual neutering operation if your new pet is still a puppy, or an amount including all of these. If you must sign an agreement to return at some point to have the dog spayed or altered, honor it. This is one of the few ways that those who care can be sure that the dog population can be kept under control. Until methods are developed for neutering young puppies before they leave the shelters, these agreements are the only control that shelters and humane societies have. The shelter operators will probably guarantee that the dog is in good health, but since many communicable diseases can be picked up in kennels and can't be prevented by inoculation, your first stop on the way home is at the veterinarian's office to be sure that the dog is in good health and to see that the dog gets whatever shots are recommended.

If you still haven't been able to find the perfect mutt, try the pet shops in your community. Many dealers do not handle mixed breeds because they can get more money for purebred dogs. However, one determined mutt owner spent $200 recently for a mutt in a New York City pet store; he wanted a particular crossbreed, and the pet-store owners were glad to oblige—although he was never able to get hold of any pedigree to prove that the dog didn't have one!

What to Look For

Caveat emptor and *cave canem*—"Let the buyer beware" and "Beware of the dog"—are two useful Latin adages to keep in mind as you look for a dog. Have your criteria for selection firmly in mind before you go, but do not simply pick the first pup you see. Here are a few pointers that the *emptor* should note:

Make sure that the place where the puppies are living is clean and spacious. If it's grimy, dirty, or cramped, chances are that the dog won't have had a good head start in life.

Ask about the puppy's history. Ask whether the litter has had human contact during its first few weeks. Dogs are naturally social animals, but if they have regular contact with only their own littermates and mother during these crucial weeks of development, they may never turn out to be good people dogs. If the puppy you want is less than nine weeks old, you will have to do this socialization yourself (see page 237 for further information).

If you have your choice of several dogs or puppies, make sure that you pick the healthiest, most outgoing one of the bunch—the dog that comes over to you wagging his tail, not carrying it between his legs. You may be the sentimental type who would rather take the sad-looking, runny-eyed runt of the litter, just because you feel sorry for him, and no one would frown on your humane instincts. But you'll probably end up with problems, which may include high veterinary bills and a temperamentally unsound animal that will never turn into the good pet you want. On the other hand, the pup may respond to your TLC and turn into the best puppy you ever saw.

Signs of good health include bright, clear eyes with an alert expression; a clean nose and ears (check inside the latter); a healthy-looking coat with no bald spots, sores, or dry skin; and an interest in the surroundings with no droopiness or depression. Signs to avoid include a distended belly, obvious symptoms of illness (see page 143), and fearful responses to you or to other dogs.

Put the pup through a series of little tests. First, clap your hands so that the pup can't see them and watch his response; deafness in puppies is not unknown and is not always easy to detect. Toss a ball or a hat near the puppy and observe his behavior.

Thomas Fall

The Right Mutt for You

Does the pup run to it, pick it up, chew it, run away with it, or ignore it? There are no effective I.Q. tests for dogs, but a bright response is to be preferred to a dull one. Put the puppy with his littermates. Does he hold his own or seem shy, passive, and easily buffaloed by the others? A bully at this stage is better than an underdog. A nervous, yippy puppy will probably become a nervous, yippy adult, but a pup full of self-confidence has a head start on becoming an ideal pet.

Although your mutt puppy won't have papers describing his family tree, and the father (if he's known at all) is most likely not going to be present, determine as much as you can about the pup's potential appearance and temperament, based on the seller's knowledge of the pup's parents. Practically speaking, size is a more important factor than good looks. People with children or those who live in small apartments are probably going to be upset when the tiny black ball of fuzz they love turns into a giant half-Newfoundland that requires a lot of room. It's impossible to tell, of course, just what you will end up with, but if you have definite ideas about what kind of dog you want—or don't want—you would be better off getting a full-grown animal and taking your chances on his past history in terms of temperament.

Generally speaking, large paws and long legs—out of proportion to the puppy's overall size—indicate that he will grow up into a medium-size or large dog. And relatively long hair may indicate a long-haired adult dog that will require more than a light touch when it comes to grooming. But there are too many contradictory stories about mutt puppies to be confident in giving out rules of paw. There are plenty of short, squat, full-grown mutts with enormous feet that remained out of proportion for life, and some very tall mutts whose short mothers just happened to mate with a Great Dane.

What If the Mutt Finds You?

Many people come by their pets simply by taking them in when there seems to be no choice in the matter. It is well to remember that the hungry stray that has found your garbage can tempting or the lonely-looking creature that begs for a pat and a kind word may, in fact, belong to someone else. Unneutered males often roam in search of fun and frolic (usually a female dog in heat) and some of them never manage to find their way home. Even if a stray doesn't have a collar or look particularly well fed, don't assume he is homeless. Collars can come loose and home may be several miles (or days) away.

If you find yourself the adopted party in such a situation, try to find out if there is an owner. Check with the pound (but don't take the dog there—not yet at least). Call the police, check the newspapers, and listen to radio programs that run ads for lost dogs. Do everything you can for a week or ten days to find the dog's owner, and if nothing results, you can then decide whether to keep the pup or not. If it's yes, take the dog to the vet for an exam and inoculations and then to the dog-licensing bureau in your area to get him a license. A collar with dog tags—identifying you as the owner and the animal as a full-fledged citizen—will help insure that the dog need never go house hunting again.

WOMAN WITH DOG
Miles B. Carpenter
Waverly, Virginia
1971
Wood, carved and painted
H., 19"
Julie and Michael Hall

*O*n the average, city dogs live two to three years longer than country dogs.

*H*eart malfunctions are three times as common in purebreds as they are in mutts.

The Right Mutt for You

Pudgie

THE MUTT WHO WENT FROM TENEMENT TO TOWN HOUSE

SMPCA

PUDGIE'S story is straight out of *Cinderella*. Her owner allowed her, as a pup, to spend most of her hours roaming the streets of Boston. Inevitably, she was hit by a car and taken to the Massachusetts SPCA hospital for surgery, where she had a pin placed in her hip. When she had recuperated and was ready to go home, a strange face arrived to pick her up, explaining that Pudgie's old owner had left town. The strange face, it turned out, was now the new tenant in the old owner's apartment and also the new owner of Pudgie. The new owner was even less reliable than the old one. Faced with an eviction notice, he decided to return Pudgie to her original owner, but instead of finding the guy at home, he found a vacant apartment in an old tenement building. Rather than look further, he simply abandoned Pudgie, tying her to the bathtub in the empty apartment. Before long, answering a complaint from neighbors about howling, Peter Oberton of the Massachusetts SPCA rescued Pudgie and took her back to the shelter headquarters.

Things began looking up for Pudgie when the veterinarian found her bone pin still in place and Pudgie no worse for wear. But, with no one to claim her, she was put into the shelter to await adoption by somebody—anybody. Happily, a ten-year-old girl, Cori Field, needed a new companion for her poodle, and when she saw Pudgie's frisky spirit and heard her sad story, Cori and her mother decided to take her home—this time to a Beacon Hill town house. The family tried to change her name to Rags, but the determined Pudgie wouldn't answer to it, so Pudgie she remains, still proud of her old name but even prouder of her new address and especially of the loving family that brought her troubles to an end at last.

ABOVE and beyond all the usual problems of owning a dog, the owner of a mutt often has the additional difficulty of defining the beast to friends who ask "What's that?" The traditional response is simply to shrug the shoulders and say "Oh, a little of this and that" or to smile and say "We call him Heinz, because he's 57 different varieties." Self-conscious mutt owners will even go so far as to describe their pets in fractions ("A quarter Labrador," "half German shepherd with a hint of collie," etc.), whether or not they actually know what the genetic ingredients are. Even if one knows the breed of the mother, the papa dog is probably long gone and his paternity may never be more than a suspicion. There's absolutely no reason, however, why your dog can't have a breed name to call his own. It just takes a little ingenuity.

One glance at the American Kennel Club's publications should give the imaginative breed inventor some good ideas. First of all, place the animal in a category—working dog, sporting or nonsporting, toy, terrier, or hound. That step should be easy enough: If the dog is big and/or strong, he's obviously a good worker, and it's just a matter of determining (or simply deciding) what kind of job the dog seems best designed to do. If the dog loves to accompany his owner through the woods or fields and seems interested in birds, he's a sporting dog. If he has no interest in chasing birds or rabbits, he's obviously nonsporting. A toy, of course, is anything small enough to be held in the lap without causing the lap undue discomfort, and a terrier is any dog that likes to dig. (The word *terrier* comes from *terra*, the Latin word for "earth," and was applied to dogs who were particularly good at chasing rodent pests right down into their own burrows.) A hound is probably the easiest classification, since it comes from the German word *hund*, meaning "dog."

Once the general category has been determined, you can get down to specifics. For example, a geographical description might give your pet a sense of ethnic belonging or that *je ne sais quoi* that often accompanies an exotic origin. Few American mongrels have traceable roots in the old country, whichever old country that might be, and so a real nationality will be difficult to assess. But even the nationalities given to purebred dogs are often imaginary. French poodles were actually German in origin, as were Great Danes. On the other hand, the German shepherd breed was founded in Alsace-Lorraine, a much-fought-over territory between Germany and France, now belonging to the latter (which is why many people call German shepherds Alsatians).

To determine which geographical origin might best suit your mutt, look for indicators like the following. Are there any foods in particular that the beast is crazy about? If Små Köttbullar and Glasmästarsill are his favorites, Scandinavia is a natural choice. A dog with a penchant for quiche Lorraine obviously has a French background. And if the animal is nuts about borscht, Russia is your answer. Look carefully at your dog. Does he have any physical characteristic that might be telling? If he's big and blond, how about Norway or Sweden? If he's slight with straight, jet-black hair, Japan and China are possibilities, or if he has a Roman nose, try Italy on for size. Also, listen to his speech pattern. Is it inflected in such a way as to give you an inkling of his

Roots
(Or, Write Your Own Registry)

roots? For instance, if his bark is "woofa, woofa," you might think strongly about Italy. If it is a guttural "arf," there's a good chance he's of German lineage.

Of course, you needn't be limited by the country category. Why not a more local appellation, such as the name of the town, street, or even the building in which the animal was born? Names like Topeka terrier, Cincinnati coon dog, Corner-of-55th-and-Park pointer, or New-York-City-Hall-Bureau-of-Vital-Statistics springer may not be elegant, but if sense of place is important, a name like that might be just the thing.

Does the dog display any behavioral mannerisms worth noting? Retrievers, pointers, shepherds, and water spaniels didn't get their names by just sitting around. Even if the behavior doesn't have any particular usefulness, you might still make it a part of the dog's name, if only to make the animal more special in your eyes. Not just any dog could be a slipper-chewing spaniel, a hydrant pointer, or a trash-can terrier.

Does your dog have any special interests? Does he chase anything in particular, letting other potential prey pass by unnoticed? Elkhounds, wolfhounds, deerhounds, bulldogs, and fox terriers know what they are supposed to chase just by reading their own pedigrees. Why not help your dog find his mission in life by calling him a burglarhound or a muggermutt? No one would want a Dodge Charger or a Chevychaser in the yard, but perhaps you could give the car-loving dog a new direction by classifying him as a ratcatcher and sicking him on pests around the garden or house.

Is your dog's appearance noteworthy? Retrievers are distinguished by being curly-coated, flat-coated, or golden; coonhounds are black and tan or blue; schnauzers are giants, miniatures, and standards; some terriers are called silky, while others are wirehaired, and some dogs are called papillons (French for "butterfly") because their wide ears look rather like wings. So consider your dog's coat, color, size, and quality in selecting his pedigree, i.e., a white rough-coated tail-waver or a black-and-blue toy nabber. Even "standard scruff" has a bit more dignity than plain old "dog."

If you are really at your wit's end about a suitable classification, get some help from the books in your library and follow the example set by Sir Walter Scott. In one of his novels, *Guy Mannering*, he invented a character named Dandie Dinmont who owned six terriers. This fictional name inspired some real-life namesakes, the Dandie Dinmont terriers, an AKC-approved breed. So as you read, take notes on famous owners of mutts and give your mutt his breed name based on your favorite character. Some of these characters have been heroes—such as Robinson Crusoe, who had a "dog Friday" as well as a man on that desert island—and some are villains, such as Bill Sikes in Dickens' *Oliver Twist*. But Sikes' dog was a noble creature in spite of his wicked owner, throwing himself off a building to his death after his ill-fated master. Dogs could do worse than be called a Crusoe cur or a Sikes spaniel.

You needn't follow our criteria for giving your dog a pedigree. You can use whatever you think is important, whatever you think will give your mutt a sense of self, whatever you think will add a touch of class to your special dog, who so richly deserves it.

Mutt —[short for muttonhead (*dull-witted person*)]
1: *a stupid or insignificant person: fool*
2: *a mongrel dog: cur*

mon-grel —1: *an individual resulting from the interbreeding of diverse breeds or strains; esp.: one of unknown ancestry* **2:** *a cross between types of persons or things*

cur —1: *a mongrel or inferior dog*
2: *a surly or cowardly fellow*

Webster's New Collegiate Dictionary

Robinson Crusoe and friend

Crossbreed Puzzle

We've all heard of cockapoos (a cross between a cocker spaniel and a poodle), but there is an infinite number of possibilities for crossbreed names open to the person who is blessed with a nimble wit and agile mind. Here are a few just to get you started.

A boxer and a schnauzer =

A poodle and a puli =

A bearded collie and a deerhound =

A chow chow and a Chihuahua =

A collie and a Labrador-Dalmatian cross =

A pointer-corgi cross and a basset hound =

A basset and a beagle =

A pug and a Yorkie =

A boulet griffon and a bouvier =

An Irish wolfhound and a whippet-Skye terrier cross =

A water spaniel and a Bedlington terrier =

A Newfoundland and a Yorkshire terrier =

A golden retriever and an Old English sheepdog =

A poodle and a chow chow =

A Boston terrier and a parti-poodle =

An Airedale and a Portuguese water dog =

A Shetland sheepdog and a Swedish elkhound-setter cross =

A Pekingese and a bouvier =

A Malamute and a pointer =

Answers:

moot point
peekaboo
Shetland sweater
Airport
Boston T. Party
pooch
a golden oldie
New Yorker
water bed
Irish whiskye
booboo
porky
bagel
porgy-and-bass
collaboratian
chowawa
beerhound
poodoo
bowzer

Bandit

THE JEFFERSON CHICKEN HOUND

Werner Rentsch

GAIL and Werner Rentsch, a young working couple, are animal lovers from way back. They have two cats, two horses, a dozen hens, a steer, and have even raised a couple of baby raccoons, which were orphaned at their weekend home in the small town of Jefferson in upper New York State. But they never got a dog, because they knew that a dog would need a lot of care and would be difficult to transport in and out of the city every weekend. Although they had friends upstate to take care of their farm animals, a dog couldn't be left to fend for himself during the week while they were working, and so they contented themselves with enjoying other people's mutts. One day, however, in the middle of a particularly cold winter, a very scroungy pup showed up at their doorstep in the country. Because they were determined not to take him in, they called the local dog-catcher, and the stray soon disappeared. But not for long. The following weekend he was back, lurking around the barn and looking with distinct interest at their flock of hens. But to their surprise, they realized that the dog was more interested in their chicken feed than in the chickens and had, in fact, been keeping himself alive by sharing their food.

They were so impressed by the dog's obvious respect for the hens and by the fact that his determination to be taken in seemed stronger than theirs to keep him out that they finally gave up and asked him in for dinner. When Sunday night rolled around, he was a full-fledged member of the family, having ingratiated himself with the cats, the horses, and the Rentsches, who named him Bandit and made room in the car for him for the trip back to the city. Being an adaptable sort, Bandit took very well to his new double life of weekend farm dog and weekday city dweller, whose only exercise was a twice daily romp in Central Park. During one such walk, another dog owner asked Werner what sort of dog Bandit was, and without thinking Werner replied: "A Jefferson chicken hound." The inquirer was so impressed that Werner decided to introduce Bandit to everyone as the best of that particular breed. The fact that he's the *only* Jefferson chicken hound in existence doesn't bother anyone, nor the fact that Bandit looks much more like a German shepherd-collie cross than he does like a basset hound.

Mixed-Breed Aptitude Tests (MBAT) for Dogs and Dog Owners

SINCE many of us have been schooled to believe that only by taking tests can we really come to know our proclivities and aptitudes, we offer you the security of that all-American standby, the multiple-choice aptitude test. In fact, we offer you two—one for you as a prospective owner and one for your dog, since it is unrealistic to overlook the fact that although you may think you have selected the right dog, the dog may not share your enthusiasm.

A special grading pencil is not needed to take the test—any old Mongol will do. Circle the appropriate letter for each question.

The MBAT for Dogs

1. If you saw a slipper, would your instinct be to:
   a. Eat it
   b. Bury it
   c. Check to see if it's your size
   d. Look at the label to see if it came from Gucci and then check to see if it's your size
   e. Take it to your owner when he / she gets home from work
2. If an intruder entered your home, would you:
   a. Smile
   b. Bite his ankle
   c. Offer him a drink
   d. Sniff to see if he's clean
   e. Bark ferociously and hope that he goes away
3. If you went into the kitchen and found a piece of roast beef sitting unattended on the counter, would you:
   a. Eat it on the spot and bury the bone
   b. Lick it all over and leave the room
   c. Check to see if it's medium rare before eating it
   d. Ignore it because of its high cholesterol count
   e. Put it in the refrigerator so it won't go bad
4. If you saw a loose puppy wandering down the street, would you:
   a. Chase him into the street in front of a car to teach him a lesson he'll never forget
   b. Chase him into a neighbor's yard and beat him up in front of a bunch of kids
   c. Check his tag before taking action to make sure his name is not too ethnic
   d. Ask him what country club his owners belong to
   e. Chase him home and stay there until his owner promises not to let it happen again
5. In the veterinarian's office, would you:
   a. Shake uncontrollably, feign timidity, and bite the vet when he gets you on the table
   b. Whine during the examination and scream bloody murder when you get your injection

The Right Mutt for You

c. Seduce the cute little bitch next to you

d. Insist that the vet scrub down the examination table twice before placing you on it

e. Remain calm and quiet, refusing to leave until the vet remembers that you also need a heartworm test

6. When you relieve yourself, do you:
   a. Aim for someone's leg
   b. Scratch at the screen door until you make a hole that you can jump through
   c. Find a little-used corner of the house and take care of things quietly
   d. Refuse to go at all until the bathroom has been wiped down with Lysol
   e. Aim for a tree growing in soil deficient in uric acid

7. If you were given a doggie toy, would you:
   a. Chew it to bits instantly
   b. Ignore it because you'd rather have something else—like a steak
   c. Check the price to see if it's worth wasting your time on
   d. Thank the donor very much but allow as how you've really outgrown that kind of stuff
   e. Play with it energetically for fifteen minutes, then put it away in your toy box

8. After you have played in a muddy area, do you:
   a. Go into the house and shake the dirt all over the place
   b. Go into the front hall and roll on the rug to avoid carrying mud throughout the house
   c. Go into the house and jump on your owner's bed
   d. Refuse to come in until you have been bathed and dried
   e. None of the above—you wouldn't be caught dead in mud

9. If you knew that it was suppertime and nothing seemed to be happening, would you:
   a. Open the refrigerator and help yourself
   b. Go next door and raid the garbage cans

c. Ring for room service

d. Write an irate letter to the management

e. Wait patiently, remembering that your time was your owner's time

10. When your owner takes you for a walk, do you:
    a. Pull like crazy on your leash so that your owner has to hang on with all his might
    b. Bite him when he tries to put a leash on you
    c. Make him follow three steps behind you
    d. Make *him* wear the leash
    e. Walk (or trot) at his left side, keeping exactly abreast and in step

Count your points: $a = 1, b = 2, c = 3, d = 4$, and $e = 5$.

Your Score: Over 50—you're not as smart as you think you are—there are only 50 possible points.

Between 40 and 50—you are an incredibly well-behaved and thoughtful animal and should probably be an owner, not an ownee.

Between 30 and 40—you are quite fastidious, genteel, and care a great deal about the niceties of life. You will need to invoke a great deal of discretion when choosing an owner, because there are many around who will not understand you or appreciate your discriminating characteristics.

Between 20 and 30—you have a very great sense of self and like to have things your own way. You, too, may have a problem finding the right owner. Remember, an owner, by his very nature, likes to have the upper hand.

Between 10 and 20—your canine instincts are strong and you could use a little help in the obedience department and are somewhat impervious to humans, but you're probably not going to have trouble finding an owner.

10 or below—you're a real dog.

The MBAT for Dog Owners

1. If a strange dog barks at you, do you:
   a. Make an obscene gesture at him
   b. Go after him with a stick
   c. Run away in fright
   d. Bark back until he shuts up
   e. Reassure the dog in a friendly tone that you mean no harm and walk away slowly

2. If you felt like a bit of exercise, would you:
   a. Promise yourself to do some sit-ups tomorrow
   b. Run over to the television and turn on the football game
   c. Take a walk in the park and leave the dog at home
   d. Walk the dog down to the corner for a six-pack and walk back home to watch the football game
   e. Take the dog on your daily two-mile jog

3. If your dog made a "mistake" on the living-room rug, would you:
   a. Throw a newspaper on top of it and walk around it
   b. Erect a run in the living room, figuring if that's where he's going to go, that's where he's going to go
   c. Tell him to get out and never come back
   d. Rub his nose in it and hit him with a newspaper
   e. Say "no" firmly, take him outside for five minutes, and keep alert the next time the dog is in the living room

4. If you had to shop for dog food, would you:
   a. Let the dog shop for his own food
   b. Not shop at all but feed him leftovers and tell him to think of all the starving Armenians
   c. Buy the most expensive, most heavily advertised food on the market
   d. Read the ingredients on the label, compare them to the canine nutritional requirement chart on page 106, and conduct a personal taste survey

5. If you found out that you couldn't keep your dog because of an allergy, would you:
   a. Ask the vet to put him to sleep
   b. Let him go, hoping that someone nice will find him
   c. Give him to your mother, because she's such a soft touch
   d. Move out of the house and let the dog stay
   e. Do everything you can to find him a good home, calling the local humane shelter as the last extreme

6. If your dog bit a neighborhood child, would you:
   a. Beat the kid for being a pest
   b. Bite the dog to let him know what it feels like
   c. Blame the neighbors for the accident, charging that the child led the dog on, and threaten to sue for abuse
   d. Introduce the dog to a dog trainer
   e. Inform the child's parents and keep the dog confined, under observation for two weeks for signs of rabies

7. If your dog looked unkempt and dirty, would you:
   a. Ignore it, 'cause that's how dogs are
   b. Tell him not to come home until he looked more presentable
   c. Run him under the hose a couple of times as he runs through the yard
   d. Take him to Vidal Sassoon
   e. Give him a good brushing, and if he's still dirty, bathe and dry him thoroughly

8. If your female dog got out while in heat and had a whirl with the locals, would you:
   a. Buy a box of cigars
   b. Wonder why your wife isn't as willing as your dog
   c. Slap a paternity suit on the owner of the winning dog
   d. Let the dog have her pups and give them to the kids to unload at school
   e. Let the dog have her pups, find each of them a good home, and have her spayed

The Right Mutt for You

9. If your dog always jumped up on people, would you:
   a. Tell them they were lucky the dog hadn't bitten them
   b. Take a "dogs-will-be-dogs" attitude
   c. Hit him on the head until he gets down
   d. Enroll him in obedience school
   e. Spend ten minutes a day teaching him not to jump up and discipline him firmly whenever he does
10. If you went away for a vacation, would you:
   a. Leave the dog at home with an open, ten-pound bag of dog kibble
   b. Tell the dog to sponge off the neighbors for a couple of weeks
   c. Leave the dog home and have one of the neighborhood kids check on him every couple of days
   d. Inspect several kennels recommended by your veterinarian and choose the cleanest and most effectively run
   e. Find a vacation retreat that allows pets and take the dog with you

Count your points using the same values on the first test.

Your Score: Between 40 and 50—you are a dog owner's dog owner and need no further coaching whatsoever.

Between 30 and 40—you have the potential for being a satisfactory dog owner, but you need to read this book.

Between 20 and 30—you're a schizophrenic type, but a few years of psychoanalysis and a thorough reading of every dog manual you can get your hands on might bring you around.

Between 10 and 20—get a cat.

Less than 10—you can't cope with yourself; your best bet would be to get a dog to take care of you.

CANE WITH DOG-HEAD HANDLE
Appalachia
Late 19th century
Wood; glass eyes
H. of cane, 35½ "; L. of dog-head, 2¾ "
Mr. and Mrs. Lawrence Kalstone

43

MOST dog books concentrate on puppies — at least their authors seem to assume that if you have a new dog, you have a very young one. Many people believe that taking on an older dog is a little like buying a used car: You are simply inheriting someone else's problems. Because we are rooters for the underdog—as most mongrels seem to be in canine literature, if not in fact—we would like to present the other side of the story. There are altogether too many dog-human relationships that turn out unhappily because the human half wasn't prepared for all the work involved in turning a puppy into a dog. Older people, families with young children, and working people for whom time and extra energy are scarce often find that the constant care required by a puppy is simply beyond them. And so they assume that they are incapable of keeping a dog and give up on the whole thing. Take heart, those of you who value your spare moments, your strength, and your patience. There is hope; there are plenty of older dogs around that would dearly love the chance to show you how gratifying owning a dog can be. If you are the sort who likes to weigh pros and cons, get out your scales.

Age Before Beauty —A Viable Alternative

A Puppy Needs:

To be fed three or four times a day

To be housebroken or paper-trained

To be taught to obey

To be kept from chewing things (out of boredom, teething pain, fear, frustration, or nutritional deficiency)

To be watched constantly or confined to places that aren't dangerous (heights, sources of heat, sharp objects, etc., etc., etc.)

A series of inoculations within the first six months

As much attention and opportunity to play as you can afford

To be handled with great care

An Older Dog Needs:

One or two meals a day

To be shown where to go and when

To be taught simply *what* you want, not *that* you want it

An occasional biscuit or bone to help keep his teeth free of tartar

To be kept from running free in the neighborhood

A one-stop annual visit to the vet for inoculations and examination (outside of emergencies)

A feeling of security and some form of daily exercise

To be handled with respect

A Puppy Doesn't Need:

To be encouraged to love you (he will anyway)

To be told who's boss (he will assume you are, unless you bend over backward to let him run the house)

To be retrained (you'll be starting from scratch)

To be spayed or altered (until he is seven to twelve months old)

An Older Dog Doesn't Need:

To be ignored; he will need reassurance and affection

To be allowed the upper hand; you must establish your dominance from the start

To keep bad habits he may have picked up en route; start any retraining immediately

To be allowed to breed (spaying or altering should be considered right away)

45

Dog Stars

OBVIOUSLY, anyone who cares a bit about astrology, and that includes a lot of us, would want to know what signs those close to us have and what characteristics those signs indicate. If we are Taurus and we know that Tauruses don't get along well with Aquarians, it behooves us to check the signs of prospective lovers or business partners, to catch trouble before it starts. And so it is with dogs, which often know us better than many people and certainly share a large part of our lives.

Mutt owners, however, are at a disadvantage. Purebred dogs usually have been raised by conscientious breeders, who have kept careful records of their birth dates, but mutts often find their owners months if not years after their natal day, which has probably gone unnoticed and unrecorded. We have, therefore, decided to include some of the dominant characteristics of each solar sign in order that the interested owner can deduce the sign of any individual dog. The sign of the zodiac in which the sun is present in the animal's chart is only one of twelve signs that affect personality and behavior; therefore, if the information below cannot be applied exactly to your own dog, keep in mind that the moon, the planets, and the rising sign may affect the overall picture or some of its details.

Aries March 21 through April 19
As the first sign in the zodiac, Aries the ram is a strong, excitable personality, who will remain a puppy all his life. As far as he is concerned, the world was made for his con-

The Right Mutt for You

venience, and if he doesn't get fed on time, you're going to hear about it. High vet bills are to be expected with an Aries; injustice is anathema to him, and many a dog has wandered home battered and bruised from fighting to help one less fortunate than himself. On the other hand, dogs born under this sign are physically strong and tough and are seldom the victims of chronic or lingering disease. There is no need to be secretive around an Aries—he detests gossip and will not talk with neighborhood dogs about his home situation. In appearance, Aries is red or gold with a large head, sharp features, and a muscular body. A full-length mirror is a must, because your Aries will probably stand around flexing.

Taurus   April 20 through May 20
Quite the opposite of Aries, Taurus is heavily built and relatively slow moving—the strong, silent type. The body is round and compact, the neck is short and thick, and the shoulders are high and square. The nose is short or retroussé, and the chin is exceptionally strong. Tauruses make excellent city dogs, because as far as exercise is concerned, they couldn't care less. There's nothing he loves more than to relax in front of the fire with a big steak bone. He will be most appreciative of your gourmet cooking and will take enormous delight in licking the sauce Béarnaise pan. Taurus can be hostile, stubborn, and blundering, but makes up for this in patience and loyalty. They are sensualists and make tender lovers.

Gemini   May 21 through June 21
Forget owning a dog born under this sign unless you have a lot of spunk and patience, for if a Gemini does not find the stimulation he needs at home, you might find him living down the street. His versatility and changeable personality make this character either a sheer delight or a big headache—but never anything in between. The Gemini is bright, alert, and curious, and has a remarkable memory. Those qualities, coupled with his natural ability to entertain, make him a wonderful performer, and he will do tricks by the hour. Sleep is something he needs a lot of but rarely gets because of his susceptibility to insomnia, so a comfortable bed is a worthwhile investment. Arthritis, rheumatism, and elimination difficulties typically plague Geminis, so housebreaking may be somewhat of a problem.

Cancer   June 22 through July 22
The dog born under this sign is one of passing moods—gay one minute and despondent the next. Cancer hates change and loves attention and home and will not be happy without a doghouse to call his own. He has enormous sensitivities, so in training, one must be careful not to be harsh or use a rough tone of voice. He can also be—as his sign denotes—crabby, but if you leave him alone, he'll soon be skipping out to get your morning newspaper again. Cancers revere the past and often collect old bones, slippers, and other relics.

Leo   July 23 through August 22
Like the lion of the same name that rules the animal kingdom, Leo the dog will rule you. His arrogance and inflated ego are insufferable, but that is quickly overlooked because of his heart—which is pure gold. Flattery will get you everywhere with a Leo, since they tend to be quite vain, and you will need to groom them regularly to keep them happy.

Leos love the good life and can frequently be found hanging out behind posh restaurants. Their voices carry far, so beware of complaints from neighbors.

Virgo   August 23 through September 22
For the most part, Virgos are a gentle lot and quite pleasant to have around. They are dependable, utterly sincere, and derive immense pleasure from serving others. If you want a dog but don't have much time to devote to him, Virgo is your answer. They are totally self-reliant and don't mind being alone. They are also fastidious, particularly about their beds and food, which may be an inconvenience as many Virgos are vegetarians and will turn up their noses at canned dog food. Dogs born under this sign abound in orderliness and will always know where their leashes are.

Libra   September 23 through October 23
At first blush, Libras may appear calm, sweet, and charming—and they can be—but there is a quarrelsome, confused, and annoying side to their nature too. If you like being stopped by strangers wanting to comment on the beauty of your dog, you can't miss with one born under this sign; an ugly specimen is a rarity. Forget using a Libra as a guard dog, however; they are almost incapable of making a decision. And don't expect them to mind well either, since they will tend to disagree with most things you say.

Scorpio   October 24 through November 21
An aura of mystery surrounds dogs born under this sign, and you will never know what they are really thinking. If that makes you nervous, don't own a Scorpio, because

they have a hypnotic gaze that will bring even the strongest of personalities to his knees. Training may be a problem: You will not be able to ply this dog with flattery or punishment—he is a total ego, sure of what he is and what he is not and what he can and cannot do. But, if he licks your hand, you can be certain that it was no mistake—Scorpios are sincere in everything. Spaying and altering are a must with these dogs—they exude passion.

Sagittarius   November 22 through December 21
It's hard to resist a Sagittarius—his flirtatious, friendly, extroverted manner is totally endearing. For the outdoorsman, this dog is a joy—he will jog along with you or chase a ball or stick endlessly. But as charming as he is, a dog born under this sign can cause you no end of problems. Keeping track of him is impossible, for he loves to travel and always has his bones packed and ready to go. And his reckless abandon in matters of the heart is likely to keep a line of irate neighbors at the front door. Be prepared for paternity suits.

Capricorn   December 22 through January 20
Ambition pervades the Capricorn character, so don't be deceived by his calm and quiet personality. He is thinking every minute—about himself and how to obtain his goals, which may include anything from a larger dog run to a collar with real diamonds instead of rhinestones. A Capricorn is hardly an exciting personality and is not a dog to entertain at cocktail parties. He is, however, a hard worker and will keep a good eye on the house. He also has good teeth, which he is

The Right Mutt for You

not averse to using to get his way. Capricorns prefer living with people who are in an upper-income bracket.

Aquarius   January 21 through February 18
Consistency of temperament is not the Aquarian dog's long suit—one minute he'll be excited and gay and licking your hand, the next, he'll be lying in the corner alone, staring dreamily off into space. You won't have trouble training an Aquarian; they are the intellectuals of the zodiac and, in addition, tend to work very hard. Dogs born under this sign will enjoy meeting your friends but are sometimes risky to have at social gatherings because they take great delight in shocking people by being unconventional. Aquarian dogs frequently need to be psychoanalyzed.

Pisces   February 19 through March 20
Pisces have a lazy, good nature and are at home in front of the fire with a tasty bone or sunbathing on a yacht. Unless you keep a constant eye on them, frequent trips to the veterinarian will be necessary, because they tend not to take care of themselves. When they're not self-absorbed, they turn their attentions to helping those less fortunate and spend much time in less desirable areas of town rounding up food for strays. Pisces can be highly emotional and can't tolerate confinement to one place for long, so never leave this dog in a kennel.

MAD dogs don't give us this name for the hot, close days of July and August, though perhaps the prevalence of mad dogs at that time of year has kept the phrase *dog days* alive. The expression originated in Roman times as *canicularis dies*, days of the dog, and was an astronomical expression referring to the dog star Sirius or possibly Procyon. The Romans linked the rising of the Dog Star, the most brilliant star in the constellation *Canis Major*, with the sultry summer heat between about July 3 and August 11, believing that the star added to the extreme heat of the sun. *Canicular days*, of course, have nothing to do with heat from the Dog Star, but the ancient expression remains with us after over twenty centuries.

Robert Hendrickson

2.
Now
That He's
Yours . . .

*T*o give a dog an unrespected name,
And hanging seems to be about the same.

Ellen Thorneycroft Fowler

Choosing a Name

GEORGE: But he's a wonderful dog, Martha, a wonderful dog.

MARTHA: George, would you please stop looking at that awful mongrel and get into bed. It's one o'clock.

GEORGE: I think he heard that, Martha. He looks hurt.

MARTHA: George, you've lost all control. Please turn out the light.

GEORGE: I will not turn out the light, and I won't go to bed. We can't rest until we've named this dog, Martha.

MARTHA: How about Herbert Schwartz?

GEORGE: Huh?

MARTHA: Herbert Schwartz . . . after my attorney, with whom you're going to be dealing if you don't turn out the light and get into bed.

GEORGE: Look, Martha, I know he's not exactly what you had in mind, but . . .

MARTHA: Not exactly what I had in mind? What am I going to tell Marge? Her poodle placed at Westminster last year, and she offered us a puppy—the pick of the litter! And what about Kay Smith, with that snooty Afghan of hers? We turned down a puppy from her too, you know. Just what do you think *she's* going to say when she sees *that?* How am I ever going to face them?

GEORGE: OK, Martha, forget it. I'll name him myself. It's all right, boy, we're going to find you a name, don't worry. *(Turns out lights.)*

MARTHA: *(Turns on light.)* George, I've got it.

GEORGE: Got what?

MARTHA: A name. Remember that dog your Uncle Terence used to have . . . the one he had the funeral for and invited the whole family? What was his name?

GEORGE: Chairman Mao. He called him the Chairman because the night he brought him home the dog ate a whole box of fortune cookies.

MARTHA: That's right. How could I forget? That dog was as crazy as your uncle is. But the point is your uncle likes your brother better than you, just because he's a banker, and he's going to be a lot more generous with your brother when his time comes. But if we were to name this creature Chairman, after Uncle Terence's dear departed, it might change the whole complexion of things.

GEORGE: That's a lousy thought.

MARTHA: I'm just trying to help.

GEORGE: A name, Martha, is a spiritual thing. A name should fit one's personality, one's appearance, one's soul. A name should call forth an image . . . it should be deeply meaningful.

MARTHA: Oh, for heaven's sake! If it means that much to you, then, what we need is a system. Names don't just happen.

GEORGE: What kind of system?

MARTHA: Well, say this dog was a French poodle. There would be any number of good French names—Phydeaux, Fifi, Toulouse . . .

GEORGE: Thank God he's not a French poodle!

MARTHA: Or if he were an Irish setter—Murphy, Flanagan, O'Hare . . . or a German shepherd or a . . .

GEORGE: Wait a minute!

MARTHA: Does he look like a well-known dog? Fala, Checkers, Lassie, Mr. Chips . . .

GEORGE: Mr. Chips wasn't a dog, Martha.

MARTHA: Does he have any special talent? Tracker, Sniffer, Racer?

GEORGE: How about Lifter?

MARTHA: Too bad he doesn't have a beautiful coat—Shiny, Silky, Puffy, Curly . . . or a terrific color—Midnight, Chocolate, Goldie . . .

GEORGE: No, Martha, the name should be inspired. *(To dog)* What do you think, fella?

MARTHA: Or if he had a distinctive personality—but Sleepy is a dwarf's name, not a dog's. And Goofus is a funny name, even for him.

GEORGE: How about Stud? You saw the way he looked at that pint-size Lhasa next door when I brought him home.

MARTHA: One stud around here is enough. If that animal had an ounce of class, we could name him after a famous literary figure—Ernest, F. Scott, Byron, Shelley. Or a musician—Beethoven, Mozart, Rachmaninoff. Or a statesman—Winston, Henry, Nesselrode. Or royalty—Prince, King, or Duke. Or a movie star—Cary, Gregory, Burt. Or a philosopher—Socrates, Plato, Russell. Or a philanthropist—Rockefeller, Astor, Guggenheim. Or a president—Lincoln, Jefferson, Monroe, Goldwater . . .

GEORGE: Goldwater?

MARTHA: Well, he should have won. If the dog were pretty, we could name him after a flower—Buttercup, Iris, Nasturtium, but he's not even fit for Dandelion.

GEORGE: That's all too contrived, Martha. It's got to be a name you feel in your bones, a name that strikes you like a bolt of lightning . . .

MARTHA: Maybe we should get out the atlas. If only you had found him in some exotic place, we could call him Sydney or Abu Dhabi. By the way, where did you pick that mutt up, George?

Now That He's Yours

GEORGE: Uh . . . on the street.

MARTHA: What street?

GEORGE: Oh, just along Prospect Street.

MARTHA: You've been hanging out at Joe Brown's Bar, haven't you? *That's* where you found that dog. At Brown's! I knew it!

DOG: Woof.

GEORGE: Did you hear that? He talked!

MARTHA: Wasting your time and money at Brown's!

DOG: Woof.

GEORGE: He spoke, Martha, he spoke! What is it, boy?

MARTHA: Shooting pool and drinking beer with those bums at Brown's!

DOG: Woof.

GEORGE: He's trying to tell us something.

MARTHA: Don't be silly. Joe Brown's indeed.

DOG: Woof.

GEORGE: We're close, Martha, we're close! He's trying to tell us what he wants to be called!

MARTHA: You *have* been drinking!

GEORGE: What is it, boy? Something we said?

MARTHA: If I ever catch you down at Brown's again . . .

DOG: Woof.

GEORGE: I've got it! Brownie, that's it, isn't it boy? Here, Brownie. Come here, Brownie! I guess that's not it. Joe, here Joe, come Joe! Nope, I guess not. Too bad. Mr. Brown would have been pleased.

DOG: Woof.

GEORGE: Mr. Brown?

DOG: Woof. Woof.

GEORGE: I knew it! Mr. Brown. That's the name—Mr. Brown!

DOG: Woof. Woof.

GEORGE: Mr. Brown, the dog of renown!

DOG: *(Smile.)*

WINSTON
Edgar Tolson
Campton, Kentucky
1967
Wood, carved and painted
L. 10″
Julie and Michael Hall

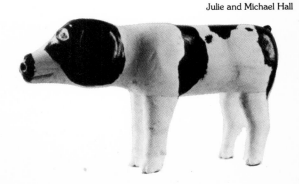

55

An Englishman and his mutt   Mary Bloom

Names of dogs end up in 176th place in the list of things that amaze and fascinate me. Canine cognomens should be designed to impinge on the ears of dogs and not to amuse neighbors, tradespeople, and casual visitors. I remember a few dogs from the past with a faint but lingering pleasure: a farm hound named Rain, a roving Airedale named Marco Polo, a female bull terrier known as Brody because she liked to jump from moving motor cars and second-story windows, and a Peke called Darien, but that's all.

James Thurber, "How to Name a Dog"

Now That He's Yours

A Rose by Any Other Name

ACCORDING to Dr. Boris Levinson, author of *Pets and Human Development* (C. C. Thomas, 1972), your dog's name may reflect your own sense of yourself, level of maturity, age, background, culture, and relationship to the rest of the world. You may give your dog a name with which you identify, something that will please or impress people and enhance your own self-esteem. Foreigners often deny their true origin and give their dogs very American names if they want to be accepted here; people who want to reject their families may select a name that will give themselves (through their dogs) an entirely new identity. Some people choose aggressive names for their animals, while others choose the names of friends or people they admire.

The first known names given to dogs were Gazelle, Black, and Firepot, chosen by an Egyptian pharaoh for three puppies more than 5,000 years ago. The Romans commonly named their dogs after friends, but often names reflected their functions—as in Cerberus (Watcher) or Hylactor (Barker) or Cainon (Killer). Children, who have little regard for history, will usually choose a name that corresponds to the dog's appearance (Blackie, Midget) or temperament (Lion, Tramp, Hero), according to Dr. Levinson, who also says that children sometimes pick names just because they like the sound and will often give an animal a human name because it resembles someone they know.

According to a survey of 116,000 dogs conducted by a radio station in 1939, 1,400 were named Prince, 1,200 Queenie, 1,000 Spot, 500 Rover, and Rags, Towser, Muggsie, and Fido had 30 each. Nowadays, it is assumed that Lassie is probably more popular for female dogs than all of these, and that Charlie Brown, Snoopy, and other folk heroes rank high up there with the leaders.

THREE-DIMENSIONAL PLAQUE
Steven Polaha
Reading, Pennsylvania
1950-1960
Wood; glass eyes
H., 8½"
Joel and Kate Kopp,
America Hurrah Antiques,
N.Y.C.

Dogmatism is puppyism come to its full growth.

Douglas Jerrold

57

Waldo

by Elizabeth Ballard

Mary Bloom

ON JULY 16th, two days after the black-out, a very sweet black dog with white markings strayed to us. He stayed in the bushes all day as it was very hot. I gave him some water and soon became very fond of him. My brother named him "Waldo." In the evening there was a storm and Waldo was terrified. I convinced my parents to let him into the house, where he cowered under a table in the den. The next day, I took Waldo to the vet. His cuts were treated and he was given a soothing flea bath. I advertised Waldo on the radio, secretly hoping he would not be claimed. No one responded to the ad, and now Waldo has become an important part of my family.

Waldo is missing his lower left canine tooth. This means that when he pants his tongue lolls out of the side rather than in front, giving him a special comical look.

He has a toy which he keeps under my bed. I drive him wild pretending to crawl under the bed to steal it. Just before I get it, Waldo rushes under the bed to snatch it up in his mouth. His favorite place to sleep in the daytime is under my bed; at night he prefers to sleep on a sofa.

Waldo has learned that he will be taken for his nighttime walk after my brother has had his bath and got into bed. As soon as Alexander gets out of the tub, Waldo starts wagging his tail and running around. Waldo is a lot of fun. I consider him one of my best friends.

Now That He's Yours

BEFORE you welcome a dog into your household, do some planning, purchasing, and decision making first.

If your mutt is a puppy, someone should be on hand during the first week, since he will need pretty constant supervision and reassurance that he is loved and has nothing to fear. A new adult dog will also need to learn the rules of the house, new schedules for walking and eating and sleeping, and like a pup, he too will need some sense of security about his new home and his new people. Although you needn't be there all the time for an adult dog, plan on being around as much as possible, at least for a couple of days.

If the dog is large, you will have to take this into account in planning his sleeping and eating areas, and if he's energetic, you must count on spending a certain amount of time each day in giving him exercise outside the house. (Every dog will need some exercise, of course, but some need more than others.)

City dwellers will have to adapt their apartments or living quarters to accommodate the dog and set up a schedule for walking him, at least three times a day for an adult dog and more for a puppy. You will also have to decide where you are going to walk him and how you plan to clean up after him. (In many cities it is illegal not to clean up after a dog.)

Preparing Your Home (and Yourself) for the Mutt

If you live in the suburbs, you will have to decide whether the dog is going to live indoors with you or in a house of his own in the yard. Since many communities have leash laws and since you will in any case want to avoid catastrophe (accidents, running away, fights, and so on), you'll also have to decide how you are going to confine the dog—by a chain-and-stake arrangement, fencing in the yard, building a dog run, or taking the dog on walks.

People living in the country may be able to let the dog run free, but if the mutt is one with hunting or herding instincts, think twice before letting him go. Neighboring farmers don't usually appreciate loose dogs around their cows and chickens, and you won't appreciate the worry that straying dogs create by taking off for hours or even days at a time. If you are getting a male dog, you may want to have him altered just to keep him from wanting to roam; spayed females, too, are far more likely to stick around and mind their own territories. But a new dog isn't going to know his territory right away, and so even in the country you will need to confine him until he gets his bearings.

Adapting Your Own Home

Although keeping a dog in your own apartment or house may not require the initial expense that building a kennel or doghouse would, this is probably the most difficult arrangement—at least in the beginning, especially with a puppy. Dogs demand far more of their owners than many people who fall for puppies in pet-shop windows or in the pound are aware of until they get those puppies home. You can't allow a pup to run loose through a house and expect this untrained, relatively ignorant little creature to know enough not to chew slippers, piddle wherever he likes, or keep out of intriguing-looking closets or off the Louis XVI chairs. Neither is it fair to assume that a grown dog is going to know the rules of a household he has never lived in. You will need to train the dog—to discipline it not to do some things, to praise it for doing others, and to keep temptation as far away as possible. This will take time and patience, and until those do's and don'ts are learned, confinement or close supervision will be necessary.

A relatively simple way to see that mistakes are avoided is to keep the dog confined to a single area at first—a whole room if you can spare it, a closed-in porch, a well-ventilated garage, a section of the house fenced off with a baby gate, or whatever you can manage. Within that space, select a spot for feeding (and use it consistently) and allow the dog to pick his own spot for sleeping. If you are getting a puppy, you will need to cover this whole area with newspaper until you have him paper-trained (see page 83 for methods of housebreaking). Dogs naturally perform all three functions—sleeping, eating, and eliminating—in different places, and once the dog has become accustomed to his living space and knows where these things are to be done, you can allow him into the rest of the house, though you'll need to keep a watchful eye out to prevent trouble before it starts. If certain parts of the house are to remain firmly off limits (the garbage can, bedrooms, the dining room, certain pieces of furniture), remove the temptation by using doors when the dog is not supervised and by using discipline when he is. If something begins to go wrong (or happens before you can stop it), simply say "no" firmly and put the dog back in his own place. Dogs are naturally eager to please, and if you're consistent about your own rules and careful to enforce them, the two of you shouldn't have much difficulty in making it through this period of adjustment.

Unlike babies, dogs need very little in the way of special furniture of their own; in fact, the less there is the better off you'll be in terms of cleaning. It's best to keep his sleeping area free of things to chew or get up on, especially if you want him to remain on the floor in the rest of the house. Contrary to popular opinion, a fancy bed isn't necessary, and many dogs will be perfectly happy on the floor if that's all they know. But most dogs like a rug or a mat of some sort, which is not only comfortable but reassuring psychologically as well. Once a dog knows that a particular object is his own sleeping pad, he'll be less likely to want to sleep on your bed. Dogs are people-oriented and would undoubtedly prefer to sleep near (or right next to) their owners, but dogs are not people and will accept their dogness with perfect equanimity once they learn where they belong.

A Home of His Own If you have a yard, you may choose to make your mutt a mutthouse. Unless you live in open country, you will also need to fence in an area around it or build a run to go with it. Here are a few general considerations to keep in mind before you start construction.

Dimensions   A dog's house shouldn't be much larger than the dog himself, just high enough for him to stand and just wide enough for him to curl up and lie down.

Heating System   Luckily, a dog is his own best heating system. All you need to do is provide insulation (insulation board lining the walls), a door (nail a piece of burlap or heavy cloth over the entrance so that the dog can push his way in and out), and a bedding of straw, hay, wood shavings, or rags, which can be easily and cheaply disposed of and replaced. The dog's body heat, plus the small size of the enclosure, will do the rest, even in subfreezing temperatures. (Don't expect a dog that hasn't been accustomed gradually to cold weather to do well if he is suddenly put outside in midwinter; he needs time to build up a thick hair coat.)

Porch   When you build the roof, make one edge overlap the side of the house, so that the dog can get shelter on rainy days or hot, sunny afternoons without having to go inside. This is a good spot to use for feeding the dog, since there won't be room to do so inside the doghouse.

Cleaning   While you're working on the roof, attach one side with hinges so that you can lift it on cleaning day. Also, line the floor and walls with oilcloth or linoleum to make cleaning easier.

Painting   Use lead-free gray or blue paint for the exterior. (It is said that flies don't like those colors.) Don't bother to paint the interior.

Water   Attach a hook to the side of the house so that a pail can be hung there; this will avoid problems of spilling. Although the pail should be removable for cleaning purposes, it will be convenient to have it accessible to a hose for refilling.

The run   The fencing should be made of sturdy wire or chain link in dimensions large enough to give the dog room to exercise, and it should be high enough to keep him from jumping out. There are several different kinds of flooring that can be used: regular or soil cement, covered or not with a few inches of clean sand; 3 or 4 inches of rounded gravel or stones (available at garden centers) over a grassless dirt base. To prevent problems with internal parasites, the run should be completely cleaned on a regular basis, so the type of flooring you select should be cleanable. Sand can be removed and replaced; cement can be hosed down and disinfected; stones can be treated with lime or chlorine twice a month. Grass will harbor worms, so keep it out of the run; plain dirt will harbor grass and weed seeds, so keep it covered. Daily cleaning is an easier chore; simply pick up stools with a scoop or shovel and place in a special pit covered with dirt and disinfectant (see page 89) or hose stool into the stones or gravel and treat the area with lime on a regular basis.

Chain-and-stake   If you decide not to build a run, the next most convenient method is the chain-and-stake arrangement, specially designed with a swivel so that the dog won't wrap his chain and himself around the stake. Many dogs dislike being tied and will protest noisily at first, but after they become accustomed to it and realize that it enables them to run, they should gradually adjust. Be sure to use a sturdy but lightweight chain and not rope (which can be chewed) or thin wire (which can cut). To keep frustration to a minimum, do not allow children to tease the dog by running or eating food just out of reach.

     If you have a small dog or a puppy, regular yard fencing may serve to keep him in, and in the warm months this is an ideal arrangement for an active pup who likes to chew.

Canine Equipment

In addition to setting up a basic living arrangement, you will also need to buy certain things before your mutt arrives. Here is a checklist followed by a brief description of the items you will want to have on hand.

Collar	Water dish or pail
Leash	Grooming tools
Food dish	Dog food

The type of collar you choose will depend in large part on the dog himself—his size and his degree of education. A chain choke collar is probably the most useful for all purposes, since it is adjustable in size and is an essential part of the training process, giving the handler a good deal of control over the dog's movements. If your dog has long hair, you may want a loose-link chain or a double chain that will lie flat without matting the fur. Don't skimp on the quality; a cheap chain is easily broken. If your mutt is particularly playful, choke collars can become entangled, and in that case, a sturdy leather collar may be preferable. If the dog is very small, a harness works well and makes leash walking far easier, since neck collars can easily slip over tiny heads.

     Chain leashes are sturdy but may be too heavy for a puppy or a small dog. Leather and braided fabric leashes are fine and nylon leashes are especially good for training purposes, since they are light but strong.

     Dog dishes must be stable and unbreakable. Active, playful puppies or active and bored older dogs will tip over an ordinary bowl. Fill a flat-bottomed bowl or pot with cool, clean water and keep it always in the same spot. Glass or pottery can be broken, but heavy flat-bottomed ceramic dishes and large enameled metal pots or aluminum pails are good. Doilies and table napkins won't improve canine table manners, but newspaper spread underneath the serving dishes will make messy eaters easier to live with.

     Grooming tools come in any number of sizes, designs, and price ranges, and your selection will be based on the type of hair coat your mutt has. Long hair will require special combs (as well as more frequent grooming sessions) and matt removers. Short hair may need only a soft brush to remove surface dirt. (See page 121 for grooming instructions.)

Last but not least, you should have dog food on hand before the dog arrives. What kind is discussed in the following chapter.

Rearranging Your Day

Newcomers to the state of dog ownership are often appalled to find that they must reorganize their lives to cope with canine needs. Dogs don't simply move in and adjust themselves to your schedules. As social creatures in the wild, unlike the solitary cats, dogs have always been accustomed to interacting with others of their own kind, and it's not surprising that in a domesticated state, dogs remain dependent on others for psychological needs, to say nothing of the physical demands that living in a non-canine situation impose. Dogs are creatures of habit and those habits must be respected.

The number of times a dog will need to be fed, walked, or given an opportunity to sleep will depend, of course, on his age, experience, and personal predilections. Set up a schedule to accommodate those functions and stick to it on a regular basis. It is possible to train a dog to adjust to one's own personal habits, but only to a point. It is unrealistic to expect an adult dog to go without eliminating for more than eight hours unless he has been conditioned to wait slightly longer, and it is unhealthy to let a dog go without exercise or food at least once daily. You will need to groom your dog's coat at least once a week and more frequently during the shedding seasons. You will have to wash his dishes daily and thoroughly clean his bedding, sleeping pad, and run at least weekly, in addition to cleaning up any soiled items or spots as soon as they are noticed.

As for long-range schedules, make a note to visit the veterinarian and the dog-licensing bureau at least once a year. You might set up a health chart for your mutt; this will be invaluable for your vet and for dog-sitters or kennel operators when you go off on vacation, and it will also serve to remind you when the dog needs his annual worming checkup and inoculations.

Just as soon as a dog comes along who . . . knows when to buy and sell stocks, he can be moved right up to the boy's bedroom and the boy can sleep in the doghouse.

Robert Benchley

Preparing Your Home (and Yourself)   **63**

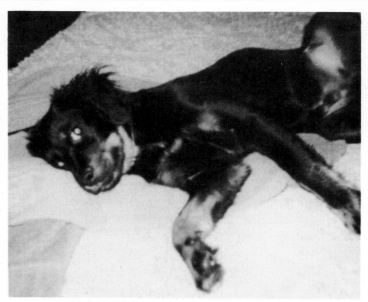

Renfield

by Cathy Rutherford and Michael Fragnito

It was apparent from the moment we first saw him that this was the puppy we had come to adopt. Looking quite small and alone, he sat on a scrap of towel in the wire and cement cage of the local animal shelter. They had classified him merely as "mixed," but it was obvious from the silky black coat and long tattered ears that strong retriever or setter heritage was present. After about thirty seconds of wiggling kisses, he convinced us to stake our claim at the front desk. It was there that we got the bad news; our puppy was a stray, and because he had been brought in only that morning, he had to remain for three days in case someone came to claim him. Because of conflicting commitments, we would be unable to return for him for several weeks, by which time he surely would have been adopted by others.

Somewhat daunted, we repaired to a nearby pub to consider the situation. Sometime during our third round of drinks, we arrived at a name for him—Renfield—and a determination to circumvent the rules and take him home with us. Back we marched to the shelter, prepared to use terrorist tactics if necessary, to carry Renfield off that day. One more mutual adoration session and in we went to confront the shelter supervisor.

Using our most diplomatic approach, we explained our circumstances again. "We *must* take this puppy home today. We won't be dissuaded . . ."

"Okay," she said, suddenly capitulating.

" . . . er, what?"

"He's yours. You'll just have to get in the car and bring him right back if someone comes asking."

Dazed by our conditional victory, we promised to somehow return should the former owner show up and whisked Rennie into the car before the supervisor could change her mind. No one ever appeared to claim him, much to our relief, and Rennie settled into our home and our hearts as if he had always been there.

Marian Duckworth (right)
and the ASPCA
Mobile Adoption Center

Mascot for the ASPCA
(New York City)
Paul Duckworth

65

THE appearance of a new dog in a household is an exciting event for everyone concerned. But that excitement and enthusiasm might not be shared by other pets, who may be terrified if not actually endangered by a bounding, inquisitive dog taking over their territory.

First of all, consider the dog himself. Obviously you don't know him very well as yet, but a few characteristics—psychological as well as physical—should have become apparent when you were making your initial decision about bringing him home. Is he large (or, if a puppy, likely to become so)? Is he bouncy or relatively quiet by nature? Is he nervous, jumping up and barking at the slightest provocation, or does he stay cool? Does he have any hunting dogs in his family tree? Watch his behavior and his reactions, both in his presence and when he doesn't realize that he's being watched. This period of adjustment is very important, for the smoother the introductions, the fewer the eventual problems. Supervision is the watchword: Don't leave the dog alone with any other animals—or even with the children—until you are sure that he can be trusted to behave as you want him to behave.

Tabby, I'd Like You to Meet Rover

Most dogs will show some curiosity about a cage containing a living creature that makes noise and moves, but as soon as they realize that there is nothing to be feared or played with, they'll lose interest and ignore both cage and bird. When you bring the dog into the room where the bird lives, pay no attention to the cage (or the dog will assume that there is something to be curious about) but keep your eye on the dog. If he shows no interest, even though he has looked the thing over, fine. Relax but keep your eye on him for at least a couple of days to be sure. If he does show interest for more than a few minutes, leaping about and barking excitedly, reprimand him with a firm "no" and push him away from the cage. Three or four attempts should be enough to convince him that it's better to ignore the bird. If the dog is still a puppy and hasn't learned to heed your commands, be patient but persistent. This is time for the dog to start learning the word "no" in any case. Then separate the bird and the dog but put them back together the following day for another lesson. When you have managed to get them together for more than two days in a row and the dog shows no reaction to the cage, you can feel sure that the lesson has been learned. If you are not sure, and you have a feeling that the dog might poke at the cage when you're not there, set up a situation by which you can leave the room but supervise him all the same (through a window, perhaps, or by using someone else to discipline the dog in your absence). If a dog is persistent enough to keep up his interest, you may have to remove the bird from temptation by hanging the cage well above the dog's head (and reach) or by putting the bird into a room where the dog cannot go. However, most dogs will become adjusted readily enough, even without being disciplined.

Caged Birds

Caged Mammals Follow the procedure outlined above if you have hamsters, gerbils, mice, rats, or rabbits. Since these animals are sometimes let out of the cage to play with the kids, be careful on those occasions to keep the dog away or to supervise very carefully, as these tiny creatures have no defenses short of hiding under the couch or escaping altogether. A rabbit that is allowed the run of the house for short periods (most people keep rabbits in cages when unsupervised since they are rarely housebroken successfully) can be introduced to the dog, though this should be done with great care and the dog should be firmly disciplined if he shows any aggression toward it. Since rabbits too have few defenses, it is best not to leave rabbit and dog together without some human to watch them.

Cats The traditional battle between cats and dogs is a myth rather than a fact, a good subject for cartoonists but having no basis in reality. Dogs and cats quickly grow accustomed to each other in the same household and are often fond of one another. There is little need to anticipate serious trouble if introductions are made sensibly and both animals are supervised during the first few days until they have become adjusted. This does not mean that one should interfere; in fact, it's best to keep cool and try to pretend that there is nothing to be concerned about. The moment a dog or a cat senses that its owner is nervous, the animal will become nervous too and probably ascribe the nervousness to the new creature on the scene. If one just goes about one's business, paying equal attention to each animal, both pets should eventually relax. Obviously, if a fight breaks out, it should be stopped (without your getting caught in the middle) and the animals separated until they have calmed down. But it is important to let them establish a kind of pecking order, and this is often done efficiently by one of the animals with a single slap on the nose of the other—not enough to injure but sufficient to establish a kind of mutual respect. Dogs naturally enjoy chasing anything that runs away, but unless a dog has been encouraged to do so, the chase usually isn't serious, and any cat worth its keep will let the dog know when it's had enough. It isn't wise, however, to allow kittens to play with lively dogs, since even in play a dog can inadvertently bite or fatally crush a kitten. A grown cat is completely capable of fending for himself.

Dogs Resident dogs may resent the appearance of a newcomer at first, and because most dogs are territorial to some extent, trouble can erupt if the new dog isn't introduced properly. Don't just bring the new mutt home and let him loose in the house while the resident dog is locked up somewhere else. Make sure that dog number one is on hand the first time dog number two turns up. The best place to make introductions is outside in the yard if you have one, since the resident dog will probably react to the newcomer by urinating here and there to show the other dog whose territory it is. (You can introduce them in the living room, of course, but it's advisable to cover the furniture with plastic!) Once this routine has been performed, more formalities are in order—a good deal of sniffing, ear flattening, and even some mild growling. Don't interfere at this point, since the dogs are establishing which is dominant and which is submissive. Signs of the latter are rolling over on the back, lowering the ears, baring the teeth (or smiling), and urinating. It is probable that the older dog with a previous claim to the household will be the dominant dog, but this isn't always the case, since some dogs are naturally more passive than others. Don't waste your time predicting; just sit back and watch. If both dogs remain aggressive, you may have a fight on your hands (see page 212 for advice on how to prevent and deal with a dogfight), but if you're careful and reassuring to both dogs, you shouldn't have trouble. Talk to the dogs, patting both to let them know that you like them both. Make sure that each dog has his own separate dishes for food and water and that they are fed at the same time. Before long, you'll find that the two animals will be fast friends. Dogs are sociable by nature, and as soon as they have set up their own pecking order, they will behave as if they had been born in the same litter.

Paul Duckworth

It is a strange thing, love. Nothing but love has made the dog lose his wild freedom, to become the servant of man. And his very servility or completeness of love makes a term of deepest contempt—"You dog!"

D. H. Lawrence

Hangdog Look

It's said that hunting dogs living in the great English country houses of the past, eating scraps tossed from the table and sleeping as close to the fire as they could get, were kept orderly by special handlers who broke up dog fights, whipped their charges and even hanged incorrigible dogs. Shakespeare, no dog lover, does refer to the hanging of dogs five times in his plays, but I've been unable to find any actual case of a dog hanging. Nevertheless, since the late seventeenth century anyone with a cringing, abject appearance, or a base, sneaky demeanor has been said to have a hangdog look. Whether real or the product of someone's imagination, the allusion was originally either to a despicable, degraded person fit only to hang a dog, or to be hanged like a dog. Nowadays a hangdog look has almost entirely lost its meaning of contemptible and sneaky and generally describes someone browbeaten, defeated, intimidated or abject—someone who looks a little like a bloodhound.

Robert Hendrickson

Now That He's Yours

Hugh Mohr

Jumbo

THE BIGGEST DOG IN STONINGTON

JUMBO belongs to the Allen family— Merrill and Judy and their children, Skipper, Howard, G. B., and Priscilla—of Stonington, Maine. He was just a little fellow when the Allens brought him home, but he's been growing ever since, and now, at age seven, he weighs almost 200 pounds.

Jumbo lives a rather sedate life, spending most of his time in the Allens' front yard. There are three or four neighbors that he drops in on every morning without fail, however, and sometimes if he's feeling particularly perky, he'll stop in at the local market for a handout.

When asked if there is a secret ingredient in Jumbo's diet that contributes to his girth, Judy Allen said, "No, he eats almost anything, but he can't stand marshmallows and bananas."

MANY people believe that veterinarians are important primarily in emergencies—to repair an injury, cure a disease, or answer anxious questions—but that's only the tip of the iceberg. Like any doctor, a vet can take better care of his patients if he has some idea of what the animal is like in its healthy state. But finding and keeping a vet in whom you have complete confidence is a two-way street; it takes some doing on both your part and his to settle into a good working relationship.

Veterinarians don't advertise (it isn't ethical), but they aren't hard to find. Most towns have at least one, and large cities usually have many, including sizable animal hospitals run by a number of veterinarians, several of them specializing in different kinds of medicine. Veterinarians are listed in the Yellow Pages, but the best way to find a good one is to ask around. Your pharmacist, local dog breeders, friends, and your own doctor are likely to be the most knowledgeable sources of recommendations.

After you've decided on a vet, make your first visit a provisional one until you assure yourself that conditions are good. Once in the office take a long look around. Is it clean? Is the receptionist courteous and knowledgeable? Do the vet's office hours correspond with your schedule? Is there reasonable order in the waiting room; are the dogs on leashes and the cats contained in some manner? If the answer to all of these is "no," pack up and leave.

Take another hard look at the examining room. Is it clean? Has the exam table been scrubbed down after the last animal? Is the vet using a sterile thermometer? Has he washed his hands?

The most intangible area of judgment is that of personality. This is where you must decide for yourself whether one veterinarian is better than another. "Better" in this case means your having confidence in the doctor's ability not only to diagnose a problem and to treat it effectively but also to care about what he is doing and to behave ethically, conscientiously, and honestly. What is important is for the vet to be comfortable around your animal and appear to really care. It may sound absurd to ask "Is the vet afraid of animals?" (afraid, not to be confused with careful), but there are such cases. Does he display a confidence with your pet that the animal is responsive to? Is he gentle but firm with your pet? If your pet acts up, does he clutch or maintain control? Remember, you're looking for someone who cares about your dog and knows his business.

As far as fees are concerned, don't be afraid to ask about them. There's no reason why you shouldn't know ahead of time what to expect. But do take into consideration the fact that veterinarians are licensed medical practitioners with four or more years of specialized training in their field. Because there are not as many veterinary hospitals as there are human hospitals (in fact, there are not nearly so many vets as there are human doctors, about 30,000 in the entire United States compared to 300,000 M.D.'s), most small-animal veterinarians, even if they work out of relatively small offices, have what amounts to an entire hospital on the premises, with radiograph equipment, a pharmacy, a laboratory, and surgery facilities. To offer you a good service costs money, so do not think that you are getting a bargain

Finding a Veterinarian

because one vet is cheaper than another. It may be that the more expensive vet cares more about giving your pet the best care possible.

Most vets will recommend a regular checkup once a year. But, even more important, a good vet will expect you to take intelligent care of your dog and to catch a minor problem before it becomes major. He won't want to hear about trivial symptoms in the middle of the night (see pages 143-148 for a description of symptoms, trivial and important), nor will he want to hear that an important symptom has been ignored or shrugged off for a day or more. He will expect you to be knowledgeable about your animal. Knowing what a dog is like under normal conditions is important; if the dog does something out of the ordinary or fails to do something routine, you should be alert to potential trouble. An accurate observation and description of symptoms and behavior are often crucial to a quick diagnosis and effective treatment, which can be literally a matter of life and death.

It would be helpful at the first visit to go armed with the following information: the dog's age, as accurately as you can determine it; its breeding, if you know it; its weight (step on your bathroom scale and weigh yourself, then holding the dog, weigh yourself again); and its sex (don't laugh—some people aren't always sure); and whatever medical history you know. If the dog is an older female, try to find out from the previous owner or the animal shelter if she's been spayed, since this is often difficult to determine after the fact. In addition to your dog, bring a stool sample so that a test can be run for internal parasites. Puppies from the best homes or dogs from the cleanest shelters can have worms, and there may be no visible symptoms.

The dog himself should be prepared too. Make sure that he is on a leash, reasonably clean, and not in an excessively excitable state. One way of keeping a dog calm is to remain calm yourself, reassuring him that there is nothing to be afraid of. (If the dog is badly frightened during the visit, the vet may suggest that he be tranquilized next time, but let him decide that.) If you are afraid that he will become overexcited at the vet's, you might give the dog a practice exam by placing him on a table with a slick surface and grooming him or giving him the once-over yourself. Any dog that has been through this routine a couple of painless times won't be unnecessarily surprised when he is lifted unceremoniously onto an exam table. Vets have a lot of experience in handling nervous dogs, but if you know that yours is likely to snap at him or may need special handling, don't hesitate to tell the vet what to expect.

When you arrive at the office or clinic, the receptionist will ask you for information about the dog. At this point, give her the stool sample so that a test may be made while you are still there. When the veterinarian is ready to see the dog, you will probably be asked to accompany the animal and to hold him during the exam. The doctor will check the eyes, ears, rectum, genital area, coat, mouth, and feet, looking for anything that seems irregular or unusual. If anything has been bothering you or the dog, be sure to mention it now. You might be concerned about whether you are feeding a suitable diet, grooming frequently enough, or otherwise providing good care. If the hair coat seems shabby or scruffy, ask about dietary supplements or vitamin pills.

The next step will be a preventive one—inoculations against diseases for which vaccines exist. If the dog is still a puppy, he will need a series of shots for distemper and perhaps also leptospirosis and hepatitis, depending on the veterinarian. While a puppy nurses, he picks up antibodies against these diseases from his mother, but as he is weaned he will require a vaccine. The rate at which these antibodies leave the puppy's system will vary, which is why the vet will probably recommend inoculations at several stages, usually four weeks, ten weeks, and around sixteen weeks. Older dogs will need this inoculation (which nowadays combines vaccines against all three diseases) once a year. If the pup is six months old or older, a rabies vaccine will also be given (and you will get a rabies tag to attach to the dog's collar). Rabies shots are required by law in all states, though whether they are to be given once every two years or only once a year will depend on the state and on the vaccine used. If you are planning to travel or to board your dog within the near future, you should ask for a health certificate (see page 129).

If possible, the veterinarian will give you the results of the fecal test at the time of your visit. If the test is positive and the dog does have internal parasites, you may be given medication to be administered at home or asked to bring the puppy back at some future date for a worming. This may take two visits, depending on the type of worm and medication used. Roundworms, hookworms, whipworms, and tapeworms are the most common forms of parasites, but there are others as well, including heartworms, which can be very serious. In some parts of the country, infestations of heartworm have become widespread; originally they were common only in southern states, but thanks to our mobile society, which usually takes its pets along with it, heartworm has moved too. This parasite is spread from one dog to the other via mosquitoes, and unfortunately, at present, no one-shot preventive exists, and medication must be given to the dog on a daily basis during the mosquito season. The veterinarian will test for heartworm by examining a blood sample. If the test is negative, he will dispense preventive medication in tablet or liquid form designed to be given in food or water. If the test is positive, the dog must undergo a series of treatments to eradicate the parasite.

Take this chance to inquire about the advisability, timing, and expense involved in neutering the dog, and in any other kinds of medical information about which you may not be clear. If the vet seems rushed, ask him when might be a good time for you to call if all your questions haven't been answered. You don't want to be a hypochondriac, but your genuine interest should be treated with the encouragement it deserves.

Harold

by Florence Sussman

One day a friend called and said that a miniature poodle in the neighborhood had become pregnant by a "traveling man" (probably one of the male terriers or the miniature schnauzer living close by).

Hearing the news, I realized I wanted a pup. That night, I spoke to my husband who loves dogs, but he said it was cruel to leave a dog home alone during the day. I thought and thought, too, and the more I contemplated it, the more I wanted a dog; I would make up for my daytime absence with extra attention at night. My husband kept saying no, but finally, after two weeks of my nagging, he relented on condition that the dog be a male. I immediately agreed to the deal.

When the pups were born, there was only one male in the litter of five, and he died after several days. Even though there were only females, I was determined to have one. I brought home one of the pups and named

her Harold, keeping her gender secret. By the time my husband finally caught on, three weeks later, it was much too late—he had fallen in love with her.

Harold is now five years old, and a great dog. We couldn't have gotten a better one if we'd paid a thousand dollars.

VIEW DOWN CORRIDOR
detail
Hoogstraten
Dyrham Park, Gloucestershire
British National Trust
England

They Shoot Dogs, Don't They?

THANKS to modern research and discoveries, we have developed methods of controlling many diseases before they start, in dogs as well as in humans. Because many of the diseases for which vaccines have been developed are fatal, dog owners are advised to take advantage of their availability and have their dogs inoculated on a regular basis as their veterinarian recommends. Because there are so many strays, it will never become entirely possible to eradicate these diseases, so don't assume that since all the dogs you know have been given their shots your dog will be immune. Some viruses can be carried on clothing, for instance, and do not require direct contact between animals. As soon as you get a dog—especially if he has come from a shelter or the streets, but even if he is the product of a kennel or pet shop—see that he gets inoculated against these diseases and is tested for worms (internal parasites) at the earliest opportunity.

Rabies   A viral disease affecting all warm-blooded animals throughout the world, transmissible to man, and invariably fatal without treatment. The virus is carried in the saliva of an infected animal and is usually transmitted by biting. Although rabies in dogs is much less common now than it once was, it is still found in wild animals in many areas, and domestic dogs can be infected if not protected by the vaccine, which is mandatory in many communities. There are several kinds of vaccine, and the vaccination routine will depend on the type used.

Canine Distemper   This, too, is a widespread disease and it may be carried by several wild species (raccoons, foxes, and skunks, for example), as well as dogs. The death rate is high and survivors may suffer permanent defects of the central nervous system. The first vaccine should be given when a puppy is six weeks old (before that, the pup is protected by antibodies in the mother's milk) with periodic inoculations after that time.

Infectious Hepatitis   This liver ailment is fatal in about 25 percent of affected animals, and survivors, who are slow to recover, may carry and spread the virus through their urine for some months after recovery. The vaccine is now available in a three-in-one shot with distemper and leptospirosis.

Leptospirosis   This disease affecting the kidneys can be transmitted to humans through the dog's urine. Vaccination can be given along with distemper shots and is recommended, since the disease can be fatal or cause permanent kidney damage.

Now That He's Yours

Tetanus This condition (called lockjaw as well as tetanus in humans) is caused by the toxin of a bacteria that affects the brain and spinal cord. Horses and cattle are usually most seriously affected and are inoculated regularly, but dogs may develop tetanus through puncture wounds. A vaccine given shortly after a dogfight or an injury may be recommended by the vet.

Tracheobronchitis Also known as kennel cough, this respiratory ailment is highly infectious, though not often serious, and can easily be avoided through one of the several vaccines available. Regular inoculation is not necessary, but it is a good idea to have the dog vaccinated before taking him to a boarding kennel or an area where many other dogs are likely to be.

Heartworm This is an internal parasite, one of the few that can be treated preventively. It has recently become more widespread, having once been common primarily in southern states, but now all dog owners living in mosquito-infested areas should be on their guard for this mosquito-carried parasite. The usual procedure is to have your dog tested for heartworm (which can be fatal) in the early spring and then placing him on a program of medication (with daily doses of capsules or liquid). These medications are not foolproof, but it would be foolish to ignore them.

The Veterinary Version of the Hippocratic Oath

Being admitted to the profession of veterinary medicine, I solemnly swear to use my scientific knowledge and skills for the benefit of society through the protection of animal health, the relief of animal suffering, the conservation of livestock resources, the promotion of public health, and the advancement of medical knowledge.

I will practice my profession conscientiously, with dignity, and in keeping with the principles of veterinary medical ethics.

I accept as a lifelong obligation the continual improvement of my professional knowledge and competence.

DOG AND CAT
Jan Griffier
Engraving after Francis Barbon
1710
Cooper-Hewitt Museum
New York

DOG LOVERS don't need any convincing when it comes to the question of which animal is really man's best friend—the cat or the dog. But there has been so much talk—to say nothing of elaborate publications—in recent years about the cat that, on behalf of mutts and purebreds alike, it seems appropriate to let the ailurophiles of the world know that we have heard their arguments and found them wanting.

Most real animal lovers accept both species on their own terms without making unfair comparisons. Granted dogs are more difficult to keep than cats in terms of care and expense. But, when all the chips are down, the dog is undoubtedly a more responsive and rewarding companion. Cats are intriguing because they tend to be solo performers and can adapt themselves to your life-style without losing their independence. But put yourself in the following situations. Which one of your beloved pets comes out on top?

1. It's been a tough week and you want to relax in bed on Sunday morning, but you've just got to find out who won last night's ball game. Which animal do you send out to the porch for the newspaper?

2. Before you start the day, you want to run down to the park for a quick jog but you need company to get yourself going. Which animal do you put on a leash?

3. One of your kids wants to play a game of catch, but you just don't have the energy. Which animal do you suggest he approach for a game?

4. You want to practice your serve but you can't get anyone onto the tennis court. Which animal can you ask to return the balls for you?

5. You've spent almost all day in the kitchen cooking dinner. You need reassurance from someone that it's been worth all the trouble. Which member of the family is going to show his appreciation by eating everything on the plate?

6. You have some friends coming over for the evening and they are a bit nervous about meeting strange animals. Which of your pets is going to shake their hands and then lie quietly at their feet?

7. You're an energy-conscious recycler and you've just finished dinner, leaving a nice big beef bone on the platter. You know you should make soup, but the family hates it, and you've already spent too much time in the kitchen today. Which animal is going to help you keep your "waste-not, want-not" instincts intact?

8. After dinner your friends ask the kids to play the piano to show what they've learned; after the recital, your guests wonder if anyone else in the family knows a trick or two. Which animal do you call on to do his stuff?

9. You are in the house alone and there have been rumors of burglars in the neighborhood. Which animal will make you feel more secure at night?

10. You're depressed and need a pair of soulful brown eyes to assure you that someone cares. Which animal do you look at first?

Dogs vs. Cats

Training Your Mutt

ARNIE Webber is not an animal trainer. He is a painter and art teacher who lives with two dogs, a cougar, a hawk, a snake, six horses, a ten-inch tarantula, assorted other spiders, and usually a varying number of transient four- and eight-legged creatures. The relationship that Arnie and his animals share is extraordinary, and that's because Arnie has incorporated his strong biases about animal training into the civilization of his own animals.

Training, according to Arnie, is not a cut-and-dried affair. As with children, you have to know the animal (or child) you're dealing with. The kind of treatment that the animal will respond to best is a little different for each one. It is, of course, a somewhat less complicated matter with purebreds; each breed has its own traits that one can allow for right at the outset. Although it is more difficult to predict, your mutt is going to have his own special personality, too. And knowing whether your dog is going to crumble on the floor when you look at him cross-eyed or has a head as hard as Mount Rushmore is vital to how you approach your civilization of him. Beyond that, Arnie says, there are certain characteristics that you must have in order to be effective with your pet: patience, perseverance, keen insight, consistency, and a genuine affection for and willingness to spend time with your dog and make him a part of your life. If you fulfill your dog's needs consistently, praise him when he's good and firmly reprimand him when he does the wrong thing, you will have a happy and usually well-mannered pet.

There are really only a few basic things you need to teach your dog to make him a compatible member of the family. The most obvious of course is that the desirable place to relieve himself is outside. There are several ways to handle this: the paper-training method and the eagle-eye approach. If you opt to paper-train your dog, confine him to a small area and cover the entire floor surface with paper. As he adjusts to this area, cover less space with paper. Gradually remove more paper until there is only one piece left and then put that by the door and eventually outside. When he eliminates on the floor and not the paper, let him know about your displeasure with a firm *no*. Most books will tell you that it is useless to reprimand your dog unless he is caught in the act of a crime or within minutes thereof because he will not know why he is being punished. Arnie says this is baloney. If you are persistent and reprimand your dog *every* time he makes a mistake, he will soon catch on. Any confusion in the dog lies in your own lack of persistence.

If you are around the house most of the time and can keep an alert eye on your dog, you will soon recognize his signals when he has to eliminate. He might sniff around a bit or do a little scratching on the rug—there will be some preliminary ritual. Whenever you see that begin to occur, immediately whisk him outside. And when he does eliminate outside, praise him highly.

Aside from understanding what *no* means, there are four basic commands your dog should know for his own benefit as well as yours: *heel, come, sit,* and *stay*. The only piece of apparatus you will need is a seven-foot leash and a choke collar. The basic procedures are thus:

J. P. Davis
Engraving after W. Shurlaw
Circa 1900

Heel Allow just enough slack in the leash so that your dog can walk comfortably next to you on your left side. If he falls behind or tries to walk too quickly, firmly jerk the leash *once* and say *heel*, pulling him back to his place beside you. Again, praise him when he does it properly, and when he gets to the point where he fully understands the command, practice with him off lead.

Sit While your dog is in a standing position, push his rump toward the ground and say *sit*. If he remains sitting, even if only for a few seconds at first, praise him. Repeat this until he catches on.

Stay With your dog in front of you and your hand raised, palm toward the dog, back up several steps and say *stay*. Again, even if he only shows the slightest inclination to stay, praise him highly and run through it again.

Come Holding one end of the leash, allow your dog to walk until the slack is out of the leash. As he reaches that point, give *one* firm jerk on the leash, say *come*, and encourage him to walk back toward you. When he appears in any way to be getting the drift of what you're saying, *praise him*. When he has this down pat while on the leash, remove it and practice with him off lead.

You needn't make training a trying time for either you or your pet. Just take about fifteen minutes every day, uninterrupted, to work with him.

There is absolutely nothing innovative or difficult about the preceding techniques. And they certainly didn't originate with Arnie Webber. Arnie's success with his animals is due to the fact that he has taken the time to know them.

With Chopper, a real hardhead with a strong fighting instinct in his lineage, Arnie

Now That He's Yours

was firm and persistent. Chopper is a pit bullterrier—a breed that has fighting blood bred into it—and Arnie has used a forceful approach throughout his training. Being aware of his dog's fighting tendencies, Arnie introduced him to people and other dogs early in life. He would deliberately take him into crowded areas, and if Chopper so much as looked like he was about to pick a fight with another dog, Arnie would reprimand him gruffly, with a slap on the rear if necessary. These training excursions continued until Chopper totally understood that fighting was off limits. In the wild, pack animals have a leader, and by asserting his dominance over Chopper, Arnie gained his respect and made himself that leader.

The extreme firmness that Arnie has employed with Chopper is tempered, however, with an enormous amount of love. The two spend a great deal of time together and Arnie takes Chopper with him wherever he goes. "You can't ignore your dog and expect him to be a well-balanced, responsive animal. It's true, a dog must understand who's boss," says Arnie, "but you have to let him know that you really care about him—you have to make him part of the family."

Batoo, Arnie's other dog, is a different story. She was a timid and frightened animal when Arnie got her at the age of three. He has never so much as raised his voice at her. Arnie was persistent, but in a calm and gentle way. It took a great deal of time and patience, but because of the assurance and encouragement that Arnie has offered her, she has become an outgoing, trustful dog. Again, Arnie was not permissive—Batoo is a well-trained dog—but his psychological approach was just the reverse of that employed with Chopper.

Arnie's dogs started out as temperamentally different as night and day. Today you would be hard put to tell which one had what background. "It has nothing to do with the method you employ," says Arnie, "it's how you employ it with each individual dog."

Mary Bloom

*Y*ou don't want an average dog, a dog that pulls on the leash, that gets into fights, jumps up on you and misbehaves. . . . The greatest dog in the world . . . is a companion who does all but speak. He will be gay or serious; he will console you in your lowest moods. He will be perfectly behaved and never leave your side. He will entertain your friends. He will rescue a child from a burning building or, if ever you are in danger of drowning, pull you from the water. He will watch your car, protect you against attack, carry your packages or umbrella, and refuse food from strangers.

Ludwig Bemelmans

Zoe
THE DOG NOBODY WANTED

ZOE HAS made the big time—with the lead role in the movie *Summerdog*, she's become a star of the silver screen. But life has not always been glitter and tinsel for this prototypical shaggy dog.

Zoe belongs to the Zabriskies—George and Sherry and their children, Oliver and Tavia—who adopted her from the New York City ASPCA several years ago. They had lost a previous dog, and George and Sherry were not really enthusiastic about getting another. But Oliver and Tavia put the pressure on, so their parents finally agreed to a new dog, but with the stipulation that they had to find one that they *really* liked at the animal shelter. George and Sherry didn't believe for a moment that the family would find a suitable pet, since it was just after Christmas—a time when the adoptable dog selection has been pretty well picked over. How wrong they were, for when they went to the shelter, there sat the irresistible Zoe. She came with a word of warning, though—Zoe had already been returned to the shelter twice, and if the Zabriskies returned her, she would be put to sleep.

It didn't take long to discover why she hadn't stayed very long in one place—she wasn't housebroken. To Zoe, the whole world, including the Zabriskies' bed, was a toilet facility. But they were stuck—they were the dog's last chance. Zoe had a permanent home at last.

About a year later, George and Sherry, documentary film makers, wrote their first feature-length script, *Summerdog*, and scraped together the money to produce it. The action revolves around the adventures of an abandoned dog, Hobo, that Oliver finds caught in a raccoon trap. Needless to say, the Zabriskies didn't go to central casting to fill the part of the dog. Nor did they have to look very far to cast several other roles—Oliver and Tavia also have parts in the film.

Is Zoe a difficult and demanding actress? Not at all. In fact, she's been nicknamed "One-Take Zoe" by the movie's director, John Clayton. The secret of her success? Cheddar cheese. Zoe will do absolutely anything for a hunk of good Cheddar. So before each scene, Sherry Zabriskie stations herself out of camera range holding a golden piece of cheese for Zoe to retrieve once she has done what is required of her.

Terry Brisbie

87

I T HAS often been said that walking between parked cars in New York City is more dangerous than crossing a busy intersection against the light, and no wonder, considering the number of dogs that defecate daily on the street or in that general area.

Stepping into dog stool is an unpleasant experience no matter how much you like dogs, and for those who don't like dogs, it can be infuriating, an affront to the senses, and not all that good for the shoes, either. Dog owners in most cities will defend to the death their right to the streets (and we once witnessed a lively row between a dog walker and a driver trying to park his car where the dog was doing his thing), but even they should beware the dangers involved, not only to themselves, but to their animals as well. Parasites are transmitted by contact with fecal matter, so that even the healthiest animal can pick up worms by treading in or sniffing at the deposit left by another dog. Unlike people, who tend to rely on calling cards or graffiti to make their presence known to the world, dogs smell each other's stool and urine—a throwback to the days when wild dogs would mark their territories by eliminating in, or marking, certain spots. So it isn't "dirty" of a dog to want to sniff, it's only canine nature. But it *is* unsanitary.

For those mutt owners who have a yard, an elaborate but very effective solution to the disposal problem is the Doggie Dooley Waste System (made by Hron Products, 555 Moore Avenue, Bellevue, Ohio 44811, and sold in many pet shops). This apparatus simulates a miniature septic system, complete with heavy plastic tank (with foot-pedal lid) imbedded in the ground over a moisture-retaining bucket that contains a chemical substance that liquefies the stool for absorption into the earth. Also included are a bucket and shovel.

Curb Your Dog!

Alternatives are few for city dwellers, but they do exist. One inexpensive and painless method is a Doggy Bag-grr, made by IDM Industries of Elk Grove, Illinois. It is a long-handled scoop with a heavy plastic frame holding a disposable plastic refuse bag. It is available in pet shops for under $5. Another similar product, invented by William Schmeieler, of Shaker Heights, Ohio, and available through Luxury Pet Products (27900 Chagrin Boulevard, Cleveland, Ohio), is designed to let your dog do the work for you. This dog potty is a long shaft with a handle for you at one end and a plastic fireplug-shape tube at the other containing a disposable plastic liner. The idea is that you place it under the dog while he's in the act. This runs under $10, and for a little more money you can even get a flashlight attachment. (Rumor has it that Bob Hope owns two of them.)

It is perhaps even more practical to paper-train or box-train an apartment-bound dog, which is certainly more convenient than walking the animal in the middle of a rainy evening. Cooperative types can get together with the neighbors to select a separate area in a block for use as a canine latrine; this will not eliminate the possibility of parasite transmission, but it will make all the non-dog-owning neighbors a lot more neighborly and the streets will be a lot cleaner.

There has been talk lately about the risk to children of stool-laden streets and parks, and this may be more than simple speculation. In any event, it behooves urban dog owners to take care of the problem in some way—if not in the eyes of the law, then certainly in the eyes of their fellow humans.

The Doggy Dooley

The Doggy Bag-grr

When the forefinger of twilight begins to smudge the cleardrawn lines of the Big City there is inaugurated an hour devoted to one of the most melancholy sights of urban life. Out from the towering flat crags and apartment peaks of the cliff dwellers of New York steals an army of beings that were once men. Even yet they go upright upon two limbs and retain human forms and speech; but you will observe that they are behind animals in progress. Each of these beings follows a dog, to which he is fastened by an artificial ligament. . . . These unfortunate dry nurses of dogdom, the cur cuddlers, mongrel managers, Spitz stalkers, poodle pullers, Skye scrapers, dachshund dandlers, terrier trailers, and Pomeranian pushers . . . follow their charges meekly. Master of the house these men whom they hold in leash may be, but they are not masters of them. From cosy corner to fire escape, from divan to dumbwaiter, doggy's snarl easily drives this two-legged being who is commissioned to walk at the other end of his string during his outing.

O. Henry, "Ulysses and the Dogman"

Now That He's Yours

Our Dog Lucy

by Tom Liebow

OUR MUTT Lucy is a lovable, ideal pet, who hasn't a mean bone in her body. We couldn't have realized seven years ago when we picked her up from the humane society what an addition she would be to our lives.

Her favorite resting place is three inches from the side of the road, stretched out on her side with her paws inches from disaster. The reason she likes that spot is to better feel the action of the neighborhood, but many is the time we received a call from a passerby offering mistaken condolences on our stricken dog.

Lucy rules the neighborhood. Just recently we had new people move in next door. Before the moving truck had left, Lucy had walked into their kitchen and helped herself to their dog's bone. She also feels that anyone's garbage is hers for the tasting. The problem is that she likes to do the tasting or picnicking on our side lawn. It's always an adventure to see what she's been sampling. In addition to bringing food home, she has arrived with pots, pans, baseball gloves, an eel, a 14-inch trout, all sorts of empty cans, containers, and cookware, and an occasional cat-food dinner.

Her foraging instincts make us think she must be part hound, but whatever she is—or does—her sweet disposition more than makes up for her mischief.

THE DOG interests of many people run well beyond the owning of a pet. They want to inform themselves but it is difficult to know which book to buy or which humane organization to subscribe to. The following is intended to offer those people some direction.

For those whose interests run to the academic, there are a great many dog books on the market; the following are felt to be worthwhile reading, either in their entirety or for specific information.

The Complete Dog Book (Official Publication of the American Kennel Club) (New York: Howell, 1972). A valuable reference book, in spite of its focus on purebreds.

Good Dog Book, by Mordecai Siegal (New York: Macmillan, 1977). Has several useful features, including a section on obesity, complete with recipes. Also a good discussion of children with dogs.

The Collins Guide to Dog Nutrition, by Donald R. Collins (New York: Howell, 1972). An excellent study that will probably tell you more than you want to know.

Informing Yourself

The Penguin Book of Pets, by Emil Dolensek, DVM, and Barbara Burn (New York: Penguin, 1978). An excellent guide for those who have more than one kind of animal in the household.

Underdog: Training the Mutt, Mongrel and Mixed-Breed Dog at Home, by Matthew Margolis and Mordecai Siegal (New York: Stein and Day, 1974). A useful guide to training, especially since it's written for the mixed breed.

The Well Dog Book, by Terri McGinniss (New York: Random House, 1974). One of the best medical guides on the market.

Your Pet's Health from A to Z, by Donal B. McKeown and Earl O. Strimple (New York: Dell, 1973). A handy reference.

Your Dog—His Health and Happiness, by Louis L. Vine (New York: Arco, 1971). One of the most complete and easily readable medical guides around.

Pets and Human Development, by Boris M. Levinson (Springfield, Ill.: C. C. Thomas, 1972). A fascinating study of the relationship between pets and people.

Understanding Your Dog, by Dr. Michael Fox (New York: Coward McCann, 1972). An interesting book on dog psychology by one of the foremost authorities on the subject.

Man Meets Dog, by Konrad Lorenz (New York: Penguin, 1953). Delightful reading, although his theories about jackal and lupus types in domestic dogs are somewhat outdated.

Travel with Your Pet, by Paula Weideger and Geraldine Thorsten (New York: Simon & Schuster, 1973). A specialized reference for traveling dog owners.

For those who would like to join a humane organization, there are many throughout the country that would love to have you on their teams. If you have time and energy to offer, check to see what sorts of groups exist locally. You will no doubt find a shelter within driving distance that will appreciate volunteer help. Groups dedicated to building low-cost spay/neuter clinics are becoming more and more common, too—another avenue to explore.

To give mention to all the humane groups that are worth your support is a book in itself. The following, however, are outstanding, as well as prototypes for many smaller organizations. **The Humane Society of the United States** (2100 L Street N.W., Washington, D.C. 20037) works to prevent cruelty to all animals—from pets to exotic wildlife—through educational programs, publicity, and legal actions. Their numerous and ambitious major goals include:
- Reducing the overbreeding of cats and dogs
- Eliminating cruelty in hunting and trapping
- Exposing and eliminating the plight of animals in research
- Eliminating animal abuse in entertainment
- Correcting inhumane conditions in zoos and other exhibits
- Stopping cruelty to food animals
- Providing technical assistance to local humane groups
- Educating children and youth to respect all forms of life
- Monitoring anti-cruelty laws and their enforcement
- Protecting wildlife

Members of HSUS receive a quarterly newsmagazine and special reports on important animal issues. Many educational and technical materials are also available at nominal charge. The Junior Membership program, KIND, is open to young people between the ages of six and eighteen, who receive an informative magazine monthly, September through June.

The American Humane Association   (5351 S. Roslyn Street, Englewood, Colo. 80110) is "a non-profit corporation dedicated to the prevention of cruelty to adults, children and animals. The Association serves 1500 humane societies throughout the United States and Canada and is the national standard-setting agency in child protective services." One of their many unique accomplishments is the Hearing Dog Program, in which they train dogs to assist the deaf. The publications and materials they offer cover a wide range of subjects, both of a general and technical nature, and are very inexpensive. Members receive *American Humane*, a magazine that is well worth the cost of membership.

The American Society for the Prevention of Cruelty to Animals (441 East 92nd Street, New York, N.Y. 10028) is the oldest humane society in the country, having served the city of New York since 1866 as the official agency for the protection of all animals. It was started by Henry Bergh, known as America's first humanitarian. It is active in the areas of humane education and legislation, adoptions, shelters, veterinary care, animal rescue, licensing, and protection against cruelty. Recently, the ASPCA created a mobile adoption unit, which takes animals that are up for adoption into neighborhoods where there are no shelters. They also own and operate the Animalport, America's first stopover for animal air travelers at J. F. Kennedy International Airport in New York, for pets whose owners leave or arrive before or after they do.

The Massachusetts Society for the Prevention of Cruelty to Animals (350 South Huntington Avenue, Boston, Mass. 02130) was created in 1868 by George Angell. It operates eight shelters throughout the state, presents extensive educational programs, and enters into matters of law enforcement and legislation. The MSPCA also owns one of the largest and most comprehensive animal hospitals in the country, Angell Memorial. Several years ago their educational affiliate, the American Humane Education Society, produced an All-American Mutt campaign—an advertising kit for use by humane groups—to bring to the public's attention the attributes of mixed-breed animals. Several of the posters contained in the kit are pictured. These are still available and can be obtained by writing to AHES at the address of the MSPCA.

If you can't decide between a Shepherd, a Setter or a Poodle, get them all.

Adopt a mutt at your local humane society and get everything you're looking for, all in one dog. The intelligence of a Poodle and the loyalty of a Lassie. The bark of a Shepherd and the heart of a Saint Bernard. The spots of a Dalmatian, the size of a Schnauzer, and the speed of a Greyhound. A genuine, All-American Mutt has it all.

And your animal shelter has lots of All-American Mutts waiting for you. There are genuine, All-American Alley Kittens, too. Just come to:

Get the best of everything. Adopt a mutt.

Jeff and Mutt.

Every year hundreds of kids find happiness when they find a genuine, All-American Mutt of their own at the humane society's animal shelter.

All-American Mutts make perfect family dogs. They're loyal, fun-loving, easy-going. And they seem to have a special gift for helping kids learn to love.

Make an All-American Mutt, or genuine All-American Alley Kitten part of your family. Just come to:

Get the best of everything. Adopt a mutt.

No one wants to hear about animal abuse.

Except us.

If you see an animal being mistreated, call us. We want to hear about it because we can do something about it.

Feeling sorry for an animal in trouble is just a waste of time. Calling us isn't.

If you see an animal being mistreated, call:

Humphrey, Browning and MacDougall
for The American Humane Education Society

3.
Mutt Maintenance

*I*f you pick up a starving dog and make him prosperous,
he will not bite you. This is the principal difference
between a dog and a man.

Mark Twain

THIS chapter is devoted to the physical mutt and to the best years of his life, which extend from that last stage of puppyhood to that first sign of old age when he reaches the age of eight or nine. Because dogs are more set in their ways than most of us, they do not require constant changes in scenery, cuisine, and daily activity; in fact, they may even suffer as a result of what we would consider a refreshing change of pace. Having arrived at a way of providing the basic essentials—a good, balanced diet, a healthy program of exercise and grooming, and periodic medical checkups—we needn't burden ourselves with thinking up new and different ways in which to indulge our canine companions. Caring for a puppy—like caring for a young human—is a difficult task since he needs a good deal more by way of food, attention, and patience than any grown mutt would ever demand. So, here come the good years, during which you can relax and enjoy your mutt. He won't need so much food to grow on, so many training sessions, so many visits to the vet. Unlike wild dogs, he will retain some puppy characteristics, such as a love of play and an enormous amount of devotion and gratitude, for which you can be grateful, but he will have become a civilized member of your domestic sphere and pay you back full measure for your loving care.

The Mutt Who Came to Dinner

The pet-food business is one of the most visible aspects of the pet industry as a whole. Every day and night our favorite television programs are inevitably interrupted by a commercial for some kind of food that was packaged for our dogs or cats. There are well over 1,000 pet-food manufacturers in the country contributing their services and products to a business whose total gross sales equal or better the gross national product of several small countries. Dog food is produced by human-food companies (Carnation, General Foods, Ralston Purina, and Quaker Oats, for instance), tobacco firms (Liggett and Myers, which makes Alpo), and dog-food specialists (Gaines). These companies invest a great deal of money in research on animal foods, and they use many hundreds of animals to test their products. Unlike many human-food manufacturers or packagers, pet-food companies are usually careful to list ingredients and proportions and nutrients on the labels. But without knowing what all those ingredients actually are and what the dog's real needs are, it is easy to fall into the trap of feeding your pet a diet that is not nutritionally sound.

Protein

Proteins are what we call the numerous and complex combinations of amino acids that occur in all living cells; some of these can be synthesized in the body, while others, called essential amino acids, must be provided in food, since we cannot synthesize them rapidly enough for cell development. If one of these essential amino acids is missing or present only in insufficient quantity in our diets, our food is nutritionally deficient, and we will suffer as a result, since that deficiency will limit the effectiveness of the protein. Protein must be digestible if it is to be effective and is

What Do Dogs Need?

usually supplied in dog food by animal and vegetable proteins from meat, milk, and soybeans.

Fat

Fat is also an essential part of a dog's food, supplying calories for proper use of protein and essential acids important for skin and coat. Fatty acids also help in utilizing fat-soluble vitamins (A, D, E, and K).

Carbohydrates

Carbohydrates—starches and sugars—are also important, both for energy and for proper elimination, since cellulose acts to absorb water and to bind waste materials. They also help to prevent protein depletion as they supply quick energy.

Vitamins

Vitamins are, of course, significant in nutrition—both the fat-soluble and water-soluble types. The former aid in the growth and maintenance of cells in the eyes, skin, mucous membranes, bones, teeth, reproduction, blood clotting, muscles, and in calcium absorption. The water-soluble vitamins, which are not stored in the body, include the B vitamins, which have to do with appetite, growth, general metabolism, and a myriad other aspects of well-being. Many people like to add vitamin supplements to their pets' diets, but these are not necessary and, in fact, can be hazardous if the animals are being fed complete, balanced diets.

Minerals

Though there is much to be learned about minerals, it is known that they are necessary in certain quantities and proportions and play a role in metabolism. Calcium and phosphorus are needed in the largest amounts (for tooth and bone primarily) and in specific relationship to each other—1.2 to 1.4 parts of calcium to 1 part phosphorus is considered an optimum ratio. (Vitamin D is necessary to the utilization of these minerals, incidentally.) Sodium and chlorine are also important (these two add up to salt), as are iron, copper, cobalt, magnesium, potassium, iodine, and zinc, as well as a number of trace minerals, such as selenium, sulfur, manganese, molybdenum, and fluorine.

Water

Water is extremely important to all life, and in dogs, about 70 percent of body weight is made up of this vital fluid. It must be available—cool and fresh—all the time.

One of the most prominent concerns of pet-food manufacturers is palatability. Obviously, no dog food is worth much if the dog won't eat it, no matter how well it stacks up nutritionally. The Gaines Research Center (among other large companies) has spent a good deal of time and money trying to ascertain what dogs really like to eat in order to arrive at some general guidelines by which they can prepare their products.

What Do Dogs Like?

Gaines found that some breeds were more discriminating than others (poodles more than Labradors more than beagles), and that smaller dogs tended to be fussier than large ones. Older dogs, too, are slightly more picky about their food, but that may be caused by the fact that they have become accustomed to certain foods. Preferences change often as a dog ages, and, of course, spoiled dogs can readily train their owners into serving only the foods they like. Appetite is certainly a factor here; hungry dogs will always eat more readily whatever is put before them than a satiated dog.

But what makes one food preferable to another? We've all been told for years that dogs are color-blind, and it follows that they would be unable to detect redness in meat, since all they see is gray. But that may not be necessarily so; in one study it was found that dogs tended to prefer white to colored biscuits, for example. Most pet-food companies readily admit, however, that the red coloring in dog food is put there for the sake of the owner, not that of the pet.

Warmth has something to do with palatability. Most dogs would rather have warm or room-temperature food than refrigerated food, which is not surprising when you consider that dogs evolved as hunters of warm-blooded prey. Texture counts, too, since chunks and gnawable foods are easier to pick up and work over. This is where dogs know what's best for them, since foods requiring some chewing are invariably good for the teeth, keeping them free of tartar. Water added to food will help release odor, which makes food more attractive, although it does tend to make food less nutritious by weight. Aroma is very important, and many dogs like their meat relatively gamy and their bones well aged. And when it comes to meat, dogs seem to prefer their meat in this order: lamb, beef, horse, pork, and chicken. Liver and other offal are attractive to dogs, especially the fatty portions, which they often prefer to lean, red meat. Dogs like fatty food generally and are equipped to digest starch. Of the cereals, they seem to prefer wheat germ, though they like soybeans, wheat, barley, and maize as well. Even such vegetables as peas and carrots will be welcomed by some animals, though fruits are less appealing. Gaines found that dogs were indifferent to salt and that they didn't care for citrus juices. Nor did they like bitter flavors such as quinine, although dogs that have been accustomed to eating sweets will develop a sweet tooth.

The research goes on in ever-more sophisticated ways, and the companies continue to search for artificial or synthetic additives that will be cheaper to manufacture and as nutritious as natural ingredients, such as onions and garlic, which are still being used as flavoring agents in some dog food.

The Mutt Who Came to Dinner

BEGGING DOG
Pennsylvania
Circa 1955
Wood, painted; glass eyes
H., 21½″
Herbert W. Hemphill, Jr.

What Are the Choices?

Many manufacturers of pet food have proven their worthiness through the years by doing excellent work in research. One can be sure that Purina, Gaines, Hills, and the other major companies put a minimum of indigestible material (gristle, tails, hair, and so on) into their foods, considering the amount of money they have put into developing it. Interested dog owners can write to these firms for complete information about their products; each booklet is full of valuable, if somewhat less than digestible, prose and charts. Even these companies put some non-nutritional ingredients, such as food coloring, chemical preservatives, and flavoring agents, in their products, for the same reasons that human-food manufacturers put them in our food. But what about cheaper brands with less recognizable labels? Or more expensive brands available only through veterinarians? How does one pick one kind of dog food over another?

Dry Dog Food

For the economy-minded, dry dog food is the answer. For one thing, it contains only about 5 to 10 percent water, compared with canned food, which may contain 75 percent water. Clearly, pound for pound you get a lot more nutrition and energy for your money. Also, because of its low water content, dry food keeps well if stored in a cool, dry place, unlike canned food, which needs refrigeration after opening.

Dry food looks like a biscuit but actually is a full-feeding product (one that supplies the total nutritional requirements of the dog) and contains a great deal more than cereal matter. Meat and fish meals, dry-milk solids, and soybean products provide protein; vitamins and minerals are also present, as are fats and carbohydrates. The difference in the various types of dry food occurs in their preparation. Dog biscuits and kibbles are usually made of a dough that has been baked and broken up into pieces or formed into the shapes of bones, postmen, or what have you. Dog meal, which can be pelleted, is composed of cooked cereal and meat meal blended together and supplemented by vitamins and minerals and fats and milled into particles and coated with fat (for palatability as well as increased calories). Expanded dry food—of which Purina Chow is an example—is made of grains, meat meals, and vegetable and dairy products, which are mixed, steamed in a pressure cooker, and whipped into a mass that is then pushed through a die (or sieve) and expanded with steam and air into porous nuggets. These nuggets are then processed to remove moisture, and they become hard and crunchy. These foods contain at least 40 percent carbohydrate (or the expanding process won't work) and may also include some binding material, such as cellulose gum. Dry foods are low in fat, and if your dog is on an exclusively dog-food diet, it is usually a good idea to supplement each feeding with a tablespoon of vegetable oil per pound of food.

Dry food is excellent for your dog's teeth and gums, as it keeps tartar accumulation to a minimum. One problem, however, is that many dogs that have not been conditioned to dry food from weaning do not readily take to a completely dry diet and find a combination of two parts dry food to one part canned food a great deal more palatable.

Canned (or wet) Food

Feeding your dog canned food exclusively is an expensive proposition, particularly if you have a large dog. Most of what's in the can is water (about 75 percent), and 25 percent is food. A one-pound can contains about 500 calories; an equal amount of dry food contains about 1600 calories.

There are several kinds of canned food, and the title of the product will indicate which is which.

All meat. The all-meat products are usually called by the name of the meat: beef, chicken, lamb, etc. By law, these foods must contain at least 95 percent of that ingredient by weight. The all-meat products cannot be used exclusively. Any all-meat diet—canned or fresh—is heavily lacking in many nutrients that your dog needs.

Complete. Products marked "complete" dinner or diet do contain all the nutrients necessary for your dog and can be used exclusively. The foods with names like "beef dinner" or "meat balls" may contain as little as 25 percent of the named ingredient, while "meat-flavored" or "dog food" may contain less than 25 percent. Any can not marked "complete" should be left on the store's shelf.

Canned foods store well, of course, although once opened cannot be kept long without refrigeration. Also, they do not allow a dog to keep tooth tartar to a minimum.

Soft-Moist Food

As the name suggests, this type of dog food is a compromise. Soft-moist foods do contain all the nutrients your dog needs and are generally very palatable, but they are expensive.

The meat ingredients are specially treated with preservatives and cooked in a pressure blender so that the amount of moisture can remain higher than in dry foods (about 25 percent). Meat by-products amount to about 30 percent of the total, which also includes soybean meal, sugar, animal fat, preservatives (to reduce the likelihood of microorganisms growing in the food), humectants (to take up water and protect it from use by bacteria and microorganisms), and vitamins and minerals. Once cooked into a homogeneous mass, the food is then extruded, and forced air dries it into a consistency suitable for packaging in various shapes and sizes—such as hamburger, sausages, and chunks of meat.

These foods are packed in individual portions and sealed in cellophane, making them easy to store and convenient for people who travel a great deal and don't like the weight or bulkiness of the other foods.

Special Diets

One way in which scientific research has been able to help dogs in recent years is to bring to light the fact that not all dogs require the same amount of nutrition in their food. Puppies, for instance, require about twice the energy and protein of mature dogs. Old and overweight dogs need less energy, while pregnant and lactating bitches need nearly as much as puppies do. Active dogs need more food than sedentary ones, and dogs with metabolic disorders require special foods that supply certain deficiencies or omit certain substances.

Some special diets are available only through veterinarians because they involve diets that have been formulated on the basis of diagnostic tests. (Only one in sixteen dogs in the United States will require a special diet, so don't assume that yours needs one unless your veterinarian recommends it.)

Dogs with the following disorders are usually put on one of these prescription diets: diabetes, heart, liver, and kidney disorders, intestinal disabilities, food allergies, obesity, and urolithiasis. The meat used in these diets is predominantly lamb, since few dogs are allergic to it and most dogs seem to prefer it to other meats. Because these prescription diets are produced in relatively small quantities, their price is slightly higher.

Commercial pet-food companies have recently made available foods designed for the particular requirements of puppies, mature dogs, overweight dogs, and aging dogs. These are handy in the case of puppies as it eliminates the necessity of adding supplements, but mature, fat, and aging dogs will do perfectly well on a mature-dog diet so long as the portions are adjusted accordingly.

Homemade Foods

The most difficult way to achieve a nutritionally sound diet for your dog is to feed him homemade foods. Although dogs are similar to humans in their nutritional requirements, they are not the same, nor can dogs tolerate some of the foods that we do, especially of the spicy sort, or the variety of foods that we demand.

Nonetheless, included here for those who like to fuss are some tried-and-true recipes from people who have healthy, happy dogs. The first, invented by Dr. Donald R. Collins, author of *The Collins Guide to Dog Nutrition*, is designed for the average dog whose owner either scorns commercial food or has none in the house.

Mixed-Breed Meat Mix

¼ pound cooked hamburger
1 hard-boiled egg, crumbled
¼ pound raw rice
½ ounce raw beef liver
½ ounce dicalcium phosphate (from pharmacy)
   vitamin-mineral supplement (from your veterinarian)

Blend the cooked hamburger and the egg. Cook the rice until it is tender in plain water (about two cups) and drain. Chop the raw liver, blend it with the rice, and stir the whole thing into the hamburger-egg mixture. Stir in the dicalcium phosphate and the vitamin-mineral supplement (using the label directions for daily dosage). Serve warm or at room temperature. Calories: 930.

Mongruel

This concoction, from Mordecai Siegal's *The Good Dog Book*, is a low-calorie, high-potency hot or cold canine cereal for the overweight dog.

3½ cups rolled oats
½ cup dry powdered milk
¼ cup sunflower seeds
¼ cup diced fruit or diced dried beef
6 tablespoons molasses
4 tablespoons salad oil
1 tablespoon water
1 heaping tablespoon desiccated liver powder or brewers'
   yeast (optional)

Combine all ingredients except the sunflower seeds and stir well. The mixture must be agreeably moist without being soggy. Grease a large baking sheet (a jelly-roll pan is perfect, allowing you to stir without spilling) and spread the cereal in an even layer. Bake at 225° F. for twenty minutes, stir well, and bake for twenty minutes more. Stir again and bake until just lightly browned. Cool for five minutes. Then stir in the seeds and store in canisters in a cool, dry place between feedings. *Cold:* serve with skim milk. *Warm:* heat equal parts of Mongruel and skim milk with a pat of butter, or serve without liquid as a dry kibble. Calories: approximately 275 per one-cup serving.

Kimmel and Foster
Engraving
c. 1900

Mutt Maintenance

Mutt Loaf

This meat-free recipe, from Francis Sheridan Goulart's book *Bum Steers*, can be used as a once-or-twice-a-week daily meal or as an extender for everyday fare with commercial dog food.

> ½ cup unsugared, unsalted natural whole-wheat flakes
> ½ cup cracked wheat or bulgur
> ½ cup uncooked oatmeal
> 1 cup vegetable broth
> 3 medium raw carrots, ground
> 1 egg
> 2 tablespoons bone meal or dry milk powder
> ¼ cup soy granules or soy grits
> ½ bunch parsley, ground
> 1 medium onion, ground
>   undegerminated cornmeal

Soak the wheat flakes, cracked wheat, and oatmeal in the vegetable broth for fifteen minutes. Preheat the oven to 350° F. Combine the soaked grains with the carrots, egg, bone meal or milk powder, soy granules, parsley, and onion. Mix well. Adjust the consistency of the mixture to resemble uncooked meat loaf by adding cornmeal. Pack the mixture into a greased loaf pan that has been lightly dusted with cornmeal and bake for thirty minutes. Cool. Cut into chunks and store in a jar in the refrigerator. Yield: 5 to 6 half-cup servings or 12 extender portions for canned dog food.

Medicinal Mutt Meal

This recipe was contributed by Jenny Baum, a veterinary assistant who also works for Louise Sanders, a breeder of bull mastiffs. It is used for dogs that are ailing or recovering from an illness, as well as for bitches that are pregnant or nursing pups.

> 1   hard-boiled egg
> ½   cup cottage cheese
> 2   pieces whole-wheat bread, chopped
> 2 to 3   cups high-protein kibble
> ½ to ¾   cup ground beef or beef liver
>   vitamin-mineral supplement

Mix all ingredients and serve at room temperature. For an ailing animal weighing approximately 50 pounds, Jenny will feed this meal twice a day; pregnant and lactating bitches get fed four times a day. For a dog twice this size, double the quantity.

How Much Food Should Dogs Be Fed? The proper amount of food depends, of course, on the dog's weight, the exercise he gets, his age, general condition, the stress he undergoes, and the weather. Dogs in cold climates need more energy (or calories) in the winter than in the summer; house pets need less energy than outside dogs; nervous animals may metabolize food faster than low-keyed mutts; and puppies will need much more than older dogs.

The chart below translates calories into a practical daily ration of food for normal, average adult dogs. Determine your dog's ideal weight (you should be able to feel his ribs easily, and there should be a "tuck-up," or waist, behind the ribs and in front of the hind legs). Then find the proper amount of calories he needs to maintain (or achieve) that weight and select the type of food you want to give him. Check the label to determine the actual calorie count. Weigh the dog occasionally (or feel for his ribs) to be sure that he isn't losing or gaining too much on the diet you have chosen.

Ideal weight (pounds)	Daily calories	Dry food* (cups)	Wet food** (cans)	Soft-moist foods*** (6-oz. packages)	Dry and wet foods combined (dry —cups; wet —cans)
5 lbs.	250	¾	½	½	⅔ dry; ⅛ wet
10	420	1⅓	⅞	¾	1 dry; ¼ wet
15	570	1⅔	1⅛	1	1⅓ dry; ⅓ wet
20	700	2⅛	1½	1⅓	1¾ dry; ⅓ wet
25	825	2½	1⅔	1½	2 dry; ⅓ wet
40	1,160	3⅔	2⅓	2¼	2¾ dry; ½ wet
50	1,350	4¼	2⅔	2½	3¼ dry; ¾ wet
90	2,150	6¾	4⅓	4	5 dry; 1 wet
120	2,900	9	5¾	5½	6⅔ dry; 1½ wet
150	3,600	11¼	7¹/₅	7	8 dry; 2 wet
175	2,635	11⅓	7¹/₅	7	8 dry; 2⅛ wet

  * Dry-food measurements are based on an average of 1,500 calories per pound; the "cup" is an 8-ounce measuring cup (though it holds far less than 8 ounces of dry food).
 ** Wet-food measurements are based on an average of 500 calories per pound; we are assuming that a can equals 16 ounces (not all do).
*** Soft-moist-food measurements are based on an average of 1,400 calories per pound or 525 calories per 6-ounce package.

Keep in mind that if you give your dog two feedings a day, the amounts listed on the chart should be divided into two portions. (They need not be equal portions; many people prefer to serve larger meals in the evening than in the morning.) If you give your dog regular treats or leftovers, you should subtract those calories from the dog's regular meals, but occasional treats can probably be sneaked in without doing any harm.

Once you have reached the ideal diet, stick to it. Even dogs that have eaten their fill will be happy for a treat, and many dogs are prone to overweight because they do not regulate their own diets or count their own calories. It is also important to note that dogs flourish on the same diet, and changing foods frequently causes intestinal upset.

Obese Dogs

Dog owners often look for excuses for obesity in dogs, just as they do in themselves. Glandular disorders may indeed promote obesity, but almost always the cause is just plain overeating. Obesity is a serious problem, causing or aggravating innumerable ailments in otherwise healthy animals. Forcing a dog to carry around a few extra pounds can put undue stress on the skeleton, the heart, and the digestive organs.

When a dog has become overweight, the simplest method of putting him on a diet is to give him less food, keeping up the proper proportions of nutrients. Some veterinarians recommend a reduction by a third, but it is probably sufficient to cut back on about 25 percent of the dog's daily ration until the desired weight is reached, gradually working back up to the ration recommended for that weight.

Underweight or Malnourished Dogs

The signs of malnourishment in a dog are pretty obvious: a dry hair coat, emaciated appearance with a distended abdomen, dehydration, scabs and sores on the skin, and possibly a sweet breath odor. The first step in such a case is to check with the vet to be sure that the dog is basically healthy. Some prescription diet may be recommended for a period of time in order to give the dog a good start with a high-calorie, high-protein ration. Or you can devise your own (see page 104). Or, simply start with the regular program of feeding based on the chart, using the dog's ideal (not present) weight as an index. If the dog appears to be less than a year old, see the puppy feeding section.

Although most starving dogs will eat almost anything, it is surprisingly common for a malnourished dog to be picky about his food, whether for psychological

DOG
Alberto Giacometti
Hirshhorn Museum and Sculpture Garden
Smithsonian Institution
Washington, D.C.

The Mutt Who Came to Dinner

Mary Bloom

reasons of insecurity or just because the dog cannot adjust quickly to a regular offering of good food. It is thus often a problem to get the proper amount of calories where they should go. Start off by selecting the most palatable, digestible food possible, which means canned or semi-moist food rather than dry. Although this may be the most expensive diet, it can eventually be fed together with dry food once the dog's appetite picks up. Work the dry food into the diet gradually as soon as the dog is getting a sufficient amount of daily calories. If the dog won't eat a full meal at one sitting (give him half an hour or so), give the food in several daily feedings, offering as much as the animal will eat. If the dog still doesn't get his full ration, supplement the food with one to three tablespoons of oil per pound of food. A particularly good food supplement at this point is fish, or fish oil, since it supplies vitamins A and D along with the fat. A vitamin-mineral supplement is important for the malnourished dog at this early stage.

Puppies

Growing puppies need about twice the calories and nutrients of adult dogs. But simply feeding a puppy twice as much dog food will not be adequate, since adult dog foods are not as digestible as foods designed especially for puppies, and the necessary nutrients will often fail to be utilized. Commercial puppy foods, whether dry, wet, or semi-moist, are best. These brands are packaged with feeding instructions according to the pup's weight and age and are based on years of research.

Most experts agree that puppies up to the age of three (some say four) months should be fed four times a day (morning, noon, evening, and just before bedtime); puppies up to the age of six months will do well on three feedings (morning, noon, and evening); puppies up to twelve months (or even as adults) can have two feedings (one-third of the daily ration in the morning; two-thirds in the evening). If the puppies eat all of their food immediately at each meal for three days in a row, it is advisable to add 5 percent more to each feeding and to continue doing so until the pup leaves a little each time.

If one doesn't have access to special puppy foods, adult food can be used, but add extra supplements as follows:

To dry food, add one tablespoon of corn oil and one tablespoon of chopped beef liver per pound of food.

To canned food, add two ounces per pound of one of the following: cottage cheese, hard-boiled egg; cheese; cooked beef, lamb, or fish; or four tablespoons of dry skim milk.

Between the ages of ten and twelve months, the puppy will begin to eat less than he is given. This is no cause for alarm, because his growth rate is slowing down and he needs less. This is the point at which one can begin to put the dog on an adult diet, using adult foods and quantities. As with any dog, regardless of age, the changeover should be gradual to avoid digestive upset.

Calorie Requirements of Puppies

Weight	Calories	Weight	Calories
1 lb.	130	25 lb.	1,650
3 lb.	343	35 lb.	2,100
6 lb.	572	50 lb.	2,750
12 lb.	943	70 lb.	3,542
20 lb.	1,384	90 lb.	4,302

How Should Dogs Be Fed?

There are various methods of feeding dogs, and your choice will probably depend on your life-style, as well as on the dog's age and condition. Many experts believe that dogs conditioned to dry food and to having food available all the time will naturally regulate their intake to their own needs. This method is called the self-feeding method, and it must be started in puppyhood if it is to be effective. Nursing puppies will call on their mother whenever they feel hungry, and assuming that she's willing, they will eat when and however much they like. This same principle applied to an older dog can be accomplished by having food around all day long in a dish or feeder (unmoistened dry food won't spoil, which is why it is the only kind that can be used in this method). Dogs that tend to be overweight or those conditioned to a one- or two-meal-a-day program can't be easily shifted into a self-feeding system, since they will overeat and must have their daily ration controlled by the feeder.

Self-feeding makes it difficult for the feeder to tell exactly how much a dog is eating and when it has gone off-feed, but the advantages are great. The feeder's time is negligible; he simply has to select the food and keep the container full and accessible to the dog. Coprophagy (the eating of feces) and nervous chewing will be minimal, and contented dogs are quieter and less likely to pick on or bully other dogs in competition for food.

For those whose dogs are not on a dry-food diet or those who want to be able to know and regulate exactly what their dogs eat, the portion-control program is the best method of feeding, and most dogs will be perfectly satisfied with one or two feedings a day. As with self-feeding, water should be available at all times, but mealtimes should be regular, consistent, and limited (pick up the food after thirty minutes if the dog has not eaten it). Just as dogs do best on one type of food every day, so they require the regular routine of mealtime for good appetite, good digestion, and regular elimination.

Another important "regular" is the place where a dog is fed. Not only are changes likely to upset a dog and make him nervous or insecure, but a dog who is taught to eat in only one place will be less apt to accept food from strangers or be attracted to an open garbage can.

It Looks Good Enough to Eat

ACCORDING to Dr. Edward H. Peeples, Jr., of Virginia Commonwealth University, in Richmond, nearly a million Americans regularly consume pet food. In 1974, the Senate Nutrition Committee reported that "one-third of the pet food purchased in slums is eaten by humans," although their data was not based on surveys but on an educated guess by the Center for Science in the Public Interest. For obvious reasons, people are reluctant to admit that they eat pet food, and it is difficult to make any kind of systematic study. Nevertheless, these experts recommend that pet-food production be controlled for safety and that information about the nutritional value and deficiencies in pet food be accumulated with human consumption in mind. Nutritionist Adele Davis was known to have remarked that ounce for ounce many pet foods are nutritionally superior to many refined and processed human foods.

THREE CHILDREN WITH DOG
Circa 1840-50
Oil on canvas
H. 41″ W. 34½″
The Newark Museum

HOOKED RUG
Found in Pennsylvania
Last quarter of the 19th century
45½″ × 53″
Thomas K. Woodard,
American Antiques & Quilts

Buttons

THE DOG WHO LIVES BY THE SEA

BUTTONS lives in Stonington, Maine, a small fishing village, with Mrs. Martha Hall, a woman who has been a resident of Stonington for longer than most folks in town can remember. Up until quite recently, Martha has lived in a one-room shack with no running water and one electric light bulb. Buttons has her own doghouse—not much smaller than the shack—right outside Martha's front door.

But life has taken a turn for Martha and Buttons. The owners of the shack that Martha lives in have decided that Martha and Buttons should live out their lives in comfort, so the one-room shack is being transformed into a four-room cottage, with a real bathroom, a real kitchen, a bedroom, and a glassy living room that overlooks the harbor. For Martha, the new home is beyond anything she ever dreamed possible, and she looks forward with great enthusiasm to being able to have a Christmas tree this year. "It's the most wonderful thing that's ever happened to me in my life," she says. "I'm going to be the queen of Ocean Street."

Buttons, however, appears unconcerned about the major changes taking place. During the renovations, Martha has moved to a small bunkhouse down the road. But Buttons refuses to leave her home. She remains in her doghouse and greets the steady stream of curious townfolk who come to see what's happening to "Martha's and Button's place."

Hugh Mohr

Run, Don't Walk

(OR, EXERCISING YOUR MUTT)

WALKING the dog has always been considered a necessary evil, one of those tedious· routines connected with owning an animal that needs to get out of the house every day. Many people who object to the chore hire dog-walkers to do it for them or let their dogs grow fat from lack of exercise. Some people simply let their dogs loose rather than supervise the exercise, and those dogs often end up hit by cars, involved in fights, or lost forever.

But if we think of walking our dogs in terms of our own fitness, the chore need no longer be something to suffer or ignore. Here are a few suggestions.

Running

If you jog a mile or two a day, take the dog along—on a leash until the dog has learned to heel properly and not to be attracted by other joggers. (Some communities ban dogs because loose animals can be a real hindrance to runners, but if you make a special application, demonstrating your own animal's good behavior, you may be granted special permission.) Even the best-trained dog will not always heel when other dogs or distractions cross his path, so be on your guard. One unleashed dog showed a good deal of common sense by refusing to jog in 100-degree weather, choosing instead to sit it out under a tree, while his dripping owner made his daily round of the park.

ATALANTA IN CALYDON
Aubrey Beardsley

Bicycling

This, too, can be a convenient way of running the dog, although the cycler should become adept at riding the bike, holding the leash, and avoiding entanglements. The dog must be trained to follow or accompany—not chase—the bike; some dogs love to chase moving objects, and other people on bikes get pretty annoyed if they are those objects.

Horseback Riding

A leash can be impractical here, but if the dog is trained to come when called, trail riding can be a good way of getting two animals exercised at once. Some dogs are frightened by horses and will bark at their heels, inviting a good swift kick in the jaws, and some horses are annoyed by the presence of dogs, but time and conditioning should solve the problem. (Remember that fox hunters and foxhounds have worked together successfully for years.)

Hiking

Most dogs, especially those with hunting-dog blood in their veins, will love accompanying their owners on trips through the woods and fields, and they can be wonderful companions, noticing birds and other creatures that we less sensitive humans might miss. Caution should be taken in the mountains and in deep woods, however, to keep the dog under control. Be sure that your dog is trained to come when called, and in unfamiliar areas, keep your dog on a leash (some parks require leashes).

Ecologists like to see some of the larger predators repopulating our woods, but dog owners should be aware of the dangers they pose. The average dog is no match for a bear, coyote, or mountain lion and can get into plenty of trouble even with the smaller but, in some ways, equally effective defenses of skunks, porcupines, and raccoons, which can even be found relatively close to home in suburban nieghborhoods. Also, a dog with a hunting instinct can quickly disappear in search of a rabbit. There are several cases on record in which small dogs were quickly dispatched by alligators whose peaceful naps were interrupted—not in the heart of the Everglades but alongside a golf course in a heavily residential area in South Carolina.

Camping out with a dog can be a marvelous experience, but be sure the dog is tied while you sleep and that his food is securely put away after suppertime so as not to lure predators. Learn some of the first-aid measures involved in removing porcupine quills and eradicating (or minimizing) skunk odors for your own peace of mind if not for actual application. Taking a dog for a walk in the woods during the hunting season can be risky, too. Even if your dog bears no resemblance to a deer or a quail, remember that hunters—especially those who go out hunting once a year—tend to shoot before they think, making no living creature safe during the hunting season. John Steinbeck, in *Travels with Charley*, describes how he wrapped Charley's tail in red Kleenex and fastened it with rubber bands in order to alert hunters.

Tennis

Most clubs that offer tennis to their members tend to discourage dogs on the premises, and with good reason. But if you have access to private facilities or to places where dogs are allowed, your mutt can be awfully useful in helping you improve your skills. Think of the energy you'll save in practicing your serves if you get your dog trained to retrieve the balls. (If you are a golfer, don't get your dog to help retrieve your drives; some golf balls contain lead, which is toxic.)

Indoor Activities

For those who don't or can't indulge in outdoor sports, Gaines has some suggestions for indoor activities that require little energy on your part to keep your dog fit. As you watch TV, during each commercial call your dog to you and tell him to sit. If there are several people in the room, have each of them call him. Or, walk around the room with him, stopping at each piece of furniture and having him sit. These up-and-down exercises help greatly to firm abdominal muscles and hindquarters, and they have application in many aspects of your daily routine—doing the laundry, dusting, vacuuming; just have the dog follow you around and sit whenever you stop.

Retrieving can also be done in the house. The ball needn't be thrown very far, but don't pick a spot where the dog is likely to run into furniture.

Whatever your exercise regimen, you are going to encounter one problem—inclement weather. Most dogs come fully dressed with a coat that should be able to withstand the cold and wet, but some dogs, because they have not been given a chance to become conditioned to bad weather, never do develop a good undercoat or guard hairs, and those dogs should be protected by some artificial means. Pet shops are full of coats and hats and pet umbrellas designed for dogs who need more than their own coat. And whether your dog uses man-made clothing or not, be sure he's warm and dry once you have him back in the house.

In some areas, salt that is put on the streets in winter to melt the ice and snow can cause discomfort to a dog's pads. There are dog boots on the market for those animals who will keep them on (and those are very few); it is more practical to simply wash off the salt with warm water.

*T*he great pleasure of the dog is that you may make a fool of yourself with him and not only will he not scold you, but he will make a fool of himself, too.

Samuel Butler

PAIR OF DANCING DOGS
U.S.
Second half of the 19th century
Wood, painted
Mr. and Mrs. Kenneth Hammitt

Games Dogs Play

IN SPITE of the increase in human exercise these days, there are still many people who would prefer to remain in one spot and let their dogs exercise around them. This involves letting the dog off the leash. If other dogs are exercised in the same area, he'll have a chance to romp and play with them. Or you may keep your dog involved in a game of your own.

Catch   For a mutt with retriever instincts, this game can be engrossing and will—if the owner is willing—continue for hours until the dog drops of exhaustion. All that you need is some space, a nice stick or a sturdy ball that can't be deflated or torn to bits by the canine's canines, and a good throwing arm. Some dogs love this even more if you are near water into which the ball can be thrown.

Frisbee   An entertaining variation on the catch theme, playing Frisbee is the favorite game of many dogs we know. A dog in New York City's Central Park once caught over 200 Frisbees in a row without missing! Be sure to check the edges of the Frisbee periodically, because a rough or sharp rim can damage the dog's mouth.

Hide-and-Seek   A dog with a hound somewhere in his past will be naturally inclined to distinguish and follow a scent, and the owner of one of these dogs can have a lot of fun laying a track (his own, of course) and then watching the dog sniff it out. You will need a friend to assist you here, to hold the dog and prevent him from seeing you (a blindfold will do, of course). It isn't always easy to get a dog to concentrate on the scent, since city parks and neighborhood lots are often replete with distracting odors, but, supposedly, there is a man who successfully trained his dog to track in the middle of Chicago.

119

Paul Duckworth

Lucy
THE ATHLETIC MUTT

A FEW years ago, Billie Jean King was given a tiny puppy, one of an unplanned litter produced by her brother's Labrador retriever. Billie Jean and her husband, Larry, are constantly on the move, traveling to tennis matches and business meetings all over the world, and they were delighted to have a pup to accompany them, especially since it, or Lucy, as they dubbed her, looked as if she would remain relatively small and be easy to transport. Lucy became an excellent and adaptable traveler, but she continued to grow until she attained the size (and appearance) of an Old English sheepdog. Nevertheless, she managed to keep up with the busy Kings, who have taken her everywhere, including to the White House. She watches Billie Jean's tennis matches and lies quietly beneath conference tables when Larry meets with his business associates, but she is also an athlete on her own. Although she takes after her now-identifiable sheepdog father in looks, she is her mother's child when it comes to sports, of which swimming is her favorite. She prefers ponds and lakes, but even small puddles are alluring. Lucy's idea of a perfect way to spend a vacation is to go river rafting in California with Billie Jean and Larry, where she has a chance to combine her love of travel with her fondness for water.

ONE OF the most pleasant responsibilities of pet-owning that is often forgotten is grooming. It is important in a dog's life not only to keep him looking good but also to give him a few minutes of your undivided attention. It also serves as a means of preventing or detecting potential health hazards. Becoming familiar with your dog's body is invaluable in spotting abnormal conditions if and when they appear.

Grooming can be enjoyable for both you and your dog if you establish a routine at the outset. Begin with daily sessions of several minutes. When the dog gets used to being handled, groom him when necessary: short-haired dogs several times a week and long-haired dogs daily.

Grooming Your Mutt

Basic Coat Care

Brushing your dog regularly will make him look better, smell better, and have fewer skin problems, and you won't have to vacuum as frequently to pick up shed hair. Coat care depends on the length of the dog's hair.

Short hair   Short-haired dogs should be brushed several times a week, but during the shedding season you may want to do it more often. A rubber curry brush is marvelous; it won't scratch, so you can bear down firmly but gently to remove the dead hair and stimulate the skin. Brush with the grain of the hair. You may have a residue of loose hair left on the coat after brushing; this can be removed with a cloth or a rubber glove.

Medium-length hair   For an effective job, you will need both a comb (double-sided combs with wide teeth on one side and narrower teeth on the other are good) and a firm bristle brush. Brush with the grain of the coat and then comb to put the coat back in order. Unsnarl mats or tangles gently with the wide-tooth side of your comb; sometimes a drop or two of oil on the mat helps. If you can't work out the mat, snip it with scissors.

Long hair   You will need a stiff long-bristle brush and a double-sided or wide-tooth comb for a dog with long hair. When purchasing the comb, select the one with the longest teeth. Long-haired dogs with heavy undercoats should be brushed daily—mats form quickly in the undercoat and tend to trap moisture under them, resulting in skin problems. Brush from the skin out, picking up the loose undercoat, and then brush with the grain of the hair to remove the loose guard hair. Comb to put the hair back in order.

Bathing

It's difficult to find agreement among experts on how often a dog should be bathed. If you regularly groom your pet, it's possible that he may never need a bath. On the other hand, if you're lax about brushing, or if a skin problem is present, or if parasites

121

decide to nest in his coat, a bath will be necessary. Then there are those unexpected accidents, such as encounters with skunks, that necessitate a bath.

Place your dog into a tub filled with water to the level of his elbows. Proceed calmly so he won't be frightened. Put a wad of cotton in each ear and a few drops of mineral oil in his eyes; this will help keep the water out. To wet him down, a spray attachment is ideal; short of that, use a sponge. Once he is wet, lather him up, scrub with your fingers, and rinse very thoroughly. A soap residue can create skin problems. If the weather is warm, it is most convenient to bathe the dog outdoors, towel-dry him, and let the sun do the rest. If the weather is cool and you must bathe him indoors, be sure he is completely dry before allowing him to go out.

If your dog does have a run-in with a skunk, sponge him with tomato juice and then bathe him well. Another remedy claimed to have merit is Massengill's douche sponged on before bathing.

Ears

Ears should be given a routine cleaning at least once a month with a cotton swab that has been saturated in hydrogen peroxide, rubbing alcohol, or mineral oil. Use a Q-tip that has been similarly saturated to wipe out the folds of the inside of the outer ear (do NOT stick the Q-tip *in* the ear). Very thick hair growing on the inside of the ear should be either trimmed or plucked out. It can cause retention of dirt, wax, and / or moisture, all of which can be the source of aggravating problems.

Possible trouble signs in the ears are inflammation of the inner part of the ear, tilting of the dog's head, foul odor, persistent head shaking, and frequent rubbing or scratching. You should consult your veterinarian as soon as possible if any of these symptoms occur.

Eyes

All you need do to routinely care for your dog's eyes is to wipe away, with a piece of tissue or cotton moistened in boric acid or saline solution, the discharge that may appear at the inside corner of each eye.

Teeth

Tooth decay is one problem that you will most likely not encounter with your dog. Calculus, or tartar—a hard deposit found at the base of the teeth at the gum line—is. The presence of dry food (kibble or meal) in your dog's diet will help to control the problem. If your dog is on a soft diet, give him dog biscuits, bones, or rawhide to gnaw on. (A regular "brushing" can also keep tartar in check if you are so inclined to do this for him. If he will tolerate it, brush with a firm up-and-down motion; if not, rub the

teeth with a piece of cotton or toweling.) A teaspoon each of salt and baking soda in a cup of water makes an excellent dentifrice.

Bad breath may or may not be a dental problem and should be checked by your veterinarian.

Nails

A dog who is outside a great deal—city or country—may never need a nail trim. A house dog, no doubt, will.

There are a number of different kinds of trimmers to choose from and the best type for you will depend somewhat on the size of your dog's nails. For a small dog, one of the following two is easy to manipulate: a small-bladed scissor with a claw-size notch or a clipper that resembles those used by humans except that it, too, is notched.

For dogs with larger nails, try either the guillotine or curved-blade variety, which both have larger openings.

With the dog at your side (your left side if you're right-handed, your right side if you're left-handed), put your arm around the dog, pressing him close to you with your upper arm, leaving the lower part of your arm and your hand free to pick up each paw. Lift the paw and remove only the curve of the nail. With dogs who have white nails, clip just short of the pink that is visible under the nail (this is a vein, called the quick). If the nails are black, trim a little nail off at a time. If you do cut too far and cause some bleeding, apply styptic.

A Bit of the Hair of the Dog That Bit You

*L*ike cures like, similia similibus curantur, *the Romans believed, like many ancient people before them, and they commonly bound hairs of a dog that bit someone to that person's wound in order to make it heal better. This was the case even if the dog was rabid, and the cure was recommended for centuries by serious medical books, about the only change up until medieval times being that the hair of the dog that bit you be burned before application. By that time it was also believed that the best cure for a hangover was a drink of the same poison that stifflicated you the night before, and the old proverb* a hair of the dog that bit you *was applied to this practice. The first mention of the phrase in this sense is in John Heywood's* Proverbs *(1546): "I pray thee leat me and my felow have a heare of the dog that bote us last night—and bitten were we both to the braine aright." Today no one puts dog hairs on dog bites, but* the hair of the dog that bit you *is still a universal "remedy" for a hangover. The practice makes some sense, too, for alcohol sedates those rebounding nerves that make hangovers so acutely painful.*

       Robert Hendrickson

Fleas and Ticks

IT'S LIKELY that either fleas or ticks or both will create the single biggest problem you have to handle during your dog's lifetime. These two parasites are formidable, and unless kept in check, can cause an unimaginable siege.

Ticks are the most difficult of the two to deal with, because of their extraordinarily high propagation rate, their resistance to insecticides, and their ability to live for long periods of time without feeding. There are numerous varieties of ticks, and some can cause severe problems. The wood tick, for instance, no longer confined to the Rocky Mountain region, infects man with Rocky Mountain spotted fever, and the spinose ear tick, found in the southwestern United States, penetrates the dog's ear canal and nestles against the eardrum. The tick you're most likely to encounter, however, is the brown dog tick.

The best tick-control method is regular inspection of your dog and removal of any ticks you might find. Pay particular attention to the dog's ears, stomach, armpits, and feet—all favorite nesting places of the tick. The most effective way to remove a tick is to first hold a small wad of alcohol- or ether-soaked cotton over it for a moment or so (this is to anesthetize the tick so it will be less resistant). Then grip the tick from the top and bottom with a pair of tweezers and slowly pull it out of the skin. Burn the tick or flush it down the toilet immediately.

If you see the beginning of a tick infestation, merely removing them from your pet is not enough, as they can live for some time in other warm spots around the house. An insecticide should be sprayed in all wall crevices and like areas, and, of course, your dog's sleeping area. Bombs or fogs are also available, which your veterinarian may carry. Care must be exercised with their use, as they are potentially dangerous.

Fleas are more easily eradicated than ticks if you act when you first discover evidence of them (the evidence being either sighting the flea itself, the presence of little black specks on your dog's skin—"flea dirt"—crusty or raw patches on your dog's skin, the result of bites, or little itchy bumps on yourself). If not nipped in the bud, however, the female flea will deposit her eggs in the house, eventually causing yet more fleas to contend with.

There are many brands and methods of protection against and for eradication of fleas, and there are dogs who may have adverse reactions to them, so, to some extent, you will need to use the trial-and-error method until you determine what your pet will tolerate. The most important point to remember before using anything is: DON'T USE PRODUCTS IN COMBINATION. This can be very hazardous.

Here are a few general pointers:

Collars Before putting a flea collar on your dog, aerate it for a day or so. Fasten it loosely enough so that two fingers can fit between it and your dog's neck. Also, check frequently for skin irritation; if there are any signs, remove the collar immediately.

Flea Tags Flea-repellent collars and tags are petroleum-based and not intended to be ingested, so if you have a small dog and see that the tag is dangling in the water bowl, remove it and try something else. Also, do not attach a flea tag to a flea collar; attach it to your dog's regular collar.

Sprays Don't spray your dog's head, and if you have birds, be careful that they do not come in contact with the aerosol.

Powders In addition to checking fleas on your dog, powders are a good means of eliminating fleas from your pet's bedding. If you are using the powder for the bedding of a nursing mother with puppies, be sure that the powder is rotenone-based; it is nontoxic and the most effective powder of those that are available commercially.

Dips Be sure to follow the dilution instructions carefully before sponging your dog with a dip. A shampoo beforehand allows for better skin penetration. If your dog is really infested, your vet can probably give you something more potent than you can buy across the counter.

Again, removing the fleas from your dog is wasted effort if they have infested the house. A bomb or fog will have to be used for a severe infestation, but short of that, the vacuum cleaner is your best weapon. Turn on the vacuum and spray nontoxic insecticide into it. Vacuum everything and every place on or in which a flea might hide—rugs, furniture, mattresses, drapes. If you can spray it all without damaging the fabric, do so. Wash your bedding and particularly any bedding your dog might have. Disposable vacuum cleaner bags should be discarded immediately, and permanent type bags should be emptied and the inside of the bag sprayed with the insecticide.

CROUCHING DOG
Possibly carved by a Long Island decoy maker
Early 20th century
Wood, carved and painted; glass eyes
L., 23″
David M. S. Pettigrew

*T*hey say a reasonable number of fleas is good fer a dog—keeps him from broodin' over bein' a dog.

Edward Noyes Westcott

Flea Facts

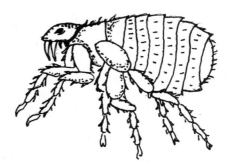

- A flea may wait as long as a year before hatching from its cocoon.
- Fleas prefer women to men.
- A flea can jump as high as eighteen inches.
- The male flea, comparatively speaking, has the largest penis in the animal kingdom (some guys have all the luck). In fact, he has two penises, one entwined with the other.
- Copulation between fleas lasts from three to nine hours (ah, to come back as a flea).

Tick Trivia

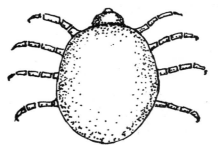

- The female brown dog tick lays up to 2,500 eggs.
- Rocky Mountain spotted fever, a sometimes fatal disease in man, is transmitted by ticks.
- Ticks can live for up to two years without feeding.
- Most varieties of ticks will attach themselves to three hosts during a lifetime, enough to tick anybody off.

EVEN the most dedicated homebodies have to leave home once in a while, and people with dogs who plan to be away for more than a day must take their animals into account, if not actually into their luggage. Ludwig Bemelmans, author of the celebrated *Madeline* books and a distinguished world traveler, was a great dog lover, and it never would have occurred to him not to have a dog or two in tow. His problem, which arose in a long-gone era of elegance, was probably a bit different from yours and mine: "You have to cross oceans on ships . . . and you must use particular ships, which don't require them to stay in the kennels. I often travel on freighters so that my dog will not be left alone."

Even if ocean liners are no longer the usual mode of conveyance for the traveler, the jet plane certainly is, to say nothing of the lesser forms of transportation such as the train, car, and family camper. All of these may be successfully used to transport mutt as well as owner (with a few exceptions), and some can even be trusted to ship the mutt on his own. (Major interstate bus lines do not have room for pets.)

Dogs are adaptable creatures and unlike cats are usually more oriented to their people than their places. If they could talk, they would probably tell you to take them along. Those who want to leave the dog behind and enjoy their vacations mutt-free or those whose dogs are not in good health or are in heat must find some means of seeing that their dogs are adequately cared for in their absence. But all of these various alternatives require preparation and information in advance, and so we have devised a set of guidelines for the traveling mutt owner.

The Mobile Mutt

A Travel Guide for the Mutt Owner

Legalities

Even if you are only traveling within the country, it's a sensible precaution to carry with you some proof that the dog has had a rabies shot within the past year and a health certificate signed by a veterinarian, just in case your dog is involved in an emergency, accident, or other incident. If you are planning to travel by train or plane, the dog is likely to be checked at some point, so be aware of the requirements of the state of destination by calling or writing to the Board of Health in the capital city.

International travel will also require a health certificate and a proof of rabies shot stamped by a federal veterinarian (your own vet will know where to find the one in your state). Check the consulates of all foreign countries you intend to visit to find out whether any other regulations apply. The United Kingdom (including Ireland) requires that all pets be placed in quarantine for a minimum of six months, which disqualifies that country for short visits with pets in tow, but France, Italy, and Germany need only the health certificate and proof of rabies shot (although the German certificate must be in German, and the Italian certificate must also include a statement from your vet that he has a license to practice). Several islands in the Caribbean also require quarantine periods, and several countries require special permits. Hawaii requires a 120-day quarantine and the state government will charge a boarding fee of at least $220 for a dog.

Airplane Travel

Airlines will usually accept pets. Check ahead and find out their rules and procedures and be sure to book a reservation, since most planes can carry only a limited number of animals. Also, be sure that your dog carrier meets with airline regulations. Because of recent protests from animal lovers about the inhumane conditions that pets have had to suffer in the luggage compartments in the past, most airlines take good care of their animal passengers; however, also ask them about the air pressure in the luggage compartment. DC-10's, for instance, are to be avoided, because the pressurization is not adequate to create sufficiently warm conditions. Also to be avoided is the yo-yo flight—the plane that makes many stops on the way to its final destination. Whenever possible, book yourself and your pet on a direct flight.

Train Travel

Train travel is rather more pleasant for dogs, since they can often accompany their owners on a leash rather than being shunted off to a baggage car. This is not always possible, however. The management of Amtrak, for instance, allows pets only in the baggage car and then only if the dog is in a secure, well-ventilated container. Metroliner and some of the newer trains don't even have baggage cars, and thus don't take pets at all. If your dog must ride with the bags, check to see if you will be allowed to visit, feed, and exercise him en route during stops. If the trip involves transfer from one train or airplane to another, be on hand to supervise. There are unpleasant stories about animals in their crates being left out in the open on cold, rainy platforms or even being lost by having been transferred to the wrong connecting cars.

Whether you travel by plane or train, you should be prepared to purchase some kind of carrying case or crate. Although the material should be light enough to be portable, it should be as sturdy as possible and well built, with no sharp, protruding edges and no lead-based paint. Active dogs will probably do best in a case just large enough to allow them to lie down and stand up but not large enough to allow pacing. The case should be well ventilated but not too open, if the dog is likely to feel insecure. (Some animals like to see something of what is going on, however, so don't keep them entirely in the dark.) Bedding should be provided—soft toweling or a blanket—and cleaned during and after the trip as necessary. If the dog is going to be fed and watered on the way by you or by an employee of the airline or train, include water and food dishes, as well as instructions and a leash in a bag attached to the side of the case. Next, mark in large legible writing on the case itself the dog's name, your name, address, and telephone number, both at home and at your destination, with any special instructions about feeding (or about the possibility of being bitten, if your dog is a nervous one). If you have a crate rather than a commercial dog carrier, mark also in large letters "Handle with Care: Dog" and "This Side Up" on all sides, since its contents may not be immediately apparent to the handler. In addition to marking the

Manufactured by Allen Products (P.O. Box 2187, Allentown, Pennsylvania, 18001) and available in many pet-supply shops, this traveling crate provides a good way to transport your dog if you are planning a trip in a car or a camper.

carrier, you will also want to make out an identification tag for the dog's collar—with name, address, and destination clearly spelled out.

It is wise to let the dog become accustomed to whatever crate or carrier you select before you travel. Let him climb in and out and give him a treat or a word of praise when he has done so. Also, give him a familiar toy to keep him company on the trip. On the day of departure, don't give him food for at least six hours before you go or water for at least two hours, and avoid travel during peak periods and days when the temperature is over 80° and humidity is high.

Car or Camper Travel

Taking a dog along on an automobile trip is usually more pleasant for the dog, since he can be with you the whole time and needn't be cramped in a small carrying case. Large wire-mesh carriers are useful, to confine the dog in the car and in motel or hotel rooms en route. Whether or not you use a carrier, be sure that the dog has enough room in the car to lie down comfortably, sufficient ventilation, and the opportunity for exercise and elimination fairly frequently (every four hours, if possible).

If your dog has never traveled with you in a car, take him on a short run to see whether he is likely to suffer motion sickness or become very nervous. If he is not comfortable on a short trip, ask your veterinarian for advice. Tranquilizers may be in order, as well as medication to control vomiting. Puppies are far more prone to motion sickness than adult dogs, but almost any dog is capable of overcoming the problem after a certain amount of conditioning to car travel. Most dogs come to love car travel.

Make sure that the following items are in your luggage:
- a leash and collar (the collar should remain on the dog, but the leash should not, since it may get tangled on the dog)
- a muzzle (most dogs won't ever use this, but some places may require its use, so have one on hand)
- a familiar object, such as a toy or a blanket, to give the dog reassurance that not *everything* is different
- a Thermos of cold water or an insulated bag of ice cubes
- a towel (to wipe off the dog or anything he might soil)
- two dishes (plastic is light) for food and water
- at least a day's worth of the dog's usual food and utensils to open the containers and mix the food
- grooming equipment
- whatever medications the veterinarian recommends (tranquilizers, heartworm medicine, etc.)
- a pooper scooper (see page 89)

On the trip itself, here are a few more things to remember.
- *Do* walk the dog as often as possible (at least every four hours)
- *Do* give the dog water as often as he will drink it
- *Do* check ahead, if you have hotel or motel reservations, to make sure they will accept your dog. The Mobile and AAA travel guides list motels and campsites that allow pets. The U.S. Department of Parks and state park services also list park campsites that allow pets. (Many no longer do.)
- *Do* keep your dog on a leash every time he leaves the car. (Dogs in unfamiliar surroundings often become confused and fail to obey commands no matter how well trained they are.)
- *Do* keep the dog from making contact with strange dogs (to avoid fights, disease, etc.)
- *Do* park in the shade
- *Don't* leave the dog in a car alone for very long, especially in hot weather, and make sure that the ventilation is adequate. The temperature inside a car can rise very quickly, to over 100 degrees even on a day of only 75 degrees. Heatstroke—even in supermarket parking lots—is not an uncommon occurrence. This is one reason wire-mesh carriers are convenient; you can leave all the car windows open (although the dog is thus prevented from discouraging burglars).

Mutt Maintenance

If you haven't made reservations ahead of time, don't sneak the dog into lodging where he isn't going to be welcomed; you may find yourself paying a fine or, worse, having the dog put out unceremoniously before you're ready to leave. Even in a dogs-allowed place, use your own dog dishes, clean up after him, and don't leave him alone in a room for the unsuspecting chambermaid. Ludwig Bemelmans found a hotel in Paris that was a dog owner's delight: "Everybody there was happy, and a special dish with water was in the corner of the bathroom. The maid had changed the fancy rose-colored eiderdown for a less costly coverlet. 'For' she said, 'he will want to sleep on your bed, monsieur. Also don't be worried about the carpet—this one is old and will be replaced anyway.'"

If you plan to visit friends, be sure they are aware that you are bringing your canine companion. Non-dog owners are not usually enthusiastic about visiting pets, and though dog owners will probably be more welcoming, their own dogs may not be as hospitable as they are. Even if a fight doesn't ensue, it is altogether too likely that the host dog will race around the house urinating on furniture just to show the visitor whose territory it really is. Keep the two dogs separated, unless the stay is to be a lengthy one, in which case they should meet on neutral ground or outdoors under supervision. And bring your dog's own equipment and his own supply of food.

Hope Rydon

The Traveling Mutt on His Own

For people who like to travel alone but want their dogs with them once they reach their destination, there are a number of animal agencies that will take care of the details and the shipping for you. These accommodating people will arrange to have the dog picked up and delivered to the airport, together with health certificates, and arrange for flight bookings, carrying cases, and someone to meet the plane at the other end. Like many convenient luxuries, the expense can be considerable, depending on the distance flown and the size of the animal, but for some people, it's the only way to go, and can be a good deal cheaper than leaving a dog in a kennel for $10 a day.

Although the agencies are well equipped to handle the ill-equipped dog, the careful owner should be sure that they are at least informed about the animal's particular likes and dislikes. Take as many precautions with the mutt traveling on his own as you would do when you are on board, seeing that he has his own carrier, food, toys, and equipment before he leaves.

The Left-Behind Mutt

There are several alternatives for people who prefer to travel without their animals or whose trips preclude the company of a dog.

For two- or three-day trips, a dog may be left at home safely enough, so long as someone comes in to feed him and exercise him at least three times a day. Sensitive or nervous dogs, however, may not do very well if they are left alone for long periods.

The ideal plan is probably a combination house-sitter/dog-sitter. Not only will the dog have someone on hand to walk and feed him on schedule, but he will also have company, which is a more important factor than most people realize. Be sure that you leave the proper food, utensils, instructions, and information about veterinarians, as well as a telephone number where you may be reached. It is common sense and probably not even worth mentioning that the person you leave in charge should be someone the dog knows and likes.

The most common way of having your dog's needs seen to is to board him in a professional kennel. This is rarely cheap, yet it is surprising how many dog owners are willing to pay large sums without being sure what they (or, more important, their dogs) are getting for the money. Dog kennels are found easily enough through the Yellow Pages, but it is not so easy to find the right one. Advertisements can be misleading, and there have been some scandals in the news in recent years involving "country clubs" for dogs that turn out to be vacant lots where dogs are chained to trees and left out in the rain. It is wise, therefore, for the owner to visit any prospective kennel and be given a guided tour. A kennel operator who refuses to show a dog owner around has something to hide, and his establishment should be avoided.

Consult your veterinarian to find out the names of good kennels. Friends will usually be happy to recommend a kennel where their dog has had good care, but be sure to ask whether the friend has actually visited and whether the dog has been there more than once before you follow up on the suggestion. Once you have a couple of good leads, call the kennels to see whether they can accommodate your dog for the time period you will be away. If so, ask when you can visit ahead of time. Here's what to look for:

1. The operator's attitude toward the dog. If he or she seems interested in the dog's individual characteristics or habits and insists on a health certificate, that's a good sign. Watch the operator with other animals and observe the manner with which he or she treats them.

2. The building itself and the kennel area. The place should be clean and odor-free, the runs relatively large with sheltered areas against the sun and weather. If there is a strong odor of disinfectant, look around to make sure it isn't being used simply as a mask for other smells that shouldn't be there. See that each cage or run is clearly labeled with the inhabitant's name and diet.
3. The food preparation area must be impeccable and well stocked with sturdy dishes and untippable water bowls. Make sure that the food is stored in such a way that pests aren't able to get at it, and if the kind of food your dog eats is not available, make arrangements for the kennel to order it or supply it yourself.
4. The condition of the dogs in the kennel. Act as if you were going to select a dog for your own, and walk around looking at each one for signs of good or bad health and temperament. If any dog seems droopy, dirty, or excessively nervous, ask the operator to explain. If the answer doesn't satisfy you, move on to the next kennel on your list.

There are other questions, too. Does the operator condone special toys and treats and will he see that they are given to the animal? Does he have an isolation area for animals that become unduly nervous within sight of other dogs—or for dogs that are ill? Does he have a veterinarian on call? Does he have grooming facilities and employees trained in using them? How often does he take the dogs out for exercise? Does he live on or near the premises—within barking distance, so to speak? Does he charge extra for any special treatment? If so, how much? Does he have a pickup and delivery service?

This last question may not be important to most people, but in large cities or in areas where good kennels cannot be found, delivery service can be an important convenience. The owner of a Scottish terrier left on vacation knowing that her dog was safely in the hands of a fine kennel, which had served the dog well on many previous occasions. Her husband returned home ahead of her and called the kennel to have the dog delivered home, but when the Scottie arrived, he seemed a bit ill. He didn't even go near his food dish but paced around the apartment nervously. A day later his wife arrived and was able to clear up the mystery—if not the dog's illness. It seems that it just wasn't her dog. By the time she recognized the fact, the kennel had realized their mistake and turned up at the door with the right Scottie and a heartfelt apology. Of course, none of this would have happened if she had owned a one-of-a-kind mutt.

STUFFED DOG
U.S.
First quarter of the 20th century
Printed fabric
H., 16″
Mrs. Steven Kellogg

The Mobile Mutt

LOSING a dog that has wandered off is a heartbreaking experience. So many questions come to mind: Could I have prevented it? Is he dead or sick? Has he found a new owner or is he fending for himself in the streets, scrounging from garbage cans and avoiding the dog catcher? Has he been stolen and sold to a research laboratory or taken to the dog pound? Not knowing the fate of your best friend is worse than knowing he has been humanely put out of his misery, because guilt has compounded your loss.

*How to Avoid
Losing
Your Dog*

1. Keep the dog confined at all times—either with a leash or in a run area with a fence that cannot be dug under or jumped over. Trusting a well-trained dog to stick close to home or to you is a risky business, for any dog can suddenly take off on the trail of a female in heat, a loose dog looking for fun or a fight, or whatever else interesting may cross his path.

2. Make sure that the dog has clear identification on his collar, not just a rabies tag and a license, but a nameplate with your name, address, and telephone number. (Collars can always come off, so this isn't foolproof.)

3. Tattooing a dog on the inside of one hind leg, which can be done by most veterinarians, is a useful means of identification, and it may also prevent dognapping, since the fines for selling or harboring a tattooed dog are considerable. There are two national registries for tattooed animals: National Dog Registry, 227 Stebbins Road, Carmel, N.Y. 10512, and Ident-a-Pet, 1509 Voorhies Ave., Brooklyn, N.Y. 11235. Many shelters also have tattooing programs, so inquire locally.

4. Another aid in retrieving a lost dog is to have on hand a good photograph of the animal and a list of the dog's vital statistics. One man lost a mutt that had lived with him for over four years and was appalled to find (after he had, happily, recovered the dog) that his guesses at height, weight, and markings had been all wrong. (He also found that there were perhaps five hundred medium-sized black mutts running loose in the Bronx, according to the number of phone calls he received.) So measure your dog (height from the back to the floor) and weigh him. Look carefully for any distinguishing markings, check the construction of ears (pricked, floppy, half and half) and the type of hair coat (curly, long, shaggy, black, spotted, etc.), and write it all down. Also write down the dog's age, sex, name, tattoo registration number, rabies tag number, license number, and breed combination, as well as the vet's name and address and the person or institution from which you got the dog.

137

How to Find Him

If you have done your best and the dog has still managed to get loose, become lost, and failed to return, here are the recommended steps to take:

1. Call the police and local dog shelter to see if he has been found and turned in.
2. Get out and carefully retrace all the areas in your neighborhood where the dog might be likely to have gone—favorite play areas, parks, streams or ponds, places where the dog may have romped with the children, or garbage dumps. If your mutt was a stray originally, go back to the place where you found him (or where he found you).
3. If you have a radio or television station that runs lost-dog ads, make sure that they know about your loss and plead with them to advertise it. One owner of a lost dog made his story so poignant that a big-city newspaper ran a story and the dog was recovered.
4. Make a personal visit *every day* to the local shelter or dog pound. Because most shelters are understaffed, they may not notice that your mutt is sitting right under their noses, and only a personal inspection of their kennels may find your dog. Although some pounds are required to keep found dogs for a week or more, in some areas there is a limit of only forty-eight hours.
5. Make up a sign containing the dog's vital statistics and a photograph and have as many copies as you feel you can post Xeroxed or photo-offset. Also hand-deliver or mail—with a personal letter—copies of the sign to veterinarians, shelters, local stores, the police, newspaper, radio, and television stations, humane organizations, post office, neighbors, and any other place you can think of. Ask these people if they have seen the dog and to keep their eyes open for him and to post your sign on their bulletin boards.
6. Check the newspapers for found-dog notices and listen to the radio.
7. Go to the local schools, camps, and to neighbors with children; they enjoy a hunt like this and often have a good deal of success. Mailmen are also good people to alert, since they are usually on the streets.
8. Get in touch with the American Humane Association (P.O. Box 1266, Denver, Colo. 80201). They have managed to get nearly a thousand radio stations to perform the public service of advertising lost pets throughout the country.

Dog Theft

Dog theft is much less prevalent now than it once was, if only because dog pounds and shelters are often the sources for laboratory animals, which is the usual destination of stolen dogs. Labs do not steal dogs, of course, but "dealers" may pick up animals that are wandering homeless. If your mutt has no collar and no tattoo, his chances of being picked up are pretty good, not just by a dognapper but by the local authorities. Stray dogs are becoming more of a menace, in terms of numbers as well as behavior, and they pose a sanitation problem, to say nothing of the damage they can cause. But dognappers can still be a threat to dogs with owners who do not take proper precautions. Teach your children to avoid strangers who inquire about their dogs; some nappers have been known to tell kids that they were doing routine inoculations on neighborhood dogs, thus rounding up a whole truckful before the children suspected any foul play. Dog thieves may also bring a female in heat into a neighborhood and let the local males round up themselves. But they tend to avoid animals that are confined, and now that it has become illegal for laboratories and pet shops to buy dogs with tattoos, thieves will leave those animals well enough alone.

The major cause for most dog disappearances, however, is not thievery but simple negligence. In most cases, loss can be prevented if the owner is careful.

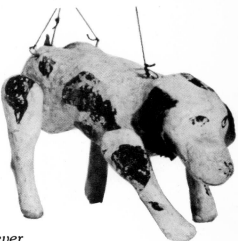

PUPPET
U.S.
Circa 1910
Wood
L., 7"
Kelter-Malcé Antiques

I have never disguised it from myself, and nobody has ever disguised it from me, that I am not a handsome dog. Even Mother never thought me beautiful. She was no prizewinning beauty herself, but she never hesitated to criticize my appearance. In fact, I have yet to meet any one who did. The first thing strangers say about me is, "What an ugly dog!"

I don't know what I am. The most of me is terrier. I have a long tail which sticks straight up in the air. My hair is wiry. My eyes are brown. I am jet-black, with a white chest. I once overheard Fred say that I was a Swiss-cheese-hound, and I have generally found Fred reliable in his statements.

P. G. Wodehouse,
"A Very Shy Gentleman"

Lassie, Come Home

A Mutt-Loving Family

Kibosh I

Kibosh II

Holly

TED AND Dorothe Brun of Mount Kisco, New York, have been mutt lovers as long as they can remember. Both of them grew up in the boat-building village of City Island, New York, where every kid on the block had a mutt of some sort; later, when they got married, they decided to keep up the tradition. Their first mutt, named Kibosh (slang for stuff and nonsense), found the Bruns on his own, but when he died at a ripe old age, they searched the local humane societies for a new mutt, and came up with two of them. The first one, Kibosh II, was as much of a people hater as Holly, a golden retriever cross, was a people lover. Apparently he had been badly beaten as a pup and at first wouldn't even allow the Bruns to put on his leash. After about a year of patient handling, however, he finally was able to trust his family and now he is more devoted to the Bruns than any animal they have ever had.

A couple of years ago, the Bruns (who also have a houseful of mixed-breed cats and a starling) had to take a trip to Florida. Rather than leave the animals at home with a house-sitter, they bought a huge camper, which they outfitted with beds and bowls, and took the whole menagerie along. Dorothe would stay in back with the cats and the bird, but Kibosh and Holly would ride up front with Ted just to make sure they didn't get lost on the way.

Hope Ryden

BOY WITH DOG, HORN, AND GUN
U.S.
19th century
Color pencil
21½″ × 17½″
Washburn Gallery

4.
Sick
as a Dog

There's an old cliché, "Sick as a dog." . . . A dog who hurts can't reason that he has felt bad before and recovered to chase cats. He can't comfort himself that this too will pass. He doesn't even care whether the doctor, the nurse or the other patients in the waiting room think he's a coward. He's sick as a dog.

James R. Kinney

AFTER preventive medicine, the best form of medical health a mutt owner can practice is to remain alert to symptoms of illness. Although it is usually not difficult to tell when an animal has been injured seriously enough to require medical attention, it is not always so easy to decide when certain symptoms are cause for calling the vet. Some early signs of illness are subtle, but the ability to recognize them quickly will often make the difference between life and death. Skim the following list quickly and keep it handy in case you notice anything out of the ordinary in the future.

Appetite loss (anorexia)   Many dogs will eat less than their full meal from time to time, but when they stop altogether—even for one meal—look for other symptoms, and if they are present, call the vet. Don't let the animal go without eating for more than twenty-four hours without making that call. If the dog starts eating strange things (paper, rope, soap, feces) and he's well beyond the stage of curious puppyhood, there may be a pancreatic problem, some digestive disturbance, or indigestion from a poor diet. Correct the diet at the next meal, but if the symptoms continue, give the vet a ring.

Sick Mutt Symptoms

Abdominal swelling   If the animal seems reluctant to lie down and there appears to be a collection of fluid in the abdominal cavity, the dog may have bloat (or gastric torsion, see page 146). Call the vet.

Bad breath   Any foul odor may indicate infection, but mouth odor can also mean tartar accumulation on the teeth (which the vet will remove) or some digestive or kidney ailment.

Baldness   Wounds, burns, and poison can cause bald spots, but the same condition can also come about as the result of a skin disease, such as mange or ringworm, a hormone imbalance, allergies, or eczema, all of which can be treated by the veterinarian.

Bleeding   External bleeding and first-aid care are discussed in the first-aid section, but internal bleeding—which may follow an accident—is not always immediately apparent. If a dog has had a trauma of some sort, keep an eye on its gums for loss of color; if the animal goes into shock, sudden death may result.

Blindness   Blindness can be caused by aging or heredity (collies, miniature poodles, and shelties may be affected), and there is no cure. Cataracts, which involve a clouding of the lens, may also cause blindness, and surgery can often be effective. A blind dog, if kept confined to a familiar room, can often do quite well, however.

Bloat   Similar to colic in horses, bloat is a condition dreaded by the owners of large dogs, since it can be fatal. Acute gastric dilation results from the accumulation of gas in the intestine, causing the abdomen to swell; the dog will usually vomit and show signs of pain. This is serious and the vet should be consulted. More serious—and often fatal—is gastric torsion, which means a twisted gut, and symptoms, which include a distended abdomen, drooling, severe pain, and dry heaves, must be noticed and reported immediately if the animal is to be saved. This can sometimes be prevented by feeding a dog small quantities of food and water at each meal and avoiding excessive exercise afterward.

Breathing trouble   Wheezing, noisy breathing, or excessive panting (not normal unless it is hot or the dog has exercised heavily) may indicate a respiratory infection or an allergy. Dogs with squat noses (pug or bulldog crosses, for instance) may inherit a breathing problem, but in a normal dog, the owner should keep alert to other symptoms.

Circling   Many dogs circle a couple of times before lying down, but continuous circling may indicate damage to the central nervous system. If the dog has in its previous life (before you) had a case of distemper, this may be a non-problematical hangover of the disease, but if not, and if the dog has recently suffered a head or spinal injury, it's worth investigating the matter with your vet.

Chewing difficulty   This may be caused by a fractured jaw, a tooth abscess, or a disease condition. If it persists and if you find no obvious reason for the problem, call the vet.

Coma   Any dog that suddenly becomes unconscious deserves a vet's attention immediately (see *Convulsions*).

Constipation   Straining or an inability to defecate may be caused by an intestinal blockage of some kind or a number of other problems that the vet will be able to diagnose. If the dog goes for more than a day without defecating, or if you see him straining, get help.

Convulsions   Violent spasms coupled with unconsciousness may be caused by any one of several serious problems—and whether a fit lasts for only a moment or for several minutes, call your vet right away. Don't do anything for the animal except keep other people away and see that he can't harm himself by falling or hitting something. Don't bother trying to hold the tongue (you may get bitten), since a dog can't swallow it anyhow. Sometimes seizures will recur throughout a dog's life—especially if the condition has been inherited or has resulted from distemper—but they can be controlled with drugs, though it may take a while before a proper method of medication can be established.

Sick as a Dog

Coughing   This is caused by some irritant to the lungs, and while the cause is often simply an irritant, it may, in an older dog, indicate heart trouble, and in any dog, it may signal a serious disease. If it persists for a day or so, call the vet. Kennel cough (see p. 173) is not serious, but other ailments—distemper, pneumonia, etc.—are.

Deafness   This is not unusual in an aging dog, but it can also be a permanent result of injury or infection; loss of hearing can also be hereditary (watch out for mutts with bullterriers, fox terriers, and Great Danes in their past), or it can be caused simply by a blocked ear canal. Many dogs get around perfectly well with impaired hearing, but it's worth checking out the cause with your vet when you visit for the annual checkup, unless the condition has come on suddenly, in which case an immediate call is in order.

Dehydration   Loss of fluid in the animal's system can be an accompaniment to shock, which is very serious indeed. It can be caused by vomiting, diarrhea, or bleeding, and immediate treatment should be sought. If you suspect the problem, pinch a fold of skin and release it; if it does not return immediately to its natural position, the animal may be in trouble.

Diarrhea   Loose or runny stool can be a symptom of many possible disorders, but if it continues for more than twenty-four hours, call the vet. Call sooner if the diarrhea is accompanied by obvious pain, lethargy, or bloody stool. Simple diarrhea will respond to the use of Kaopectate or a limited diet.

Dribbling   A housebroken dog that suddenly begins urinating uncontrollably is probably an older female and can readily be treated with hormone tablets. If the dog is male and relatively young, you might think about retraining him.

Drooling   This is to be expected on a hot day when the dog is panting, but if the animal is obviously not frightened or excited or exhausted, and the symptoms of nausea are present, there may be an infection or injury present and the dog should be treated. Check for cysts, foreign bodies in the mouth, and fractures.

Ear problems   Unusual discharges, odor, shaking of the head, or swellings (called hematomas, the accumulation of blood in a pocket in the ear) should all receive a vet's attention. There may be infection caused by ear mites or some other problem.

Eye problems   If a dog's eyes become puffy or enlarged, bloodshot or cloudy, and if he blinks, squints, or has a noticeable abnormal discharge, get a vet to look at him. None of these may be serious, but leave it to the doctor to diagnose the problem, since early diagnosis may prevent eventual blindness. If you know that the problem is caused by some irritating substance or a foreign body, you can try to flush it out with water. If the third eyelid—a membrane that protects the eye—becomes inflamed and protruding, it may necessitate surgery. Be glad your dog is a mutt when it comes to eye problems, of which you should have few. The bulging eyes of the Peke and the droopy eyelids of the St. Bernard and the cocker spaniel won't trouble you.

Flatulence   Like bad breath, this condition is unpleasant to be around, and it may also indicate trouble, in this case, gas in the intestine. This is rarely serious—if caused by gulping food—but occasionally may indicate a disease of the digestive tract that deserves attention.

Headshaking   This may indicate the presence of parasites or infection in the ear and can cause hematoma (an accumulation of blood under the skin). Head tilt is more serious and may be the result of a tumor, a brain injury, or distemper.

Hiccups   These are not unusual in small puppies, but if they are persistent, the dog should be checked.

Hoarseness   An inability to bark or difficulty in barking may be the simple result of too much barking or coughing, but it may also indicate a mild infection. If the dog has been barking because of frustration at being cooped up, try letting him out once in a while.

Jaundice   Yellow coloring in the mouth, ears, or eyes may indicate a disease process in the liver or the circulatory system. It should be taken seriously.

Licking   Although a dog will lick a wound or sore spot to soothe irritation, the activity, if prolonged, can do more damage than good. If licked patches become raw, get a vet to check out the cause; it may be anal gland trouble, parasites, or some other problem requiring treatment.

Limping   Check the dog to see that there is no cut or splinter in the foot; if not and if the condition persists, the cause may be an injury or a disease of the bone or nervous system.

Nasal discharge   A cloudy discharge may mean anything from a respiratory ailment to a serious disease, while a bloody discharge can signify an injury, abscess, or the presence of a foreign body. Mutts with spaniel blood in their veins may suffer from a disease called hyperkeratosis as they age, signaled by hardened nose and foot pads. There is no known cause or cure, but massaging with oil will soften the tissue.

Paralysis   This is a serious symptom and may be the result of an injury to the spine or head, a fracture in a limb, a brain tumor, or a serious disease. Get medical help right away.

Scooting   When a dog rubs his anal glands along the ground, the problem may be parasites, anal gland trouble, or some kind of irritation. Infection may result if the vet doesn't diagnose the cause.

Scratching   Like licking, scratching is the dog's way of relieving an itch or irritation, and it can be equally damaging if it persists. Fleas may be the cause, or anal-gland problems, or one of a number of skin diseases, but the scratching itself may cause further trouble by promoting infection and attracting parasites.

Shedding   This is a seasonal condition, most noticeable in long-haired dogs, but excessive shedding, resulting in baldness, may be cause for alarm. Stress can cause shedding, as can a poor diet, but if these situations don't appear to exist, have the dog checked for other causes.

Shivering   This is a normal reaction to cold, but not in dogs, who may in fact be suffering from fear or pain. Check further for other symptoms if you suspect the latter.

Sneezing   If no irritant is apparent, and the sneezes are accompanied by pus or a bloody discharge, the problem may be disease and needs attention.

Straining   (See *Constipation* and *Urinating*)

Swelling   So many disease conditions may cause swelling that we recommend you check out the situation with the vet. Abscesses, bloat, tumors, dropsy, and other problems may be the cause.

Temperature   A dog's normal temperature ranges from 101 to 102° F. If the dog seems feverish and the temperature is much higher than 102°, call the vet. Pregnant bitches may often show subnormal temperatures a day or so before whelping.

Thirst   Excessive thirst when the dog hasn't exercised heavily or been drinking or eating salty substances can be a sign of urinary disease or diabetes. Have it checked out.

Tongue problems   A swollen or ulcerated tongue may be caused by a bite or sting, but it may also indicate disease. Whatever the cause, get the vet to diagnose and treat it, since the ailment may interfere with proper eating and drinking.

Urinating   Any abnormal urination—excessive urination or failure to urinate—should be cause for concern, since it may indicate urinary disease, tumors, or prostate infection. Bloody urine, incontinence, or straining should be checked by the vet as well.

Vomiting   Dogs vomit readily and there may be no reason for alarm, but if the vomiting continues for more than a few hours, when blood is present in the vomit, or when it is accompanied by other symptoms, call the vet. Simple vomiting may be treated by withholding food and water for a day to rest the stomach, which may have been upset by some indigestible substance, nervousness, motion sickness, or over-eating. Prolonged or violent vomiting, however, may be a symptom of serious illness or poisoning.

Wheezing   (See *Breathing trouble*)

Mary Bloom

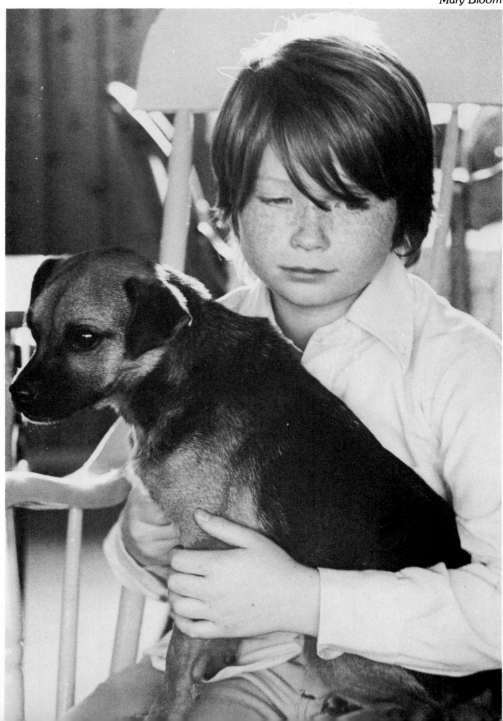

Emergency Treatment

A REFERENCE TABLE FOR HANDLING EMERGENCIES

AFFLICTION	*TREATMENT*
Bites and Stings	Apply warm compresses of bicarbonate of soda. If the animal has an extreme reaction, treat him as if in shock (page 162) and get immediate medical attention.
Burns	
Superficial	Wash with bicarbonate of soda, apply Vaseline, and bandage, if possible.
Severe	Get immediate medical attention. Treat for shock, if necessary (page 162).
Chemical	Alkali—wash with acid, i.e., vinegar. Acid—wash with alkali, i.e., bicarbonate of soda. Cover with a moist bandage.
Convulsions	When convulsion subsides, sedate animal and get immediate medical attention.
Drowning	Make sure tongue is out of throat. Turn dog upside down and allow water to run out. Apply artificial respiration or mouth-to-mouth resuscitation (page 159). Treat for shock once dog starts to breathe. See vet immediately.
Electric Shock	Turn off current. Apply artificial respiration or mouth-to-mouth resuscitation.
Frostbite	Allow to thaw slowly. Apply Vaseline and loose bandage.
Heart Attack	Symptoms: Dog will gasp for air and become unconscious. Tongue may turn blue. Apply artificial respiration and give a stimulant. When consciousness is regained, treat for shock (page 162). See vet immediately.
Heatstroke	Symptoms: Weakness, dilated pupils, panting, inability to stand. Get animal into fresh air. Place in cool tub or sponge with cool water. Apply ice pack to head. See vet immediately.

Poisoning General symptoms: Crying or whimpering, abdominal pain, vomiting, shaking, heavy breathing.

General treatment:

Corrosive acid ingestion: Administer milk of magnesia or a mixture of 4 teaspoons of baking soda to a glass of water.

Alkali ingestion (i.e., sink-drain cleaner): Administer vinegar or lemon juice.

Both treatments should be followed by giving the dogs as much olive oil, milk, or raw egg white as you can.

All other poisons: Induce vomiting immediately with one of the following emetics:
• Equal parts of hydrogen peroxide (3 percent) and water;
• One teaspoon of table salt in one cup warm water;
• One tablespoon of mustard powder in one cup warm water;
• Soapy water.
If vomiting does not occur within ten to fifteen minutes, repeat. Once the dog has vomited, administer one of the following antidotes:
• Universal antidote (can be made up in advance by a pharmacist): two parts activated charcoal, one part light magnesium oxide, one part kaolin, one part tannic acid;
• Two parts heavily burned and crumbled toast, one part strong tea; one part milk of magnesia;
• Two to three tablespoons of activated charcoal in a cup of warm water;
• As much milk and raw egg white as the dog will take.

Porcupine Quills See vet immediately. If you are miles from medical attention and the dog can be handled, cut the ends of quills with scissors to release the air pressure from them and remove with pliers.

Snake Bite Muzzle dog. Apply tourniquet above bite. If fang marks are obvious, cut a small X through each one. If they are not, cut several small X's at approximate point of bite. Squeeze out blood and venom. Apply ice packs or cold compresses.

Stroke Symptoms: Partial or total paralysis.

Get immediate medical attention.

Suffocation Apply artificial respiration or mouth-to-mouth resuscitation (pages 161 and 162). Get immediate medical attention.

Swallowed Foreign Objects Get immediate medical attention.

Temperature

Below 99°   Wrap dog in warm blankets or heating pad. Administer a stimulant (e.g., brandy). Get immediate medical attention.

Above 102°   If temperature persists for over twenty-four hours, get immediate medical attention.

Unconsciousness   Use a stimulative inhalant, i.e., smelling salts. Apply artificial respiration or mouth-to-mouth resuscitation. See vet immediately.

Vomiting, Severe   Remove drinking water from dishes and replace with ice cubes. Get medical attention immediately.

Wounds

Incisions   Allow to bleed for a moment. Wash surrounding area with germicidal soap. Bandage with sterile gauze. If serious, apply compression bandage. After several days, remove bandage and apply Vitamin A and D Ointment twice a day. If incision is large (over an inch), see vet.

Lacerations

Simple   Wash with peroxide and water. Do not bandage. After several days, apply Vitamin A and D Ointment twice a day.

Serious   Wash with peroxide and water. Bandage loosely. Get immediate medical attention.

Punctures   Pour hydrogen peroxide into wound. Wash surrounding area with germicidal soap.

Plants Poisonous to Animals

Autumn Crocus	A°	Jimson Weed	A°
Bittersweet	L,St,B°	Larkspur, Delphinium	L, Sd°
Black Locust	L,Sd,St°	Lily-of-the-Valley	A°
Boxwood	L,St°	Lupine	A°
Buttercup	St,L°	Mistletoe	B°
Caladium	A*	Monkshood	A°
Castor Bean	A°	Mountain Laurel	A°
Daffodil	A°	Mushrooms (some)	A°
Daphne	A*	Nightshade	A°
Dumbcane	A*	Oleander	A°
English Ivy	L,B°	Philodendron	A*
Euonymus	A°	Poinsettia	A*
Foxglove	A°	Pokeberry	A°
Golden Chain	A°	Privet	L,B°
Holly	L,B°	Rhododendron, Azalea	A°
Hyacinth	A°	Tobacco (nicotiana)	A°
Hydrangea	A°	Wisteria	A°
Jerusalem Cherry	A°	Yew	A°

Key

A   All parts of the plant
B   Berries or fruit
Sd   Seeds
St   Stem, twigs or bark
L   Leaves
*   Do not induce vomiting —give milk or water to wash esophagus
°   Induce vomiting

Poisons

Poison	Common Sources	First Aid
Lead	linoleum, lead paint chips, plaster, putty, varnish, ceramic glazes, golf balls, pesticides	Induce vomiting. Usually a progressive poisoning.
Ethylene glycol	car antifreeze, Sterno, windshield de-icer	Give vodka in milk.
Petroleum distillates	paint and paint thinner, paint remover, kerosene, gasoline, benzene, furniture polish, floor wax, lighter fluid, motor or fuel oil	Corrosive. DO NOT induce vomiting. Give milk or water to wash esophagus.
	turpentine	Induce vomiting. Give milk or water.
	carbon tetrachloride	Induce vomiting. DO NOT give milk, fats or oils, ONLY water.
Arsenic	paint, herbicides, pesticides	Induce vomiting. Give milk or water.
Red Squill Warfarin (d-con) ANTU Thallium Sodium Fluoroacetate (1080)	rodenticides, pesticides	Induce vomiting. Give milk or water.
Metaldehyde	snail bait	Induce vomiting. Give milk or water.
Strychnine	rodenticide	DO NOT induce vomiting. Give milk or water.
Chlorinated hydrocarbons	insecticides, pesticides, weed killers, such as chlordane, lindane, methoxychlor, heptachlor, toxaphene	Induce vomiting. DO NOT give milk, fats or oil, ONLY water.
Organophosphates	insecticides, pesticides, malathion, dichlorvos, fenthion, ronnel, parathion	Induce vomiting. Give milk or water.

Poison	Common Sources	First Aid
Weak alkalis	soap, laundry detergent, shampoo	Induce vomiting. Give milk or water.
Strong alkalis	lye, caustic soda, drain cleaners, ammonia, grease solvents, washing powders, some metal cleaners and polishes	Corrosive. DO NOT induce vomiting. Give milk or water to wash esophagus.
Weak acids including oxalic acid	household chlorine bleach, some disinfectants, some metal cleaners and polishes	Induce vomiting. Give milk or water.
Strong acids	some metal cleaners and polishes, sulfuric acid in car batteries (some Lysol and pine oil products should be treated as strong acids)	DO NOT induce vomiting. Give milk or water to wash esophagus.
Copper sulfate	toilet bowl cleaners (dilute) toilet bowl cleaners (undilute)	Induce vomiting. Give milk or water. DO NOT induce vomiting. Give milk or water.
Phenol (carbolic acid)	household disinfectants and antiseptics, hexachlorophene, Lysol and pine oil products, carbolated vaseline, fungicides, herbicides, tar, creosote	Induce vomiting. Give milk or water. Cats are particularly sensitive to phenol.
Phosphorus	non-safety matches, fireworks, striking surface of match boxes	Induce vomiting. DO NOT give milk, fats or oil, ONLY water.
Naphthalene	moth flakes and balls, insect repellents	Induce vomiting. DO NOT give milk, fats or oil, ONLY water.
Human medication	aspirin, amphetamines, barbiturates, iodine, paregoric	Induce vomiting. Give milk or water.
Other household products	aniline dyes in leather polish, dyes in some crayons, ink and glues, nail polish remover, nicotine in cigarette filters and tobacco	Induce vomiting. Give milk or water.

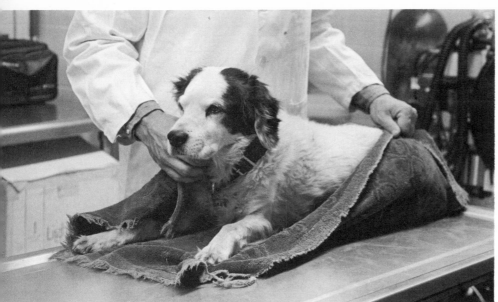

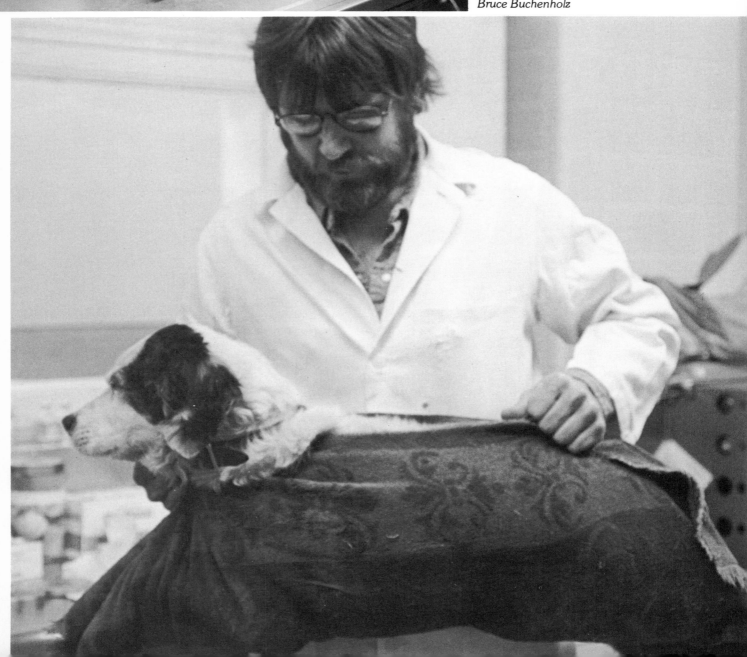

First-Aid Techniques

HANDLING an injured animal properly may mean the difference between life and death. Though accidents can happen at any time, most of us are totally unprepared to deal with this situation in either humans or dogs. Since what you do between the time your pet is injured and the time you get to a vet can be of crucial importance, it is worthwhile to familiarize yourself with a few basic animal-handling techniques.

The most important thing to remember when dealing with an injured animal is to keep calm. Hurt pets are often confused by pain and shock and may display a far different temperament than they normally do.

First Aid for an Injured Animal

1. Call the vet immediately. This will give him time to make the necessary emergency preparations.
2. If the dog is skittish or hysterical, restrain him with a loose noose around his neck.
3. Apply a muzzle—always—even if the dog seems calm (see *Muzzling,* page 158).
4. If bleeding is profuse, put a pressure bandage directly over the affected area (*Pressure Bandages and Tourniquets,* page 160). If this does not stop the bleeding, you may need to apply a tourniquet.. Many veterinarians do not have blood on hand for transfusions, so the less blood lost now, the better off your pet will be ultimately.
5. If a limb is obviously broken, apply a temporary splint. This can be done by placing any straight object next to the limb and wrapping a towel or other cloth around it and the limb to keep the leg motionless. Do not tamper too much; excessive movement and stress can cause further damage.
6. If the dog has stopped breathing but you can still detect a heartbeat, apply artificial respiration (*Artificial Respiration,* page 161).
7. Cover the animal with a blanket, towel, coat, or whatever is handy to prevent shock.
8. To move the dog, spread a blanket or coat as close to the spine as possible. Carefully roll the dog over onto the blanket. You can then pick the blanket up by the four corners and transport the animal.

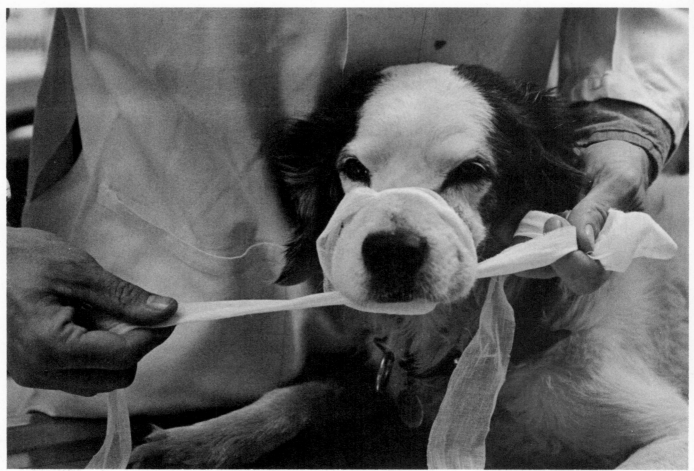

Muzzling Many people think that muzzling an animal—especially your own loving pet who has never even bared his teeth to anyone—is ridiculous. It isn't. Even the gentlest dog, under stress, is capable of taking a chunk out of your arm. Before trying to move an injured dog, your own or someone else's, muzzle him. If it appears, however, that the dog is going to vomit, wait a few minutes before putting the muzzle on. If he starts to retch after it has been applied, remove it immediately and put it on again after he has finished.

   If you would like to buy a muzzle to keep on hand for emergencies, your local pet store probably stocks them, but you can make one yourself.

1. Use a piece of gauze, a strip of sheet, your tie, a knee sock, the skirt of your dress—any piece of cloth that is several inches wide and about two feet long, depending on the size of the dog.
2. With one end of the cloth in each hand, lay it across the dog's nose, as close to the eyes as possible.
3. Wrap the cloth completely around the snout and tie firmly (but not too tightly) underneath the jaw.
4. Pull the ends back on each side of the dog's neck and make a final tie behind the neck.

Sick as a Dog

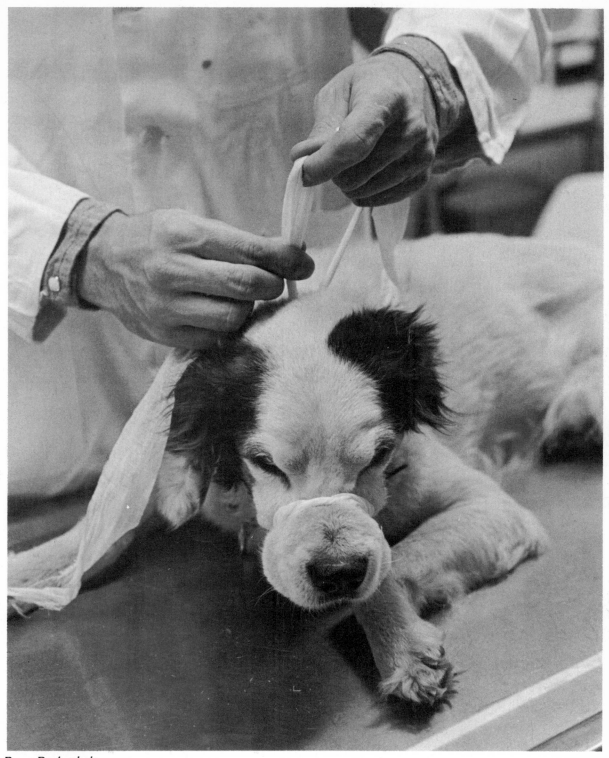

Bruce Buchenholz

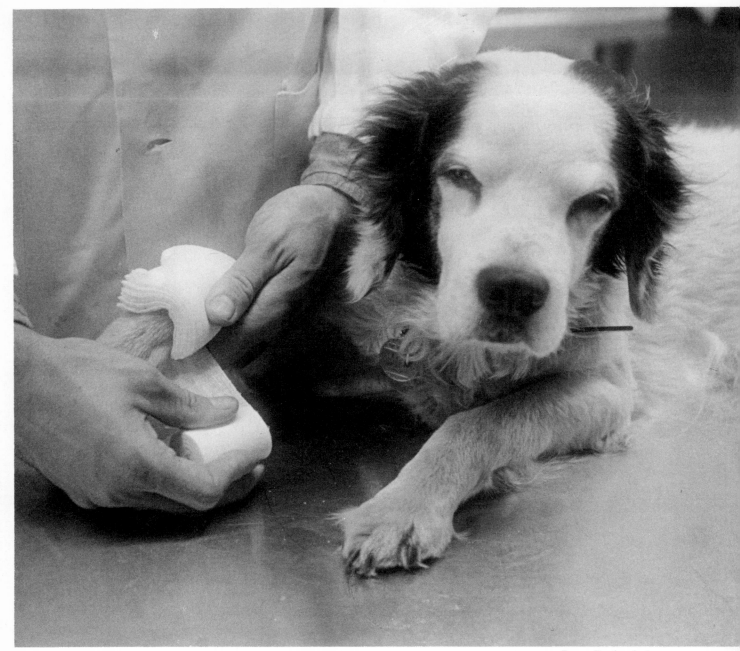

Bruce Buchenholz

Pressure Bandages and Tourniquets If there is a source of water nearby, cleanse the wound as best you can before applying the bandage. The pressure bandage can be made from whatever cloth is available, folded over several times to form a pad. Place the pad over the wound and apply pressure with your fingers. Continue this until the bleeding stops. If your fingers get tired and the wound is conveniently located, you can place the pad over the wound and then wrap a bandage around that.

Sick as a Dog

Don't use a tourniquet until it has become apparent that a pressure bandage is not going to do the job. This will happen in the case of a severed artery, when the blood will be spurting, not just running, out of the wound. The theory and apparatus of tourniquets are simple, but this method of controlling bleeding must be used cautiously. To make the tourniquet, loop a strip of cloth around the leg, above the wound, and tie it in a loop about twice the size of the dog's leg, making sure there is a good tight knot in the cloth. Insert a stick or another straight object in the loop and twist it, tightening the loop around the leg until the bleeding stops. Keep it tight for seven or eight minutes, then loosen it slightly, just enough to allow a small flow of blood for a minute or so. Retighten it and continue this procedure.

Should you find yourself faced with profuse bleeding and a broken limb simultaneously, ignore the break and try to stop the bleeding. It's not a problem you'd hope to run into, but if you don't get the bleeding stopped first, what happens to the leg will be academic.

Artificial respiration should be given if your pet has stopped breathing but still has a heartbeat. The idea is to keep air moving in and out of the lungs until the dog can resume normal breathing on his own. There are several ways, manually and by mouth, to accomplish this:

Artificial Respiration

1. Place the dog on his right side with his head and neck extended.
2. Reach in his mouth and pull his tongue out. The tongue is generally quite slippery, but a piece of cloth will help you to grasp it.
3. Stick your finger as far back into the dog's throat as possible and remove any excess saliva or other material that may have accumulated there.
4. Putting your two hands on his chest above his ribs, press your weight firmly down to push his chest together. Press down on the chest for two seconds. Release for two seconds and lift the right front leg up as far as it will go (this helps to expand the lungs and chest somewhat). Return the leg to its normal position and repeat, until the dog starts breathing himself. A chant—push 1, push 2, leg up, rest 1, rest 2, leg down—might help to keep you going.

A more effective method of artificial respiration is mouth-to-mouth (or more accurately mouth-to-nose) resuscitation. Sometimes—if you suspect the dog has cracked ribs for instance—this will be your only alternative. So, if this situation occurs, forget yourself for the moment—as far as we know, no one has ever contracted a terminal illness from administering mouth-to-mouth resuscitation to a dog—and proceed as follows:

1. As before, pull out his tongue and clear his throat.
2. Cover his mouth with one hand to prevent air from coming out.
3. Make an airtight tube with your other hand and place it over the dog's nose or place your mouth directly over the dog's nose and blow gently into his nostrils.

4. Remove your mouth, take a breath, and blow again, continuing this pattern about every five seconds (two seconds to blow in, one second to rest, two seconds to let the air release).

   If there are two of you, a third alternative is available. While one person is using the manual method (forget about moving the leg in this case), the other can be using mouth-to-mouth; when the person working on the chest is in the release part of the cycle, the other person is blowing air directly into the dog's nose.

   As long as the dog's heart is beating, it is worth the effort to continue artificial respiration. It may take a long time —possibly an hour —but you may be saving a life.

Shock There are many reasons for shock to occur, but chances are that if your pet has been injured traumatically, he will go into shock. To diagnose this, check the dog's gums; if he is in shock they will be pale and grayish. He may also be breathing shallowly and irregularly, have a barely discernible heartbeat, and possibly dilated pupils. Above all, keep the pet warm, covering him with blankets or even using hot water bottles or a heating pad. If he is unconscious or semiconscious, that is about all you can do. If he is not, however, a stimulant could help a great deal. Whiskey, warm coffee, brandy, a mixture of honey or syrup or sugar with brandy or whiskey are all good stimulants and might save the dog's life. If they are available, smelling salts can also be used.

Administering Liquid Medicine The most reliable way of giving liquid medicine is the lip-pouch method. Measure the medicine in a spoon or, better yet, an eyedropper or syringe. Grasp your dog's lower lip, just forward of the corner of his mouth, and pull it out, away from his teeth, thereby forming a pouch or pocket. Pour a small amount of medicine into the pouch and close his lip. The medicine will trickle through his teeth and down his throat. Repeat this procedure until the entire dosage has been given.

Force-Feeding Check with your vet first to find out if there is anything your dog should or shouldn't be eating. If the food to be given is of a hamburger consistency, roll it into small balls, force his mouth open as you would if administering a pill, and shove the food deep into the throat. Close the mouth, lift the muzzle, and stroke. If the food is semiliquid in nature, spoon it onto the back of the tongue and repeat the stroking procedure.

Pilling Your Dog Standing on the right side of your dog, grasp his muzzle, above the nose, with your left hand and squeeze his lips against his teeth, your thumb on one side and your fingers on the other. Squeeze as hard as you must to force him to open his mouth. With your

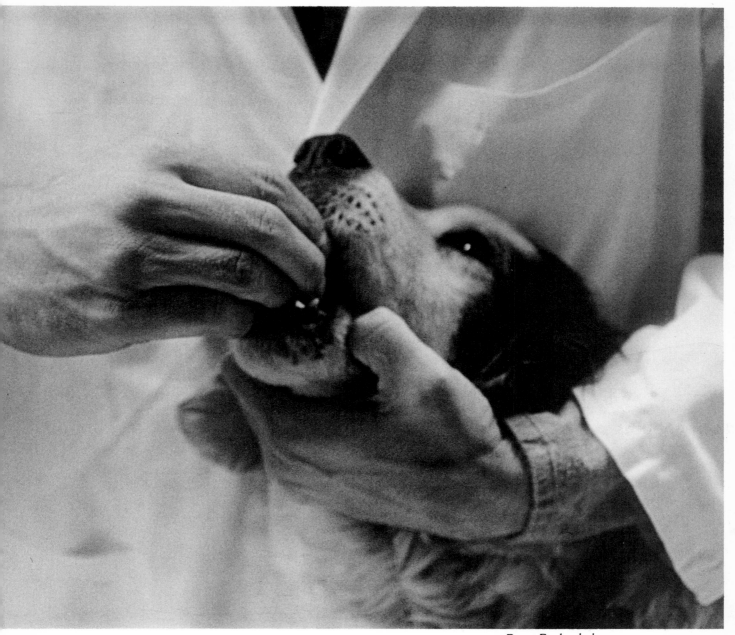

right hand, place the pill as far back on his tongue as you can; don't toss it—place it. Close his mouth firmly and hold it shut. Lift his muzzle and stroke downward on his throat or blow in his face, causing him to gulp.

First-Aid Kit

Hydrogen peroxide (3%)
Sterile gauze rolls
Sterile cotton
Alcohol
Mustard powder
Kaopectate
Vitamin A and D Ointment
Vaseline
Germicidal soap
Mineral oil
Milk of magnesia

Baking soda
Rectal thermometer
Vinegar
Muzzle
Stick for tourniquet
Razor blade, small sharp knife, or scalpel
Scissors
Smelling salts
Universal antidote (see page 152) or activated charcoal
Q-tips

The Do's and Don'ts of Home Nursing

AT ONE time or another, it is likely that you will have to play Florence Nightingale to your dog. For that eventuality, we offer the following short course in home nursing.

DO

- Give your dog only medicine prescribed by the vet.
- Give medications on schedule.
- Keep your dog comfortable, making sure that his bedding is clean and dry.
- Let your dog rest quietly.
- Keep your dog inside, except possibly to eliminate.
- Keep constant tabs on your dog's temperature (a normal temperature is around 101 degrees).
- Report any sudden change in condition to the vet immediately.
- Encourage your dog to take liquids—no matter how little—to avoid dehydration.

DON'T

- Give your dog old medicine or human medicine.
- Make up for a missed dose by doubling the next dose.
- Allow your dog to lie in drafts or hard areas where sores are likely to develop.
- Handle your dog unnecessarily.
- Let your dog overexercise inside or outside.
- Allow your dog to run a temperature for more than twenty-four hours without notifying the vet.
- Hesitate to hand-feed your dog if he is refusing food, provided he is not nauseated.

Sick as a Dog

Lady

THE MUTT WHO BEGAN AS A TRAMP

LADY'S background is a mystery. She was found in a Korvette's parking lot in Yonkers, New York, and taken to the Mount Vernon dog pound where the employees isolated her from the other dogs because her temperament was so nasty. In fact, no one could touch her because she would growl and snap, and, needless to say, the chances that she would be adopted were very slim. Mary Bloom, a photographer, just happened to be visiting the pound the day after Lady arrived and when she heard about Lady's reputation, she had a suspicion that there might be something physical—not psychological—the matter. She adopted Lady and took her to a veterinarian, who discovered several tumors, which he removed right away. After Lady recovered, Mary groomed her, and what appeared to be a standard French poodle crossed with an English cocker spaniel began to show through, along with a perfectly delightful personality. When an older woman who had recently lost her own cocker spaniel came to visit Mary, Lady immediately went to her and put her paws on the woman's lap. The woman obviously reminded Lady of some good soul in her checkered past, and Lady reminded the woman of her cocker. The two have been constant companions ever since.

Mary Bloom

165

A Medical Glossary for Mutt Owners

THE following list of diseases and ailments, arranged alphabetically within sections devoted to different parts of the canine physiological structure, is intended as a general guide only. There are many good dog-health books available with more detailed information (see page 92). This glossary is not designed to enable the reader to attempt diagnosis at home, but these definitions will give the mutt owner some idea of what the veterinarian is dealing with and how serious certain symptoms may be.

EYES

Cataracts A clouding of the lens of the eye, which may be caused by diabetes, aging, injury, or infection. Surgery is possible but far less successful in dogs than it is in humans. Cocker spaniels, Afghans, and miniature poodles seem more inclined to cataracts than other purebreds, so be on your guard if your mutt has any of those genes.

Conjunctivitis (pinkeye) An infection of the conjunctiva, the membrane that covers the white of the eyeball and lines the eyelids. This may be accompanied by a sticky discharge. There are many causes possible (wound, foreign body, allergy, congenital defect, disease), and treatment involves correcting the cause, cleaning the affected area, and using antibiotics.

Corneal ulcer A sore on the surface of the eyeball, especially common in dogs with protruding eyes. Many causes (wounds, disease, foreign bodies, etc.) are possible, and treatment may be simply an application of antibiotics or, in more complicated cases, the use of surgery.

Glaucoma A disease of the eye that may result in blindness if not diagnosed quickly. Symptoms include listless behavior, enlarged eyeball, cloudy cornea, bloodshot eyes, and pain. Mutts with cocker spaniel or basset hound blood may be more susceptible than others.

EARS

Hematoma An accumulation of blood just under the skin, which may be caused by violent headshaking (due to ear mites perhaps) or an injury. The swelling may dissolve without treatment or it may require surgery, but the underlying cause should be determined.

Otitis A bacterial infection causing inflammation of the ear canal, caused by foreign bodies, water in the ear, allergy, parasites, tumors, or the conformation of the ear (narrow ear canal, droopy ears, dense hair growth). Otitis can be treated with antibiotics.

Parasites Mites, lice, fleas, and ticks may all find their way to the ear and should be eliminated as soon as possible before infection results (see page 125).

167

SKIN DISEASES

Acne A breakout of blackheads, which eventually form pustules, on the skin, usually around the upper lip and chin, seen most often in puppies. Caused by an infection, acne can be treated with antibiotics and a thorough cleaning of the affected area.

Allergy An extreme reaction to various substances, usually chemicals, pollen, dust, food, and such, which may cause hives, dermatitis, asthma, anemia, and other diseases. Treatment will not cure but may control the problem.

Eczema An open skin sore (or "hot spot") caused by scratching or licking, which, in turn, is caused by anything from fleas to allergies. The main form of treatment is to control the source of the itch itself and to keep the animal from making matters worse by irritating the area.

Fleabite dermatitis An extreme reaction to fleas that causes itching so intense that a sore is formed, usually in the abdominal or tail area. Treatment involves ridding the animal of fleas and applying a soothing ointment to the irritated area to reduce the need to scratch.

Flea-collar dermatitis This is caused by an allergy to the toxic matter in the flea collar, resulting in sores around the neck. If these become infected, healing may take several weeks. Remove the flea collar and see the vet about treatment.

Hives Bumps or spots on the skin caused by an allergy. Not serious, and the dog's itchiness can be controlled with medication.

Mange An infection caused by mites, which takes two major forms: sarcoptic mange (or scabies), which causes itching but can be easily treated; and red, or demodectic, mange, which is common in young dogs and not contagious, unlike sarcoptic mange. Red mange may be complicated by bacterial infection and progress to an incurable condition, causing loss of hair, chronic skin irritation, and the eventual formation of scales. The animal may build up a resistance to the disease so that it cannot be controlled with antibiotics, anti-parasite medication, and baths.

Pyoderma A general term referring to a skin infection that produces pus. It may take several forms: juvenile pyoderma in puppies; impetigo; lip-fold pyoderma (common in spaniels); and vulvar-fold pyoderma. Pyoderma may also cause calluses on the leg, infections in the base of the claws, and abscesses between the pads of the foot. Treatment includes bathing the affected area and the use of antibiotic ointments. Extreme cases may require internal use of antibiotics or even surgery.

Seborrhea Caused by metabolic disorder, this is a common disease in dogs, usually found on the back and abdomen in the form of reddened bald areas, dry scales, or an oily, odorous condition. The disease can be controlled, but it will usually recur in spite of shampoos, antibiotics, and cortisone.

Warts These minor tumors are common in older dogs and are not serious; consequently treatment needn't be given unless the dog is bothered by their presence.

MOUTH DISORDERS

Gingivitis Inflammation of the gums caused by a bacterial infection that can be brought on by the accumulation of tartar on the teeth, which must be removed before the condition will improve. Advanced gingivitis is called pyorrhea and can affect other parts of the body if not treated.

Glossitis Inflammation of the tongue resulting from bacterial infection, which may also cause ulcerations. The condition may be brought on by bites, injury, tartar on teeth, burns, or the presence of foreign bodies.

Papillomatosis A viral disease affecting young dogs and causing whitish warts on the lips and tongue. These can be removed surgically, but the condition will usually disappear without treatment within one to three months, and the exposure will immunize the dog against further infection.

Stomatitis A bacterial infection in the mouth, symptomatized by drooling, loss of appetite, bleeding gums, and ulcerated lips and tongue. Treatment involves use of antibiotics. (See also *Gingivitis* and *Glossitis.*)

Tooth problems The loss of deciduous teeth in young dogs is usually not accompanied by discomfort, but a premature loss of teeth may involve pain if the new teeth are not sufficiently developed; a loss of appetite or digestive upset may occur if several teeth are lost at once. In older dogs, tooth loss can be caused by accident, but periodontitis, or alveolar periostitis (a bacterial infection usually associated with the accumulation of tartar and gingivitis), is far more common. This can be prevented by regular tooth cleaning and tartar removal. Other dental ailments may be caused by the presence of disease (distemper, for one) or as a side effect of certain drugs.

DIGESTIVE DISORDERS

Acute gastric dilation A serious condition, usually called bloat, involving distention of the abdomen and resulting in death if not diagnosed and treated promptly. The onset is rapid, usually within two hours of eating, and the animal may suffer pain, restlessness, and nausea. If caused by gastric torsion (twisted stomach), the animal will quickly go into shock and may die within a few hours. Milder cases may be caused by overeating, ingestion of spoiled or dry food or indigestible material; the dilation—indicating a rapid accumulation of gas—should be treated

quickly. Recurrence of the disorder can be prevented by correcting feeding methods (i.e., giving small quantities at a time, preventing the excessive consumption of water) and by preventing exercise immediately after eating.

Acute gastritis A general term referring to digestive upset, usually caused by the ingestion of foreign material or spoiled food, overeating (especially in puppies), or sudden changes in diet. Acute gastritis is usually caused by eating an irritating substance and is characterized by vomiting, which will often remove the cause, and increased thirst, since dehydration will set in quickly. The vet should be notified immediately. Chronic gastritis will involve sporadic vomiting, poor condition, and variable appetite; there may be any number of different causes, and the veterinarian should diagnose the condition and prescribe appropriate treatment.

Constipation Difficulty in evacuating feces, which may be caused by an obstruction, either mechanical (as in a tumor, parasites, enlarged prostate, fracture of pelvis, etc.) or digestive (intake of bones, large quantities of dry food, hair, etc.), or by the presence of abscesses, neural dysfunctions, etc. Mild cases may be treated with an enema of warm water to remove the hardened feces, but the condition should get a vet's attention.

Enterocolitis An infection of the intestinal tract, which may be acute or chronic, caused by bacterial infection, systemic diseases (such as distemper, salmonellosis, etc.), or the ingestion of irritating substances. Acute enterocolitis will cause sudden explosive diarrhea and vomiting (if the cause is ingested irritants), while chronic enterocolitis may involve no abnormal signs except for occasional diarrhea. Diagnosis of the underlying cause and appropriate treatment to remove it and to control the diarrhea should be attended to right away.

Esophagitis Although inflammation of the esophagus is not common, it may be caused by the intake of foreign bodies. Difficulty in swallowing will be the first sign, followed by regurgitation and drooling. The cause must be removed before treat- ment—which may involve a soft or liquid diet, drugs, topical anesthetics, and control of saliva flow—can begin.

Liver disease Acute or chronic, liver disease affects dogs of any age, causing gradual deterioration of the liver. Symptoms include digestive problems, loss of weight, weakness, dark feces, and anemia in the chronic type; and, in the acute form, vomiting, diarrhea, abdominal pain, and refusal to eat. Treatment will vary, depending on the type of disease and its severity, but special diets and medication will undoubtedly be necessary.

Motion sickness As with children, this problem is common in puppies and rare in adult dogs. Although medication can control motion sickness (nausea, vomiting, drooling), it is best to prevent it by not feeding the dog just before traveling and by conditioning him to travel at an early age.

Peritonitis An inflammation of the abdominal lining, causing vomiting, diarrhea, pain, and fever. Treatment includes the use of antibiotics and, in extreme cases, surgery to drain the abdominal cavity.

Pharyngitis Inflammation of the pharynx, usually caused by infection in nearby areas, such as the mouth, tonsils, or nasal cavities, but also occurring in conjunction with a systemic disease (distemper, etc.) or as the result of the ingestion of a foreign body. Refusal to eat (even if the animal seems hungry), gagging, attempt to vomit, regurgitation of foamy white material, and eventual cough or impaired breathing are the usual signs.

URINARY SYSTEM

Cystitis Inflammation of the bladder, caused by various things (virus, bacteria, injury, improper diet). Affecting older animals, the symptoms include frequent urination, dark or bloody urine, restlessness, and vague signs of stiffness and pain. Treatment may be prolonged, even lifelong.

Nephritis Inflammation of the kidneys, which can take both acute and chronic forms, caused by poisoning or disease. Chronic nephritis is more common and is incurable, although it may be controlled by special diet. Symptoms include watery urine and excessive drinking of water.

Stones (calculi) The formation of stones may occur in the bladder, kidneys, ureter, or urethra, and usually causes infection. Bloody urine, frequent urination, straining, thirst, and loss of appetite may all signal the presence of stones, which can be removed surgically.

Uremia A condition, not a disease, involving the buildup of toxic substances in the system, caused by kidney failure, blockage, poor circulation to the kidneys, or bladder rupture. Symptoms are vomiting, dehydration, a urine odor in the mouth, lethargic behavior, and convulsions. The condition is very serious and immediate treatment must be given if the dog is to survive.

INTERNAL PARASITES

Coccidia A parasite of the digestive system, transmitted through feces and causing coccidiosis. The symptoms include bloody diarrhea, loss of appetite, and depression. Coccidiosis can be easily prevented by cleanliness; once contracted, the disease can be controlled with medication.

Heartworm A parasite, transmitted by mosquitoes, that affects the circulatory system. (See page 77.)

Hookworm A parasite that feeds on blood and intestinal tissue. Very serious in puppies or extreme cases, hookworm is transmitted through feces. It can be controlled in sanitary conditions, but medication, generally administered in two stages, is usually necessary to eradicate the adult stage of the worm. Black or bloody stools are early signs, but severe cases will cause diarrhea, anemia, and coughing (when the worm reaches the lungs).

Roundworm A common parasite of the digestive tract, often visible in stool or vomit, causing symptoms such as reduced appetite, coughing, and dull coat. Two wormings may be necessary to eradicate roundworms, and routine fecal examinations are recommended.

Tapeworm A common intestinal parasite, not often serious, although difficult to diagnose and eradicate. Symptoms are subtle—loss of appetite, loss of weight, and nervous behavior, though tapeworm segments are sometimes visible in stool.

Whipworm A parasite of the colon and cecum that can cause colitis if not controlled. Bloody stool and diarrhea may indicate whipworms, which are not easy to detect, although they may be eradicated with medication and are discouraged from recurring in sanitary conditions.

BACTERIAL INFECTIONS

Abscesses The accumulation of pus, often caused by a wound, such as a bite or deep puncture, not uncommon between the toes of dogs, in the anal glands, sinuses, roots of teeth. The abscess must be drained surgically and treated with antibiotics to reduce the infection.

Brucellosis Most common in breeding kennels (where mutts are unlikely to be), this disease can be transmitted through urine, vaginal discharge, aborted material, etc., or any contaminated substance. The usual result is abortion in pregnant females.

REPRODUCTIVE SYSTEM

Abortion The loss of a fetus is not common in dogs, but since causes vary, the bitch should be seen by a vet to prevent recurrence.

Eclampsia (puerperal tetany) A serious disease in the nursing bitch, accompanied by calcium deficiency, high fever, heavy panting, spasms, and pain. Treatment includes the use of calcium gluconate and cortisone, which must be given quickly if the animal is to survive.

Mastitis Another ailment affecting the nursing bitch, involving inflammation of the mammary glands, which become hard, hot, and painful to the touch. If an abscess develops, it will have to be drained, but a simple case can be treated with antibiotics and hot- and cold-pack applications.

Metritis An inflammation of the uterus that will appear occasionally after birth or estrus. It can be acute, accompanied by loss of appetite, depression, and vomiting, in which case spaying may be indicated, or it can be chronic, without symptoms, causing the animal to become sterile, to abort, or to give birth to weak puppies.

Leptospirosis (see page 79)

Salmonellosis The bacteria salmonella can cause severe gastric problems or it may be carried by animals that show no symptoms at all.

Tetanus (see page 79)

Tonsilitis Infection of the tonsils, usually in puppies, causing gagging or vomiting, high fever, and bad breath. Antibiotics and soft foods may help eliminate the symptoms, but surgery may also be recommended.

Prolapse of the vagina This occurs when the vaginal wall protrudes from the vulva, as it may do in large dogs after delivery or during estrus. It will usually disappear on its own, but surgery is recommended to prevent the condition from recurring.

Prostate gland infection (prostatitis) A common condition in older dogs, involving an infection or abscess. Symptoms are weakness, a tender abdomen, straining, and the presence of pus or blood at the tip of the penis. Treatment with antibiotics may be successful or not; castration is often recommended.

Pyometra A more serious ailment affecting the uterus, causing it to become enlarged with an accumulation of pus; there may be some signs of discharge and distended abdomen or there may be more noticeable symptoms, including loss of appetite, vomiting and drinking much water. Surgery is the usual treatment.

Vaginitis An uncommon condition in dogs, this may be signaled by vaginal discharge, which can bring on excessive licking or the attention of male dogs. Treatment is not often very successful.

MUSCULAR-SKELETAL SYSTEM

Arthritis This condition involves an inflammation of the joints, which occurs in aging dogs, although in some animals arthritis is hereditary. The animal will walk with difficulty and pain, although a bit of exercise may alleviate the problem momentarily. Damp, cold days are worse than dry, warm ones. There is no cure and the condition will gradually worsen, but medication can be given to relieve pain.

Disk disorders As dogs age, the elasticity in the cartilage of vertebral disks will become more rigid and may, if jarred, slip through a ligament, causing pressure on the spinal cord. Paralysis, pain, and difficulty in moving are the usual results. Medication or surgery may help improve the condition, as will rest and therapy. Mutts with poodle, dachshund, Pekingese, and cocker spaniel in their past may be more prone than others. Obesity and excessive strain on the spinal cord will often exacerbate or bring on the condition.

Dysplasia A joint disease, resulting from an improperly formed hip joint, which is often a cause of arthritis and is probably inherited, since it is present in the dog from birth. As the dog ages and grows, the problem—difficulty in walking, wobbly hindquarters—will become noticeable. There is no cure, but the animal can be treated to relieve the pain. In some cases, a dog can be treated surgically, but this is not common. A dog with this disorder should be prevented from gaining too much weight. Elbow dysplasia, which affects the front legs, is most common in German shepherds; the lameness is soon followed by arthritis and a general deterioration of the forelegs.

Hernia A weakness in the muscle wall that allows internal organs or fat to protrude. Hernias of the navel may be found occasionally in puppies; older dogs may suffer hernias in the abdomen or in the area near the anus and may require surgery. The hernia will be visible as a bulge under the skin.

Legg-Perthes disease An uncommon condition causing lameness in the hind leg and eventual arthritis, usually found in young poodles. Rest and cortisone may improve the condition, although surgery may be recommended.

Myositis An inflammation of the muscle tissue resulting from an injury and causing great pain. Treatment includes cold compresses on the affected area, antibiotics, and rest.

Osteochondritis A bone disease causing painful lameness, usually in the shoulder area and usually in large dogs. The condition can be diagnosed by X ray, and though the cause is unknown, the condition responds well to treatment and surgery.

Osteomyelitis Another bone disease, difficult to cure but not very common, usually following a fracture or injury. Antibiotics and surgery are usually recommended.

Panosteitis A more common bone disease, particularly in young, large dogs, causing lameness and pain when the limb is handled. The cause is not known, but the dog usually recovers.

Rickets (osteomalacia) A no longer common disease, caused by a deficiency of calcium and phosphorus. It results in lameness, enlarged joints, and bowed legs. Treatment can prevent further deterioration.

173

GLANDS

Anal glands   When these glands become impacted or infected, abscesses can form, causing the area to become inflamed. The dog will try to relieve the pain by biting and licking at the area or scooting on his tail. The vet will clean or drain the area and treat the animal with antibiotics. In extreme cases, surgery to remove the glands may be recommended.

Cysts   These growths may be caused by the rupture of glandular ducts. They can occur in the jaw (salivary cysts), or beneath the skin (sebaceous gland cysts). Removal of the cyst is the usual procedure.

Diabetes mellitus   An incurable but controllable disease involving the animal's inability to secrete sufficient insulin to maintain the blood-sugar balance. Symptoms include increased appetite and thirst and urination; treatment may involve diet control and daily injections of insulin.

Pancreatitis   Inflammation of the pancreas, not uncommon in older or obese dogs. The acute form is marked by sudden vomiting, fever, and depression and will require immediate treatment; the chronic form, symptomatized by large fatty stools and loss of weight but not appetite, may respond to a special diet.

VIRAL INFECTIONS

Canine distemper   (see page 78)

Infectious canine hepatitis   (see page 78)

Rabies   (see page 78)

NERVOUS SYSTEM

Encephalitis   Inflammation of the brain. Rare in dogs, encephalitis may accompany distemper, rabies, and other diseases.

Epilepsy   Chronic occurrence of seizures in a dog can be diagnosed as epilepsy, although the condition is not exactly the same as the disease in humans. It occurs most frequently in young miniature and toy poodles and can be controlled by anticonvulsant medication. False or symptomatic epilepsy is used to describe several metabolic diseases that resemble epilepsy; causes may be dietary deficiency or abnormal digestion and treatment will involve appropriate changes in diet. (See *Convulsions,* page 144).

Hydrocephalus   Water on the brain, also rare, but occasionally found in puppies as the result of a birth defect.

Spinal-cord disorders   See *Disk disorders,* page 171.

Tumors of the brain   Uncommon in dogs, brain tumors are most often seen in boxers and Boston terriers and aged dogs. The animal will have difficulty moving and will be depressed. Circling, pacing, repetitive barking, and seizures may also be apparent.

RESPIRATORY SYSTEM

Asthma   A rare condition in dogs, causing wheezing and heavy and difficult breathing.

Bronchitis   A respiratory ailment symptomatized by coughing, which may be caused by allergies, chemical irritants, parasites, lung or heart disease, and congenital or hereditary defects (particularly in poodles), but is usually accompanied by other diseases. Can be treated with antibiotics, antihistamines, cortisone.

Emphysema   A rare and incurable lung disease, which may be caused by a long siege of bronchitis or asthma. Most common in older animals, treatment usually involves simply making the dog comfortable by suppressing coughs and wheezing with medication.

Kennel cough   Tracheobronchitis is a contagious disease affecting the trachea and is often spread rapidly in kennels. Coughing is the primary symptom, and coughing fits can look serious, although the disease is not too dangerous, lasting only a week or two.

Pneumonia   Inflammation of the lungs, usually caused by bacterial infections, parasites, a tumor, wounds, heart disease, etc. Symptoms are heavy breathing, fever, and coughing. Treatment includes the use of antibiotics and, in some cases, oxygen therapy.

Rhinitis   Inflammation of the nasal passages, caused by chemical irritants, allergies, distemper, root infection in canine teeth, foreign objects, and tumors. Treatment includes cleaning the nasal passage, the use of steam to improve breathing, antihistamines, or cortisone.

Sinusitis   Inflammation of the sinuses, accompanying infection of the respiratory system or caused by abscess in a tooth. Treatment, which may be prolonged, usually includes the use of antibiotics and in extreme cases surgery to drain the area.

CIRCULATORY SYSTEM

Anemia   Lack of red blood cells, a condition (not a disease) usually brought about by severe blood loss, externally or internally. A dog may fail to produce red blood cells as the result of disease, or the cells may be destroyed by bacterial infection or an allergic reaction called autoimmune-hemolytic anemia. Anemia causes an animal to become sluggish and weak; diagnosis is complicated and difficult.

Heart disease   A catchall term that refers to any abnormality in the heart or circulatory system; it is not uncommon in aging dogs. Symptoms include dry coughing, difficult breathing, sluggish behavior, and fatigue after only mild exercise. Treatment is possible through diet control and medication and may be successful if the condition is diagnosed early on. Heart failure may result, either in a chronic or an acute form, though the latter is rare in dogs.

Lymphosarcoma   A tumor in the lymph nodes, usually seen first in the neck area in older dogs. Other symptoms include difficulty in breathing, loss of weight, fever, and decreased appetite. Euthanasia is recommended, since the disease is almost always fatal.

Only His Vet Knows For Sure

Cosmetic Surgery

YOU MIGHT overhear a conversation about cosmetic surgery while cheering on a Great Dane at Westminster, but it's not likely to be idle cocktail-party chatter among a group of mutt owners. Nevertheless, it does present a dilemma to some owners of purebred-looking mutts and deserves a small amount of attention.

When dog owners speak of cosmetic surgery, they are commonly referring to one of three procedures: dewclaw removal, tail docking, and ear cropping. The word *cosmetic* as it applies to dewclaw removal is almost a misnomer; it is cosmetic in that the standards for some breeds require it to be done if a dog is to be shown, but beyond that, it also has a very practical application. Dewclaws are those appendages found partway up on the inside of a dog's front legs (comparable to human thumbs). Occasionally a dog will be born with dewclaws on all four legs and sometimes with no dewclaws at all. The problem is that they get in the way—when a dog scratches or rubs his face, the dewclaw can scratch or damage his eye. They present further problems in that they frequently get hung up on objects—fencing, underbrush, even rugs—and become torn or disjointed, causing no small amount of discomfort. The best time to have dewclaws removed is when a pup is two or three days old; they heal very quickly and the amount of pain involved is minimal. That will undoubtedly be impossible in the case of your pet, so talk to the vet on your initial visit and get his opinion. It may be that your dog could go through life without ever having a problem, but if you own an outdoor type, whose chances of ripping a dewclaw are great, it's not a bad idea to have the dewclaws removed. The younger your pet, the less traumatic the surgery.

Tail docking is a procedure that is also performed at the age of two or three days and is required by the standard set for a number of breeds. Why would you want to have a mutt's tail docked? You won't unless perhaps you have a dog that looks strikingly like a poddle or a schnauzer, and you'd like to complete the picture. It's a relatively minor operation if the dog is only a couple of days old, but it is not an insignificant one as the dog gets older. At the age of two or three months, there is relatively little risk involved (with the exception of the anesthetic, which is the biggest risk in most surgery), but recovery will be painful and annoying to your dog. It might be best to try to overcome your sense of the esthetic and leave your dog's tail alone.

It is true that the sight of a Great Dane smartly posing with his ears erect is nothing short of spectacular, but we can't think of a single reason why anyone would crop a mutt's ears—even to make it look like a Great Dane (our sensitive and sensible friends in England don't crop any dogs' ears regardless of breed). Ear cropping is painful (it is not done until the dog is two or three months old), takes a substantial amount of time to heal, is enormously aggravating to a dog, and exposes the ears to a very strong possibility of infection.

 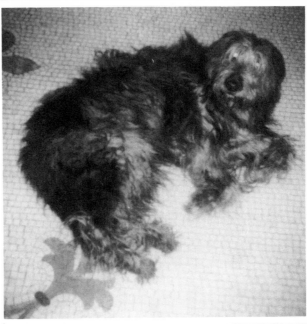

O'Brian

by David Moon

This is O'Brian. He is a dog. I explain because I am so often asked, "What is that?," and my answer is simply, "That is a dog."

This is a dog with a sense of humor, who has laughed himself right out of his class at obedience school. By and large, humor is a fairly meaningless quality in a pet.

O'Brian has never done *anything* obedient. He has never come when he is called. He is about as useful as a cat.

He eats and we are friends. On the whole, we find our arrangement satisfactory.

177

5.
The
Mental
Mutt

There has always been considerable difference of opinion as to whether or not a dog really thinks. I, personally, have no doubt that distinct mental processes do go on inside the dog's brain, although many times these processes are hardly worthy of the name. I have known dogs, especially puppies, who were almost as stupid as humans in their mental reactions.

Robert Benchley

ALTHOUGH it has been said—by no less than Captain Arthur Haggerty, the well-known dog trainer—that "dogs, next to humans, are the most domesticated creatures on the face of the earth," a great deal still has to be learned about canine psychology. Behaviorists have studied dogs in the wild, veterinarians have dealt with psychosomatic illness, and many dog trainers have begun to think of themselves as canine psychologists, but much of what they know still doesn't apply to the ordinary, well-adjusted house dog. Because domesticated dogs are so uniquely close to humans, we can often see a lot of an owner's personality projected onto his dog, and this phenomenon does make it possible to determine something of what makes Fido tick. But there is a lot more than meets the eye in analyzing the normal dog.

Under-standing Your Mutt

We know from studies of wolves that dogs by their very nature have certain charac-teristics as social animals and that dog communication is carried out primarily through gestures of various meaningful kinds. There are dominant dogs and submissive dogs, and on first meeting they can quickly sort out relative status by acting in special ways. These gestures can also be seen in domestic dogs. A submissive dog will flatten his shoulders, put his tail between his legs or wag it, bare his teeth in a kind of smile, roll over on his back, or urinate nervously, while a dominant dog will bare his teeth aggressively, snarl, growl, bark, stare, or, with pricked ears, take a rigid stance or a crouch. Raised hackles (hair along the neck and back) also indicate a dominant or aggressive dog, or a fearful one (we raise our hackles when we have gooseflesh); this is nature's way of making a dog look bigger and more imposing than he normally does.

Natural Canine Traits

Dogs are also naturally equipped with sensory organs unlike those of other species. By comparison with humans, dogs have twice the peripheral vision, although they cannot focus clearly at a distance. This equips the dog well for seeing a moving object as it crosses the path of vision, though the dog may not be able to determine right away whether he is seeing a cat, a car, or a rabbit. Although the extent of color blindness in dogs is still undetermined, we know that they are sensitive to different tones or degrees of lightness even though they can't distinguish between some colors. Dogs can hear better than we do (though less well than cats) and are especially sensitive to pitch and the consistency of rhythms. Dog whistles, for exam-ple, are audible to dogs but are too high pitched for the human ear. Nevertheless, dogs can't discriminate different tones as well as we can (where music is concerned, dogs have tin ears), but they can localize sounds better than we can and they have good memories when it comes to hearing and remembering footstep rhythms and other vibrations. Because they have fifty times the olfactory membranes that we do, dogs are far more sensitive to faint odors and are more discriminating, capable of distinguishing between different scents—food, other dogs, a bitch in heat, territory, etc. Dogs also have good scent memory, a trait that in some breeds has been developed to a high and very useful degree.

181

Breed Traits   The natural social and physical makeup of the dog isn't the whole story. Dogs vary considerably—more so than any other species—in terms of size, appearance, and natural abilities, and this is because humans have bred them for numerous purposes, exaggerating certain traits and eliminating others. In recent years, however, we have employed dogs less for these specific purposes and yet have kept up the specialized breeding—more for the sake of show and snobbery than for actual usefulness. It is the rare keeshond or bouvier who pulls a canal boat, and we have yet to see a French poodle hunting for his livelihood. The dogs still used for the purposes for which they were bred—hunting, herding, and sled pulling—are the exceptions rather than the rule. The most popular job for the American dog is unquestionably that of house pet and companion, a job for which very few dogs (the miniature poodles and other tiny breeds, for example) were actually bred.

We all know (or should) that show dogs, guard dogs, laboratory animals, and seeing-eye dogs aren't very good house pets (if they were good around the house, they wouldn't be good at their jobs), but often we try to adapt a particular breed for our own personal use. Luckily, dogs are among the most adaptable creatures we know, and most of them make good pets once they learn what is expected of them. But many do not, and the problems that result can be serious and heartrending.

Some of these problems are caused by specialized breeding for the sake of fashion. As the distinguished animal behaviorist Konrad Lorenz points out in his book *Man Meets Dog*:

> . . . there is no single breed of dog the originally excellent mental qualities of which have not been completely destroyed as a result of having become "fashionable." Only where, in some quiet corner of the world, the dog in question has gone on being bred for use and without any deference to fashion has such destruction been avoided. . . .

Certain congenital defects do recur in certain breeds—hip dysplasia in some large breeds, spinal weakness in dachshunds, and so on. But there are temperamental defects as well. An aggressive temperament coupled with a huge body, as in a St. Bernard or a mastiff, can be a dangerous defect indeed, especially in a household. Dogs with strong territorial instincts, such as the husky, have been accused of viciousness because they have bitten people who stray onto their territory. But vicious is the wrong word here, since it implies a vice; what has occurred is not the fault of the dog but that of the breeder who has failed to eliminate the trait in the dog's genetic makeup or has sold the dog to the wrong people. Owners should always be aware of their dog's natural canine and bred-in traits before making their choice.

Obviously one can't always tell exactly what has gone into a mutt in terms of genetic heritage (what looks like a beagle may be something else altogether), but there are simple tests that one can do (see page 30) to determine innate instincts and traits if they aren't immediately apparent.

The Mental Mutt

Knowing a dog's breeding and natural instincts, however, still doesn't prepare us to know a dog. Individual dogs may be brighter than others, more alert, more inclined to training, or they may be slow-witted, mischievous, and unpleasant to have around. Although a certain amount of this can be ascribed to individual characteristics, there is a great deal we can learn about a dog simply by knowing how it has been treated by humans in the past. (Or conversely, we can often determine how a dog has been treated by the way he behaves.) It is easy enough to tell that a dog who cowers when you raise your hand has been beaten or that a dog who is frightened of men rather than women has seen abuse from one sex but not the other. But things are rarely that simple. Many obviously abused dogs, seemingly overcome with gratitude for good treatment, never react in fear and trembling from their new owners, and some well-treated animals will suddenly react in an undesirable way for reasons that aren't at all apparent. This is because abuse doesn't always take the form of a beating; sometimes a well-meaning person can abuse an animal by doing exactly the opposite, by overindulging it in a misguided attempt at being kind. Or a neurotic person, using the dog as a target for all his neuroses (on purpose or inadvertently), can quickly turn a perfectly healthy animal into a bundle of similar neurotic symptoms.

The writer John Steinbeck, a dog lover all his life, had this to say about overindulgence in *Travels with Charley*:

> I yield to no one in my distaste for the self-styled dog lover, the kind who heaps up frustrations and makes a dog carry them around. Such a dog-lover talks baby talk to mature and thoughtful animals, and attributes his own sloppy characteristics to them until the dog becomes in his mind an alter ego. Such people, it seems to me, are capable of inflicting long and lasting tortures on an animal, denying it any of its natural desires and fulfillments until a dog of weak character breaks down and becomes the fat, asthmatic, furbound bundle of neuroses. When a stranger addresses Charley in baby talk, Charley avoids him. For Charley is not a human; he's a dog, and he likes it that way. He feels that he is a first-rate dog and has no wish to be a second-rate human.

Not all dogs are as self-confident as Charley was, however. In fact, many experts believe that domestic dogs are simply immature versions of the wild dog, made to feel more submissive and dependent than they intrinsically are, to suffer what Michael Fox calls the "perpetual puppy syndrome." These dogs, he says, "will develop a whole range of emotional disorders when their relationship with the owner is threatened, as it is by the birth of a child, by the introduction of a new pet, or by separation for some reason from the owners." Dogs that are dependent on their masters are probably easier to train and more responsive as companions, but as Lorenz points out, too much indulgence, instead of creating a faithful animal, will have the opposite effect of creating a dog that is friendly to everyone. This kind of dog will carry puppy problems well into adulthood—chewing shoes, urinating in the house when nervous, and otherwise acting like a baby dog.

Individual "Man-made" Traits

A more dangerous set of symptoms is that shown by the fearful dog, who may bark ferociously so long as he is tied or confined but will cower in terror when released. This dog is highly likely to bite—not out of aggressiveness, but out of fear and a lack of self-confidence. An unusually frightened dog is to be avoided by anyone for whom that dog shows fear, or a painful bite may result.

A more predictable, but no less dangerous, animal is the aggressive dog who has never learned to obey his owner. Many people overindulge their animals as puppies, letting them get away with everything short of murder and allowing them to go untrained and undisciplined. Love is important to a pet dog, but respect is perhaps even more so, for without it, a dog can easily take the upper hand and bite the hand that feeds it in the process. Lots of people have big, tough dogs for the sake of protecting themselves and their property, but they are terrified of the animals, and the dogs know it. Some dogs may be submissive with their masters but dominant with other people—those who fear the dog or those who are smaller and less masterful with the animal. The incidence of dog bites is rising every year—because there are more dogs around, more dogs serving double-duty as guard and pet, and because people don't know how to handle them. These dogs can be trained, of course, but too often people are forced into destroying them because they have caused too much damage or injury or because the owners don't realize that the aggressiveness is simply dog nature allowed to go uncontrolled. Even if we can't always control ourselves, we can certainly learn to control our pets—and if we can't, we shouldn't have them.

Some dogs, according to trainers who specialize in canine problems, will pick up neurotic behavior directly from their owners. As Mordecai Siegal puts it, "there are dogs that pace, dogs that suffer from insomnia, dogs that fear strangers, dogs that fear other dogs, dogs that are sexually attractive to specific humans, and even dogs that suffer mental breakdowns." But, he notes, "there are no known canine chain-smokers."

Some neuroses in dogs can't always be explained. Very often we ascribe human emotions to dogs that are jealous, for instance, or spiteful enough to urinate in the house when they have been left alone against their wishes. Although too much anthropomorphism is—like too much of anything—ill-advised, it is true that dogs do share many of our fears and feelings. A "one-man" dog, entirely dependent on one person, may well resent the presence of someone else who "intrudes," in the dog's eyes, and breaks up the usual routines or monopolizes his master's attention and affection. Dogs often resent the birth of a child in a family where they have hitherto been the "babies," and such animals should be treated with the greatest of care and supervision. Patience and common sense on the part of the owner to the "jilted" dog will overcome most problems, but a refresher course in basic training may be necessary, too. One needn't take a "spiteful" dog who doesn't like being left at home everywhere one goes, but some adjustments can be made to cure the problem. Some people, for instance, will get pets for their pets, just to keep them busy and happy when they are left alone; racehorses often have mascots, and there's no reason why a frustrated, lonely dog shouldn't have another dog or a cat around to keep him

The Mental Mutt

company if he must spend many hours on his own. Toys may help, of course, but extremely dependent dogs usually need something more.

Dr. Mark W. Allam, former dean of the University of Pennsylvania School of Veterinary Medicine, believes that it is possible to retrain a neurotic dog into an acceptable one if it is put into an environment different from the animal's home and treated with great care and patience by an expert. Older dogs are more difficult to retrain than younger ones, and some dogs may never be retrained at all, since the owners are unlikely to change once the dog returns to the household, no matter how much money has been spent to "cure" the animal.

Many people who do not have the time or believe they do not have the expertise will turn their canine problems over to an expert, a trainer who can, using basic methods (most of which are outlined in the numerous books available on the subject of dog training), take a misbehaving mutt under his wing and turn him into a model citizen. But only if the owner is retrained as well—how to treat the dog and how not to—can this often expensive procedure be effective. The fees charged by these trainers—many of whom call themselves dog psychiatrists—can be very substantial indeed and the dog will revert almost immediately to his old self if the conditions that brought the problem about in the first place are not changed, or if the owner doesn't learn how to control the animal as well as the expert does.

One of the reasons that neurotic dogs are common is that there are so many neurotic people owning them, but unless a dog is in danger of losing his home or inflicting harm on people or other animals, his neurosis may be perfectly acceptable. A dog who makes a pest of himself because he wants attention all the time may be the perfect companion for someone who needs someone to love. A hypochondriac animal may simply have picked up on the fact that his owner craves the opportunity to fuss and play nurse. It is certainly true that some people need dogs as much as dogs need people, and those who have trouble getting along with other people often find happiness and fulfillment in a symbiotic relationship with their pets. If other people find the relationship—or the dog's behavior—unusual or even "sick," it may be quite normal and rewarding for the individuals involved.

After all, not all human problems are avoidable or even treatable. Lonely and bereaved persons can benefit greatly from the companionship of a dog, not only at home but also outside it, where the animal can break the ice very quickly. Those who remember Walt Disney's *Lady and the Tramp* will recall that it was the meeting of the two dogs that brought the owners together. John Steinbeck, on his camping trip across America, found that "in establishing contact with strange people, Charley is my ambassador. I release him and he drifts toward the objective, or rather to whatever the objective may be preparing for dinner. I retrieve him so that he will not be a nuisance to my neighbors—*et voilà!* A child can do the same thing, but a dog is better."

Mary Bloom

Understanding Your Mutt   **185**

"Willie, I know how desperate you must feel."

Charles G. Lewis
Engraving after Edwin Landseer
Date unknown

I'm OK, But I'm Not So Sure About You

Scenario: The Park Avenue office of Dr. Joyce Mothers, a group psychologist of some note. A number of mutts meander into the room and take seats.

WILLIE: Ouch! Slugger, stop it, stop it! That hurts! Let go of me . . . stop biting me! Look! Look what you've done! You've broken the skin and I'm bleeding—my tail is bleeding. Oh, dear . . . look what *I've* done. Oh, I just want to go home. *(Wailing.)* What an awful day.

ARTIE: Ha, ha, ha. Slugger, you're a card. You shoulda seen the expression on Willie's face when you nabbed him on the tail. His eyes got as big as saucers and then he peed. What a riot!

SUSIE: Artie, you shut up. Don't encourage that sadistic brute.

Willie, poor Willie, are you all right? Your little tail looks so sore. Let me wash it off for you. Don't pay any attention to those two. They're mean and they're bullies.

WILLIE: Thanks, Susie. But I'm going home. It's so embarrassing to pee all the time. When I get excited I pee, when I get upset I pee, when somebody yells at me I pee. Life is just too much to handle anymore. I'm leaving. There's nothing anyone here can do for me except make matters worse.

SUSIE: No, wait . . . don't go. Here comes Dr. Mothers. She'll help, Willie, really she will.

DR. MOTHERS: What's all the commotion about? I could hear you all the way down the hall.

SUSIE: Dr. Mothers, that oaf Slugger bit Willie on the tail. Look at it . . . it's all swollen. And then Willie peed, and now he says he's going to leave. Well, Slugger's the one who should leave—and Artie, too . . . he's not much better. They're nothing but a disruption to the group.

DR. MOTHERS: Friends, could we all sit down. You, too, Willie . . . please stay.

Slugger, this group is your last chance. Your parole officer felt that we might be able to help you with your chronic biting problem. We know your puppyhood was difficult and that biting was your only defense then, but then is not now. If you're not going to try and let the group help you in a reasonable way, I'll have to make a recommendation I don't want to make—that you be sent away for obedience training, which means that you'll be slapped sharply across the muzzle every time you bite and that when you are out of the house you will be muzzled at all times.

Willie, as far as you're concerned, I know how desperate you must feel. Your problem is humiliating and embarrassing, and it's not one that can be solved overnight. We must, through patience and time and kindness, make you understand that we can be trusted—that you needn't be fearful or apprehensive about your relationships with others. You have every reason to be a bundle of nerves—your former family was despicable, teasing and yelling and poking at you all the time. But your new family loves you and they are kind and considerate. It will take time, Willie, but you *will* stop piddling. Just give everybody a chance.

WILLIE: I hope so, Dr. Mothers . . . oh, I hope so.

DR. MOTHERS: Now, group, where were we when we ended last week?

SUSIE: Kenny was going to tell us about his problem.

DR. MOTHERS: Kenny, go ahead.

KENNY: Well, this will probably sound silly, but it isn't silly to me. I'm sorry to bother you all, but I don't know where else to turn. In fact, that's all I do—turn. I chase my tail around and around until I'm exhausted. It's not that I like my tail that much or even that I want to catch it, and I hate to sound like a complainer, because I'm really very grateful for the good food I get and the cage I have to live in, but I think maybe I'm going crazy, and so does my family . . . they think . . .

CARL: Cage? Did you say cage? You mean to tell me that you live in a . . . cage?

KENNY: Well, sure. Doesn't every dog? It's a little cramped, and sometimes I get nervous, but . . .

CARL: No wonder you chase your tail. I'd chase my tail too in your spot. You're claus . . . clauspo . . . claustro . . .

DR. MOTHERS: Claustrophobic. Carl is quite right, Kenny. Behavior such as chasing one's tail or attacking spots on the floor is a natural manifestation of being cooped up in tight quarters. Speak to your family . . .

CARL: Yeah, get on *their* tails and tell 'em you don't want to live like a prisoner no more.

BEN: Woof, woof, woof.

DR. MOTHERS: Do you have something to say, Ben?

BEN: Oh, no, Dr. Mothers.

DR. MOTHERS: OK, then.

Ginger, your family called me yesterday. I understand you've chewed up another couch pillow.

GINGER: That's right! I did it and I'm glad! If I want to chew on a drape or eat the couch leg, then I'm going to do it and there's nobody

The Mental Mutt

that's going to stop me. If they think they're going to leave me alone in the house, then they're dead wrong, because I don't like it one bit, and they're going to be sorry for it. They think that I'm not very smart and that I can't be trained, but boy, do I have them fooled. It just makes me mad, mad, mad when they leave without me, and if they do it again I'll chew up the rest of the couch pillows.

SAM: If you were my dog, I'd throw you out on your ear. You're an infantile, spoiled brat. You have the nicest family anybody could ask for, and just because they leave you home alone once in a while you destroy stuff. You don't take them with you everywhere you go. Fair's fair. People have rights, too, you know.

BEN: Woof, woof.

ARTIE: If you don't shut up, Ben, I'll slug you in the kisser.

DR. MOTHERS: Boys, that's enough.

Ginger, I hope you were listening to what Sam said. You are behaving very selfishly. Do any of the members of the group have any ideas about what we can do for Ginger?

ARTIE: Yeah, tell her to jump in the lake.

SUSIE: Well, sometimes when my family goes out, they leave the radio or TV on. It's really very soothing and makes time go so fast that you hardly even miss them.

BEN: Woof, woof . . . Ouch! Get your paws offa me, Artie!

ARTIE: I told ya to shut up, Ben.

Well, Ginger, I'll tell ya what I'd do to ya—I'd beat your head off.

DR. MOTHERS: That might be a bit drastic, Artie, but it certainly sounds as though Ginger should be sternly reprimanded whenever she does something destructive.

GINGER: It won't make any difference. I'll still chew, chew, chew.

DR. MOTHERS: Well, then, the only remedy is to confine you to an area of the house where there is nothing you can destroy—say, the basement or garage.

ARTIE: That's lettin' her have it, Doc! Jeez, I gotta move my seat. Carl, you stink! What'd you have for breakfast—baked beans? Ya sure have some case of gas!

SAM: That's no case of gas . . . it's his breath!

ARTIE: His breath?! His breath?!!

CARL: Oh, I knew this would happen. I told you, Dr. Mothers, I told you. Oh, I can't talk about it, I can't deal with it. I'm leaving right now.

ARTIE: When you leave, pick up some mouthwash.

189

DR. MOTHERS:	Artie!
CARL:	*(Sobbing.)*
DR. MOTHERS:	Group, Carl suffers from coprophagy.
ARTIE:	He suffers from stinkin' is what he suffers from.
DR. MOTHERS:	Artie, the group is getting very tired of your aggressive, insensitive behavior.
SLUGGER:	Yeah, ya better watch it, Artie. Ya know what they did to old Flip a coupla years ago because his family decided he was too aggressive and a bully? They cut off his ba . . . they castrated him. Do ya believe that?
ARTIE:	*(Crossing his legs.)* You gotta be kiddin'!
DR. MOTHERS:	It's quite true, Artie, that in many cases of aggressiveness in male dogs, castration is indicated. More often than not, it has quite a calming effect.
ARTIE:	Calming! Killing is more like it! But, listen, I ain't bein' a wise guy when I say that Carl stinks. It's a fact!
DR. MOTHERS:	Yes—about Carl. Carl's problem—coprophagy—is the practice of eating one's own stool.
ARTIE:	Oh, jeez.
SLUGGER:	I think I'm gonna be sick.
CARL:	Stop, please stop.
DR. MOTHERS:	Group, we're here to help, not to hurt.
SUSIE:	Carl, why would you want to do a thing like that?
CARL:	*(Sobbing.)* I don't *want* to do it. I can't help myself.
DR. MOTHERS:	The experts don't agree on what causes Carl's problem. Some feel it is a dietary deficiency, others think it's a mental problem, and still others attribute it to an enzyme deficiency.
FRED:	I'd like to say something here. Ya know in my racket—being a stray, that is—ya run into all kinds. I met a guy once who used to do the same thing. Well, his folks took him to some big, fancy vet and he told him that there's stuff that can be added to food that makes it really taste bad when it comes out the other end, if ya know what I mean. Well, my buddy tried it—every time he ate, his folks added mono . . . monos . . .
DR. MOTHERS:	Monosodium glutamate.
FRED:	Yeah, right. They added monosodium glutamate to his food. An' ya know what? He hasn't touched a pile of sh . . . poo . . . stool in three years. Every once in a while he gets that old gleam in his eye and he salivates a little, but the old mouth stays shut.
BEN:	Woof, woof.
GINGER:	Ben, your barking is really annoying and disturbing. You never contribute anything to the group. You just bark whenever you

The Mental Mutt

feel like it—to hear the sound of your own voice. I wish you'd cut it out.

DR. MOTHERS: Yes, Ben, it is distracting. We know you're lonely and bored most of the time at home, and that's probably why you bark, but people would pay more attention to you if you didn't make so much noise. I understand your neighbors are complaining and threatening to call the police. Your family is going to have to muzzle you if you don't quiet down. I don't think you want that to happen.

SUSIE: Is that thunder? My God, is that thunder I hear? Oh, no. Please not that. *(Panting, crawls under chair.)* I can't stand it, no, not thunder. *(Chewing at herself.)* Anything but thunder.

SAM: What's the matter with her?

ARTIE: She's hysterical again . . . really goes off the deep end during a thunderstorm.

SUSIE: *(Trembling.)* Please, Dr. Mothers, do something . . .

DR. MOTHERS: OK, dear, I'll . . .

WILLIE: Oh, Susie, please don't get upset. It makes me so nervous to see you distraught . . . please, please . . . oh, I knew it, there I go again. Oh, darn, I've gotten the chair all wet. Oh, I want to go home . . .

DR. MOTHERS: Willie, pull yourself together. Susie, it'll be all right. Kenny, will you stop chasing your tail and get me some paper towels?

ARTIE: I'll get 'em, Dr. M. Here they are. Hey, who chewed up the towels?

GINGER: I'm leaving.

ARTIE: Ginger, for cryin' out loud!

BEN: Woof, woof.

ARTIE: Ben, will ya shut up. Here ya are, Dr. M.

CARL: Scuse me, I have to go take care of something.

DR. MOTHERS: Carl, don't leave . . . Ben, will you please be quiet . . . Artie, would you please wipe up Willie's mess . . . and stop Ginger from chewing up that chair. Slugger, would you please get your teeth out of my leg . . . Susie, darling, it's going to be all right . . .

191

Cleo's vanity was one of the most disarming things about her. Praise her mawkishly and she fairly melted with gratitude. She was an insufferable poseur. When I came home from work late at night and lounged for a few moments before going to bed, she would sit up erect on the couch, throw out her chest grandly, and draw her breath in short gasps to attract attention. When everyone in the room was praising her—although with tongue in cheek—she would alternate the profile with the full face to display all her glory. "The duchess," we used to call her when she was posing regally in the back seat of the open car. But she was no fool. She knew just how much irony we were mixing with the praise and she did not like to be laughed at. If she felt that the laughter was against her, she would crowd herself into a corner some distance away and stare at us with polite disapproval.

From Robert Benchley's story "Cleo for Short"

An Eccentric Quartet

One morning [Mutt] foolishly pursued a cat into the ex-schoolteacher's yard. He was immediately surrounded by four ravening Huskies. They were a merciless lot, and they closed in for the kill. Mutt saw at once that this time he would have to fight. With one quick motion he flung himself over on his back and began to pedal furiously with all four feet. It looked rather as if he were riding a bicycle built for two, but upside down. He also began to sound his siren. This was a noise he made—just how, I do not know—deep in the back of his throat. It was a kind of frenzied wail. The siren rose in pitch and volume as his legs increased their r.p.m.'s, until he began to sound like a gas turbine at full throttle.

The effect of this unorthodox behavior on the four Huskies was to bring them to an abrupt halt. Their ears went forward and their tails uncurled as a look of pained bewilderment wrinkled their brows. And then slowly, and one by one, they began to back away, their eyes uneasily averted from the distressing spectacle before them. When they were ten feet from Mutt they turned as one dog and fled without dignity for their own back yard.

From Farley Mowat's The Dog Who Wouldn't Be

The Mental Mutt

NINEPIN GAME PULL TOY
Maine
Early 20th century
Papier-mâché, polychrome, gesso
L., 20″, H., 12″
Ms. Molly Epstein

The first dog I remember well was a large black and white mutt that was part German shepherd, part English sheep dog, and part collie—the wrong part in each case. With what strikes me now as unforgivable whimsey, we called him Ladadog from the title by Albert Payson Terhune. He was a splendid dog in many respects but, in the last analysis, I'm afraid he was a bit of a social climber. He used to pretend that he was just crazy about us. I mean, if you just left the room to comb your hair he would greet you on your return with passionate lickings, pawings, and convulsive tail-waggings. . . . However, all this mawkish, slobbering sentiment disappeared the moment he stepped over the threshold. I remember we kids used to spot him on our way home from school, chasing around the Parkers' lawn with a cocker friend of his, and we'd rush over to him with happy squeals of "Laddy, oleboy, oleboy, oleboy," and Ladadog would just stand there looking slightly pained and distinctly cool. It wasn't that he cut us dead. He nodded, but it was with the remote air of a celebrity at a cocktail party saying, "Of course I remember you, and how's Ed?"

From Jean Kerr's Please Don't Eat the Daisies

Our dog was scraped out of a sand hole full of mongrel puppies by a mower on a naval airfield when the hot war was our way of life. We named him Captain, for even as a white-and-tan ball of fluff, with his pointed black ears and vertical tail, he was one of the lords of the earth. . . . Without a doubt Cap understood every word in the English language in ordinary use, and a good many common only in naval parlance. He would respond to conversation that he overheard while pretending to be asleep, and he knew the meaning of many words that we spelled out to fool him. We often kidded him for not learning to talk—much to his discomfiture. He frequently tried, but never quite made it.

Glenn Matthew White, "Toodles Doesn't Understand"

193

Communicating with Your Dog

It has been shown that although dogs can learn to discriminate between as many as 75 or 100 words, they can produce no more than one or two recognizable sounds themselves. Therefore, in order to hear what your dog has to say, it's more effective to keep your eyes open and be alert to his gestures rather than to his voice, although you needn't learn those gestures yourself in order to get your point across.

WHITE DOG WITH RED-BROWN
SPOTS
Alton Foundry
Lancaster, Ohio
Late 19th century
Iron, painted
L., 8¼″
Mr. and Mrs. William Gilmore

The dog should not try to lead a man's life, any more than the man should be treated like a dog. When a doting person gets down on all fours and plays with his dog's rubber mouse, for example, it only confuses the puppy and gives him a sense of insecurity. He gets the impression that his world is unstable, and wonders whether he is supposed to walk on his hind legs and learn to smoke cigars. Dogs treated in this way become acutely self-conscious about not having any clothes on and develop a neurosis about their tails.

From Corey Ford's essay "Every Dog Should Have a Man"

Imus

by Douglas Firestone

Date of Birth: January 1, 1976

Birthplace: Springfield, Mass.

Lineage: Highly questionable. Mother; supposedly cocker spaniel. Father; your guess is as good as mine. (Possible background: springer spaniel, terrier, beagle, and whatever strikes our fancy on any given day.)

Distinguishing marks: Mostly black with four white paws, white chest, white tip of tail.

Residence: Formerly Middletown, Ct. Now East Setauket, N.Y.

Hobbies: Favors barking at birds and chewing twigs. Also chews rawhide "bones." Fetches, but won't give up item once it's been fetched; licks noses; stays up nights figuring out new ways to get attention and twist all who meet him around his paw.

Talents: Speaks when spoken to, rolls over, shakes hands, sits and lies down on command of "What do you have to do?"

Words Understood: Above commands plus: cookie, carrot, pillow, bone, ball, bed, car, out, go up, go down, come here, want to do this or that? Example: "Want to play with your bone?" etc.

Physical Condition: Excellent.

Emotional State: Imus does not fully understand that he is a member of the canine persuasion. When he sees the neighborhood children, he cries to be with his friends. When, however, he sees another dog, he behaves as any child would at the thrill of playing with a real puppy.

Habits: Rolls in the dirt when inspired by the proper scent. Digs holes until evenly coated with dirt, but cleans himself with speed and thoroughness. Hates being bathed.

Other Activities: Swims when thrown in, usually to the nearest pool ladder.

Name of foster parents: Doug and Sue Firestone.

Children and Dogs

IT DOESN'T take an expert to see the very real advantages there are in the dog-child relationship, yet it is good to know that the experts confirm the fact that having a dog is a valuable and important experience for a child.

Dr. Boris Levinson, in his book *Pets and Human Development,* describes the way in which children may benefit at all stages of growth from the presence of a pet. In this day and age of broken homes, alienated groups in society, and disorder in the streets, pets give people a way of opening up, of trusting other living beings, of giving love and affection without fear. And for children, these responses can be instilled from the earliest years with the assistance of a pet dog. Clinical observation has shown that families with pets have fewer problems than those without. Pets are often a successful means of uniting parents and children simply by being a love object for the whole family, and they can give the child a sense of responsibility in homes where chores have gone by the board.

Very young children can learn about the world around them from an animal, learn to sort out their own identity ("me" and "other") and to distinguish firsthand between the creatures that surround them ("dog," "cat," "mother," "father"). Small babies, always attracted to dogs, explore their fur, ears, and tails by touching, pulling, and watching the dog's reactions. Toddlers can be taught not to hurt the dog. By respecting his feelings and pains, they can begin to understand that other living creatures have them, too. Children learning to walk and play can find playmates in a pet dog, a noncompetitive animal that simply enjoys the child without judging or disciplining him. Children who do not have siblings can quickly advance their motor skills and coordination by interacting with a playful dog.

Dogs are also wonderful teachers of other aspects of living: birth, death, illness, and aging. In fact, the illness and death of a pet may be the child's first experience with these inevitable facts of life, and although sadness will be unavoidable, a child who learns to deal with loss and grief at an early age is far better prepared for the tragedies of life than one who meets them later on. With the help of the parents, a child can learn the basics of caring for the ill and the ceremonies of life from birth to death when the family dog is affected.

A dog can teach a child to have a sense of responsibility and caring and can give him a feeling of self-confidence for having been able to make decisions. Dogs can be companions, protectors, and status symbols for children who are learning to relate to their peers and to the rest of the world outside the family. And they can help a child develop special skills. An interest in drawing, painting, or photography will take on extra meaning if the family dog can be persuaded to pose. Money management can be instilled as a child learns how much it costs, say, to feed a dog or to visit the veterinarian; if the child receives a small allowance as recompense for taking care of the dog, he'll get an idea of the value of his own time and effort. A child who wishes to learn more about his dog can be encouraged to take the time to read up on the subject. Dogs will help sedentary children get exercise and can teach budding psychologists something about behavior by learning to come, sit, stay, and heel. But perhaps most important, a dog will enable a child—especially a lonely or disturbed one—to feel loved, no questions asked.

Dogs, too, will benefit. For one thing, dogs need exercise and they love to play, and kids are great at providing opportunities for both. And dogs as a species can benefit by having helped individuals learn to love them and care for them properly.

The amount of a child's responsibility for his pet depends on both the maturity of the child and the temperament of the dog. Toddlers, of course, can't be expected to take on much responsibility when it comes to taking care of a dog, but they can be helpful in preparing food and cleaning up the dog's dishes and sleeping area. Older youngsters, who can be more actively helpful, are able to feed, walk, and brush the dog. Don't, however, allow the child to take part in these activities unless you are certain that the dog is reliable. It is not unusual for a dog to be possessive about his meals and snap at someone he feels is interfering. Nor is it unlikely for a dog to snap at someone who is too

BOY AND DOG
Painter unknown
Circa 1845
Newark Museum
New Jersey

197

rough while brushing him. And don't let your child walk the dog unless you are sure the dog will not take off after another animal or a person. In general, don't subject the child or the dog to a situation that neither is equipped to handle.

A dog can be aggressive out of fear, jealousy, territorial instinct (as when a child threatens his food or his property), and in excessive play when a dominant animal may choose to exercise his dominance. In the selection of the dog, avoid one that you know to be aggressive, either through heredity or previous treatment (a guard dog and a pet dog can rarely be combined in the same animal), and avoid any excitable or nervous animal that may react badly under stress. Children should be taught to recognize signs of aggression and fear and to deal with them appropriately. They should also be encouraged to train their animals to assert their own dominance over them and keep them under control, especially when a situation gets slightly out of hand.

A child may fear dogs because of their size, strength, or manner, or because of some bad experience with animals; some parents can instill this fear in children inadvertently. A gradual program of introducing a child to a puppy or small dog and then to a larger animal should help overcome this fear, but any fearful child, who may arouse the instincts and the hackles of a strange dog with aggressive instincts, should be taught how to behave with such animals to avoid trouble. (See page 210.) A fearful child should also be taught what can be harmful or painful to a dog and be told that such treatment is dangerous as well as wrong. A child may deliberately abuse his pet, pulling his tail, poking at him, or chasing him. Such a child should be supervised closely or the dog should be removed. Some kids mistreat dogs without meaning to, as in simple neglect through oversight or ignorance, and these children, too, need supervision and assistance. If you see your child mistreating an animal, be firm in explaining the difference between play and abuse and in outlining the possible consequences. Teach the child not to tease the dog, which can be anything from causing actual pain to surprising the dog by sneaking up on it. Sudden loud noises and sneak attacks from the rear can cause any hypertense dog to react in self-defense. And even a dog that isn't hyper-anything but only hungry may turn into a child molester by trying to grab a piece of food from his hand. The child's natural inclination is to hold the food up high, but this is only part of the game to the dog, who will jump up to get it. If the kids must eat in front of the dog, tell them to do so quickly and quietly; if the dog seems to threaten them, it's better to let the dog have the food.

It may be heartwarming to watch a child and his pet sleep together on the child's bed, but because there are some parasites that can be transmitted from one to the other, it isn't recommended. Kids can pick up fleas and ticks as easily as their dogs can, and roundworm can also affect humans who have had contact with the animal's feces. (Most children won't play with a dog's stool, but they can be licked in the face or come into contact with contaminated fur and areas where the dog sleeps and plays.) There would be no harm in letting the dog sleep at the foot of a child's bed, however, so long as the spot is cleaned regularly.

Most important, supervise your child's relationship with his pet until you are confident that a rapport is established and that both are trustworthy and friendly.

A dog teaches a boy fidelity, perseverance, and to turn around three times before lying down.

       Robert Benchley

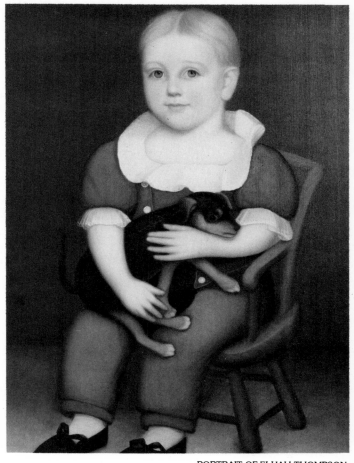

PORTRAIT OF ELIJAH THOMPSON
U.S.
Circa 1838
Oil on tulipwood panel
30″ × 24″
Private Collection

The ideal age for a boy to own a dog is between forty-five and fifty. By this time the boy ought to have attained his full growth, and, provided he is ever going to, ought to know more or less what he wants to make of himself in life. At this age the dog will be more of a companion than a chattel and, if necessary, can be counted upon to carry the boy by the middle and drop him into bed in case sleep overcomes him at a dinner or camp meeting or anything. It can also be counted upon to tell him he has made a fool of himself and embarrassed all his friends. A wife could do no more.

       Robert Benchley, "Your Boy and His Dog"

Grits

Did you know that a mutt presently has tenure in the White House? Meet Grits, Amy Carter's all-American dog who lives in the White House kennel and periodically cruises the broad lawns of his Pennsylvania Avenue mansion.

Grits, despite his name, is not a southerner. He was born in Washington, D.C., one of a large litter that arrived on Election Day 1976. His mother belonged to Mrs. Meeder, a teacher at Stevens Elementary School. After Jimmy Carter won the presidency and Amy started school at Stevens, Mrs. Meeder, believing Grit's birthday no coincidence, promptly gave the pup to Amy.

Because Grits has to carry out his new position as White House pet with extraordinary diplomacy, he was sent to obedience school to learn the rules of puppy etiquette. Now he consorts with some of our country's most important figures as well as foreign heads of state, and his picture has appeared—along with his distinguished family—in periodicals all over the land.

PORTRAIT OF ANDREW JACKSON
TEN BROECK
Ammi Phillips
New York
1834
Oil on canvas
39″ × 34″
Private Collection

COME ONE! COME ALL!

THE GREAT MUTT-OF-THE-YEAR SHOW

BRING YOUR DOG (ON A LEASH)
AND YOUR FRIENDS AND FAMILY
FOR A CHANCE TO COMPETE IN
TESTS OF WIT, STRENGTH, BEAUTY, AND TALENT IN
THIS FIRST ANNUAL SHOW FOR NON-BREEDS

PLACE: THE SCHOOL   **TIME:** SATURDAY
OCTOBER 10
10 A.M. TO 4 P.M.

RAIN DATE: SUNDAY
OCTOBER 11

RIBBONS FOR
• BEST PERSONALITY
• BEST LOOKING
• BEST IN SHOW
• BEST OF MUTT
AND MORE!!

PRIZES!

FUN!

GAMES!

REFRESHMENTS!

FOR INFORMATION AND ADVANCE REGISTRATION, CALL
GEORGE AND MARTHA McDEVITT AT 222-3333.
FEMALES IN HEAT NEED NOT APPLY • THERE WILL BE A SMALL FEE (50¢)
— FOR EACH CLASS —

Leonard Henderson

Showing Off

NOTHING is tougher on a mutt's ego than to walk into the house of a purebred friend and see blue ribbons decking the walls and trophies sitting on the TV. It's not sour grapes because his pal won the prizes; it's the fact that the organizers of most dog shows are narrow-minded and restrict the entries to purebred dogs—yet another blatant example of dog discrimination.

Well, there's no reason why your mutt or any other should have to suffer this injustice. If purebreds can have shows, so can mutts. And, here's how.

Planning the Show

1. **Corral a committee** to organize the event.
2. **Pick a day** (and a rain date in case the weather doesn't cooperate) at least a month away, so that people can do some last-minute training.
3. **Pick a place**—your own backyard or a neighbor's, a local park or a vacant lot or field or you might even try the school grounds or the church—and get any necessary permission.
4. **Make some posters** to announce the show, give the time, place, and your name and telephone number. Ask people to register with you a week ahead of time, so that you can begin to set up classes and buy prizes. If funding is a problem, ask entrants to pay a fee for each class. Get local shops, the vet's office, and the school to let you put the poster on their bulletin boards or in their windows.
5. **Buy a notebook** and keep records of early registrants and any fees that are collected. These can be used to buy prizes or pay for other items that you will need, but be sure that you know just who has paid and who has not.
6. **Select officials** and determine their duties.

Steward   The steward will register the dogs, seeing that every entrant gets a number and a program. He will also direct entrants to their proper places, collect entrance fees, see that each dog is on a leash, and that no dog is in heat.

Ringmaster   The ringmaster will make sure the ring is in good shape, announce the classes, maintain order in the ring, and announce the winners.

Judges   Gauge the number of judges you will need by the number of events you are planning. Three judges, at least, will probably be necessary.

Veterinarian   It's wise to have him on hand (or on call) in case of emergency.

Parking attendants   (if needed).

Clean-up committee   To clean up after the show.

Caterer   Ask the Good Humor man if he'd like to come to the showgrounds during the show, or ask people to make food and sell it or give it away.

7. **Collect prizes.** While you are making the rounds with your posters, ask shopkeepers if they would like to donate prizes. They might like the publicity of having their names mentioned when the prizes are awarded.

Suggestions for prizes:
- blue ribbons
- rawhide "bones"
- collars
- leashes
- dog biscuits
- food dishes
- gift certificates at the local pet shop or veterinarian or supermarket
- T-shirts with the dogs' names written on them (to be done at the show with a felt-tip pen)

8. **Make a list of the supplies** you will need the day of the show.
- rope and posts to mark off the ring
- trash baskets for the showgrounds
- extra-heavy paper for signs and numbers
- one or more clipboards and paper for the judges
- special equipment for the classes (see below)
- programs (one master copy and access to a copying machine)
- string
- a table
- a megaphone for the ringmaster
- a cashbox for entrance fees
- pooper scoopers
- pencils and paper for the steward

Preparing for the Show

About a week ahead of time, when you have an idea of how many people and dogs are going to show up, use your leftover poster paper and make numbers for each handler to wear during the classes. Cut out circular or square pieces about ten inches across and number them from one on (making sure you have a number of blanks for last-minute entrants). Punch holes at the top of each card and put strings about two feet long through each hole (for handlers to tie around their waists). Mark the entrants' numbers in your notebook.

At this point you can make a program, listing the name and number of each entrant, the titles for each class, the rules, and the time of day you expect each class to take place. If you have ten or more entries in a class, allow at least half an hour for it and about ten minutes between classes. If you think the show will run more than three hours, plan a half-hour break at some point to give people a chance to rest, eat, and groom themselves or their dogs. Make copies of the program, enough for each entrant and some extras for onlookers, judges, and last-minute contestants.

The Day of the Show

Have your committee arrive at the showgrounds at least an hour ahead of time.

See that the grounds are reasonably clean and that trash baskets are placed here and there.

Rope off a canine latrine area somewhere near the edge of the grounds and make a sign so that everyone will know that this is the place.

Make the show ring by using posts, sinking

them every six feet or so, and surround them with long pieces of rope or chicken wire. Ropes are not foolproof, in that a dog with a bad case of stage fright can always duck out; chicken wire is better and inexpensive. Leave a gap for the in-gate and out-gate.

Set up the steward's table, indicating it with a "Register Here" sign.

If you are having refreshments, organize the refreshment area in a spot away from the ring.

In case of emergencies—such as a dogfight—be sure that someone responsible (a parent, veterinarian, or policeman) who has had experience with this sort of thing is on hand. Buckets of cold water will be useful.

The month was November, the place was the Guild Theatre in New York City, and the occasion was a real live mutt show, staged as a promotion for the movie Summerdog. *It was chillingly cold, but that did not deter a flock of mutts, with owners in tow, from being on hand and exhibiting a true competitive spirit.*

The panel of judges was an all-star cast of mutt lovers—actresses Peggy Cass and Sandy Dennis and director of the New York Humane Society, Robert Perper. Prizes were awarded to the biggest, the smallest, the fattest, the thinnest, the most mixed mutt, and the mutt who most resembled its owner. Pictured here are some of the contestants in action.

Kristen Sternberg

The Show

Use your imagination and design classes that will be as varied as possible—for the sake of the dogs and their special talents and for the amusement of the spectators. One or two classes can be based on appearance, a few on intelligence, and the rest on fun.

Here are some ideas, together with rules, but don't let these inhibit you from thinking up new ones.

Size Class

PRIZES: Two, one for the largest dog, one for the smallest.
JUDGES: One.
EQUIPMENT: Yardstick.
RULES: Each dog will be measured from shoulder to ground. (High hair or thick fur doesn't count.) An alternate way to measure could be by weight, involving the use of bathroom scales. Each handler must weigh himself, then pick up the dog and weigh himself again, subtracting the difference. If the dogs are large, though, a yardstick is a lot more practical.

Bruce Buchenholz

Obedience Class

PRIZES: Three, one for each dog that most successfully and rapidly obeys the following commands: sit, heel, and stay.

JUDGES One.

EQUIPMENT: None.

RULES: Every entrant must line up in front of the judge, who will then go down the line, ask each handler to remove the leash and then to make the appropriate command. If more than one dog performs the command correctly and promptly, a runoff should be held. For *Sit,* the handler stands in front of the dog, makes the command, and the dog sits. For *Heel,* the handler stands in front of the dog and speaks the command. The dog must walk around handler to his left side and sit down. For *Stay,* the handler first commands his dog to sit and stay, then moves at least ten feet away and calls the dog to come. The dog must stay seated until called and then must move promptly to the front of the handler and sit down.

Trick and Treat Class

PRIZES: One prize for each dog that performs one of the following tricks most successfully (six tricks, six prizes, and so on): roll over, speak, sit up (on hindlegs), fetch (you will need an object, such as a ball for this), back up, jump an obstacle (going away from the owner), find an article by scent. For the last you will need three objects wrapped in a piece of cloth, two of them odorless and the third smelling like meat; the dog must select the scented cloth and return to the owner with it.

JUDGES: One.

EQUIPMENT: Objects to be fetched; obstacle to be jumped.

RULES: Like those for obedience class, one animal being judged at a time.

Fun and Games Class

PRIZES: One for each dog-and-handler combination that wins each of the categories listed below.
JUDGES: One or more.
EQUIPMENT: See categories below.
RULES: See categories below.

Stay and Come Each handler commands his dog to stay and then walks twenty feet away. The handlers line up in a row and call their dogs to come at the same time. The dog who makes it back to his own handler first is the winner.

Steeplechase Set up at least six jumps around the edge of the ring, making them very wide but not too high. (A rope strung between supports is the easiest.) Handlers and dogs on leashes start at the sound of a bell and run together over the whole course to the finish line.

Egg and Spoon Each handler loops the leash around one wrist and in that same hand holds a spoon with an egg on it. When the bell sounds, handlers with dogs on the other end of their leashes run together around the ring until only one egg is left in the winning spoon.

Musical Wheelbarrows Enough wheelbarrows (or carton boxes) for everyone in the class, minus one, are lined up in the center of the ring. The music plays and everyone walks his dog around the ring on a leash. When the music stops, each dog must get into a wheelbarrow. The leftover dog is eliminated, and the game is repeated until there is only one winner. When two or more dogs get into the same barrow, the tie goes to the smallest.

Duck Duck Dog Each handler with a dog on leash sits in a circle on the ground, except for one team, which is "it" (so appointed by the judge). "It" walks around the outside of the circle, patting each handler on the head, saying "Duck," "Duck," and so on until he picks the one he wants to be "It," whose head he pats, saying "Dog." The new "It" jumps up with his dog and chases the first "It" around the circle, trying to tag the handler before he can sit down in the vacant spot with his dog. If the first handler gets tagged, he becomes "It" again; if he gets back to the vacant spot untagged, "It" remains so until he, in turn, catches someone. Anyone who is "It" for three times in a row is out, and the game continues until there are two left, both of whom are named winners.

Bruce Buchenholz

Kristen Sternberg

Mixed-Breed

PRIZES: Two, one for the dog that is the least obvious combination of breeds and the other for the most obvious.

JUDGES: Three.

EQUIPMENT: None.

RULES: Each judge must guess the combinations for every dog in the class. The dog with the most correct guesses is winner of Best of Breed, and the dog with the most wrong guesses is Worst of Breed, or Best of Mutt.

Look-alike Class

PRIZES: One, for the dog most resembling the handler.

JUDGES: As many as aren't afraid of making enemies

EQUIPMENT: None

RULES: Clothing may be worn by the dog.

Best in Show

The prizewinners from each class compete in the final class, which is judged on the basis of temperament and general condition. In other words, the steadiest, best-mannered, best-groomed, and healthiest-looking mutt is the winner.

Canine Congeniality Award

Have everyone watching vote (by clapping or yelling) on the most popular dog, who will be given the Canine Congeniality Award.

Notes: If you want to avoid hurt feelings for the losers, you can give every entrant in every class a little prize—such as a small pack of dog treats.

Kristen Sternberg

Bruce Buchenholz

The Menacing Mutt

DON'T assume that just because you, and especially your children, are good with animals that you are invulnerable to dog bite. The statistics for dog bite are on the increase, especially in cities, and it is estimated that over one million Americans are bitten by dogs every year—running up medical bills of over $50 million. According to Dr. Alan Beck, of New York City's Bureau of Animal Affairs, about 60 percent of these bites involve children. Most dog bites occur on the legs (about 50 percent), with the rest involving the arms, hands, and body. At least 10 percent of the bites require stitches, but many doctors prefer to use other methods of closing wounds, so that the 10 percent figure doesn't accurately represent the severity of the usual dog-bite wound. Curiously enough, most dog bites are inflicted by pet dogs rather than strays (though not usually on immediate members of the pet's family) and often in the vicinity of the dog's home. And very few—as little as 2 percent—of the bites are aggravated by the victim. The increasing statistics are probably due to the fact that more people are getting larger dogs and failing to train and confine them.

How to Avoid a Dog Bite

The first step is to learn the signs of both aggressive dogs and those who bite out of fear. The former will stand erect, hair raised on the neck and back, with lips drawn over the teeth, through which will come a distinctive snarl or growl—a warning of worse to come. The fear-biting dog is less predictable, since he will probably cower and put his tail between his legs as if he were showing submissive behavior. Don't be taken in. Instead of fleeing as you approach, this dog will usually stop as if to hide, and if the person closes in or otherwise threatens, the dog will bite.

The second step in preventing an attack is to give the dog every chance not to bite by not threatening it. Don't walk into a strange dog's territory unless the owner is standing nearby and has control over the dog. Don't touch a dog you don't know, for it may assume that your raised hand is about to strike. If you must pass near the animal, speak to it in soothing tones, with some authority in your voice, and cover up any nervousness you may really feel. It doesn't matter what you say so long as the dog interprets it as a reassurance that you mean it no harm. Don't look the dog straight in the eye; staring down is a game that dogs play naturally, and a strange dog may interpret this as a threat.

If the dog continues to look menacing, slowly move away, facing the dog until you are well out of his range. Do not turn around and walk off rapidly—or worse, run—because the dog will only chase you. The idea is to let the dog think that he has won and that you are no longer a threat to him. Don't let your ego get the upper hand here—it's better to lose the psychological battle than it is to risk a bite. If you own the dog, though, you'd better get some expert help, since losing a battle like this with your own dog may also lose you a war.

People who ride bicycles or who jog for exercise should take special precautions, avoiding private property and areas where you know that loose dogs are present. A dog likes nothing better than a speeding obstacle to chase, and if the animal is small you may be able to outrun him, but if he is large, you may have trouble. Carry a dog repellent with you, put a horn on your bike, or otherwise equip yourself in case of trouble. Cyclers can often prevent attack by placing the bike between themselves and the dog and yelling "Go Home" or pretending to throw something. Joggers will be excused from embarrassment if they choose to jump on a car or in a tree to avoid attack. People with children in tow should not lift a child up to prevent dog bite; the dangling legs will only offer a temptation to jump up.

If you must enter someone's property to deliver something or present yourself for some reason, make sure that the owner is not only there, but there with a leash on the dog. (Famous last words before a dog bite: "Oh, my dog wouldn't *dream* of biting anyone!") If no one is there and the dog is not confined, come back later.

Teach your children to avoid strange dogs, but teach them also not to tease their own pets, especially during mealtime or when an otherwise mild-mannered bitch has her puppies on hand.

Dealing with Dog Bite

If the dog should lunge at you, in spite of all your precautions, be quick about folding your arms across in front of your face and kick the dog in the chest as hard as you can. If you are bitten on the arm, don't pull away, for the dog's teeth, which are designed to tear and lacerate, will do more damage if you resist. If possible, feed your sleeve to the dog by taking off your coat or jacket. Use any handy object, such as an umbrella or a pocketbook, as a weapon.

If you are bitten, report the incident to the dog's owner and make certain that the dog has been vaccinated for rabies within the past year. Also report a bite to the Department of Health; they will send the owner a card and ask him to observe the dog and return the card after ten days. If the dog is not wearing a collar and there is no owner in sight, make a mental note of his physical description and report the incident to the police. Luckily, the incidence of rabies has decreased so markedly that no cases of rabies in man caused by dogs have been reported in over a decade. There are still 200 to 300 cases of rabies in dogs reported each year, however.

Be sure to take care of yourself by washing the wound thoroughly with soap and water and applying a topical antiseptic. A tetanus shot is a good idea. If the wound is an open one, allow it to bleed, but control excessive bleeding with direct pressure and get yourself to a physician.

How to Stop a Dogfight

MOST DOGS are curious and pleased to see one of their own kind and would rather play than fight, after a preliminary session of sniffing and tail wagging. In fact, dogs often have a natural system of preventing fights by indicating through gestures which ones are dominant and which submissive. But things can get out of control if the dog has had little experience with other dogs or is naturally aggressive and meets up with another aggressive animal. Male dogs will be quick to defend territory or argue over a female in heat; females will fight over puppies; and dogs with mastiff, bullterrier, chow, and German shepherd blood are more apt to be tough than hounds that are bred to be kept in packs. If you have any doubts at all about your own dog's predilections, be sure to keep him on a leash when you walk him in an area where canine confrontations are likely to occur. It's not a foolproof method, but it will at least give you the upper hand.

If you are alone and a fight breaks out, you can try the traditional method of hitting the dogs with whatever is at hand—a broom, shovel, or a bucket of water. Best of all is a hose turned on full blast until the dogs' tempers cool. If you have a large dog who's prone to fighting, you should take the precaution of carrying a walking stick with you.

If there are two people on the scene, each one should grab the hind legs of each dog at the same time and pull them apart or grab each tail and pull the dogs up and away from each other so that their hind legs cannot touch the ground. Timing is all important here, and one should be very careful never to get between the fighting animals. Whatever you do, don't rush in, where angels fear to tread, without thinking; it will only cause you to come out the loser in what, after all, isn't your battle at all.

Aggressive posture (left) and conciliatory stance (right)
Charles Darwin
1872

When a dog approaches a strange dog or man in a savage or hostile frame of mind he walks upright and very stiffly; his head is slightly raised, or not much lowered; the tail is held erect and quite rigid; the hairs bristle, especially along the neck and back; the pricked ears are directed forwards, and the eyes have a fixed stare. These actions . . . follow from the dog's intention to attack his enemy, and are thus to a large extent intelligible. As he prepares to spring with a savage growl on his enemy, the canine teeth are uncovered, and the ears are pressed close backwards on the head. . . . Let us suppose that the dog suddenly discovers that the man he is approaching is not a stranger, but his master, and let it be observed how completely and instantaneously his whole bearing is reversed. Instead of walking upright, the body sinks downwards or even crouches, and is thrown into flexuous movements; his tail, instead of being stiff and upright, is lowered and wagged from side to side; his hair instantly becomes smooth; his ears are depressed and drawn backwards, but not closely to the head, and his lips hang loosely. From the drawing back of the ears, the eyelids become elongated, and the eyes no longer appear round and staring.

Charles Darwin, The Expression of the Emotions in Man and Animals (1872)

Jennifer O'Neill

A STAR AMONG MUTTS

BEST known as an actress, whose starring role in *Summer of '42* launched her on a film career, Jennifer O'Neill is equally active as a supporter of the humane movement. Not only does she have four mutts of her own, each one rescued from a humane society, but she has also been working with a committee to set up a low-cost spay-neuter clinic in Westchester County to help bring the animal population under control. In addition, she is active in New York City's ASPCA mutt-adoption program. With Jennifer at a fund-raising event for Animals by Choice, Inc., are her cat, Oscar (from the Los Angeles SPCA), Samantha (from the Briarcliff SPCA), Frank (from New York's ASPCA), and Sally (from the SPCA in Westport, Connecticut). (Jennifer's latest film, in which she co-stars with Anthony Quinn, is James Michener's *Caravan*.)

NINEPIN GAME PULL TOY
Maine
Early 20th century
Papier-mâché, polychrome, gesso
L., 20", H., 12"
Ms. Molly Epstein

6.
The Facts of Life

The Wimple Saga

Ten years ago, so it is told,
There lived a family named Wimple
In a house with a couple of kids and a cat
And a dog called Mr. McDimple.

One day when Wimple returned from work,
The house was in a panic.
"It's McDimple," they cried, "he's disap-
        peared,
And all of us are frantic."

"Now pull yourselves together, dears,
There is no need to cry."
Just then old McDimple walked in,
With a devilish look in his eye.

"Where have you been, McDimple, old pal?
Your behavior is untoward."
McDimple just smiled and gave them a wink
And plopped himself down on the floor.

From that day on, every couple of days,
McDimple would just disappear.
And then he'd return, without a word,
But a grin from ear to ear.

Frankly, the Wimples were worried.
Why did McDimple leave home?
They gave him three squares, lots of love,
        and a bed.
Why, oh why, did he roam?

One day there came a knock on the door—
A man named Mr. O'Bubble.
"I want to see your mongrel," he screamed,
"He got my Fifi in trouble!"

"Calm down, O'Bubble," Wimple replied,
"I'm sure there's some explanation."
The phone rang, then, and a lady yelled,
"Mr. Wimple, I'm Mrs. Carnation."

"That mutt, that vile, old cur of yours,
Has been here night and day.

He's fathered the pups of my dear little
        pooch,
What have you got to say?"

Before Mr. Wimple had time to respond,
The postman arrived with a cart
Of irate letters from incensed folks,
Demanding that Wimple depart.

"Your dog," they read, "has ravaged the
        place,
Impregnating every last virgin.
You've got twenty-four hours to get out of
        town,
You and that miserable urchin."

Wimple sat down with his head in his hands.
He couldn't believe the whole scene.
But he packed up his family, the cat, and the
        dog,
And moved them all to Racine.

Their stay in Racine lasted maybe six
        months,
When they went through the same old to-do.
So they packed up again and hopped in the
        car
And headed for Kalamazoo.

From Kalamazoo they moved to Maine,
From Maine to North Dakota,
Then Indiana to Idaho,
Arizona to Minnesota.

And so it went on—and on—and on.
Many moves did the Wimples betake,
From town to town and state to state,
Leaving legions of pups in their wake.

One can't say where the Wimples are now,
But, for sure, they're still moving around.
So keep your eye out for a dog with a
        smile—
McDimple may soon hit your town.

EVERYONE is aware of the high dog population in this country, and nearly everyone knows about the appallingly large numbers of dogs that must be destroyed each year by humane societies because they have no homes and no hope of finding owners. These are man-made statistics, of course, resulting from the negligence of dog owners, who allow their pets to breed indiscriminately and to produce litters of unwanted puppies.

We believe that any dog—male or female, purebred or mongrel—should be neutered early in life unless it is a show specimen or a purebred animal of particular excellence owned by a licensed breeder. Too many popular breeds have deteriorated over the years because of uncontrolled breeding by amateurs or by puppy mills that turn out thousands of animals a year for the pet-shop trade with little regard for improving the breeds and a lot of regard for cold cash. (Bitches on these farms are usually kept in tiny cages and are bred as often as nature allows; their health and their quality don't matter, so long as they have a pedigree.)

Many argue against neutering dogs, but the millions of dogs put to death annually provide a counterargument that is difficult to dispute. Here's how the arguments go.

Leading Your Dog to the Alter

Argument: I feel that it is unnatural to keep a dog from doing what comes naturally.

Counterargument: Keeping a dog in a human dwelling isn't exactly what Mother Nature intended to begin with, and since domestic dogs are entirely dependent on us, their creators, it is our responsibility to take over the controls when it comes to breeding. It has been observed by behaviorists that wild dogs tend to regulate their own populations by allowing only the dominant bitch in the group to breed; the low-ranking bitches do not generally have pups at all, and if they do, the dominant bitch will often attack them. The process of natural selection enables the wild pack to carry on only the strongest of its genes to future generations.

Argument: Neutered animals become obese, a condition that often shortens their lives.

Counterargument: Neutered animals that become overweight get that way by over-eating, just as humans do. Because they use up less energy by not roaming and fighting (both of which are effective life-shorteners), they require less food and their diets should be regulated accordingly. Also, veterinarians tell us, spayed females are less likely to develop uterine cysts, infections, and breast cancer as they mature. And because castrated males aren't constantly on the prowl for females in heat, they become better pets around the house, which makes a longer lifespan more probable.

Argument: An animal that isn't allowed to breed becomes frustrated psychologically, and neutered animals become dull and uninteresting.

Counterargument: What a dog doesn't know won't hurt him (or her). Frustration in a dog may be caused by many things—lack of exercise, lack of attention or stimulus, abuse, and so on, but a dog that has never bred is not likely to feel frustrated unless, in the case of the male, he is confined within sight of a bitch in heat, or in the case of the female, she is locked away but in sight of ardent suitors. These circumstances are frustrating in the extreme. Neutering solves these problems by making the dog more content with its lot and less interested in getting out.

Argument: A litter of puppies will be a wonderful learning experience for the children.

Counterargument: There are plenty of less costly and more effective methods of giving your children a sex education. There is no question that the miracle of birth is a very exciting event to observe. But most dogs prefer to whelp late at night or very early in the morning when disturbances and distractions are at a minimum, and many bitches become very upset if people—especially excited children—are present. If the presence of an owner is necessary because the dog is in trouble, most sensible parents would prefer to have the vet on hand and not the kids, for whom the experience might be an upsetting one. As for the nursing process, children generally become familiar with it in one or two sessions, and after that it's back to the playroom. And the parents are left with a litter of pups that will need veterinary attention, extra food, special care, and new homes, which may not be easy to find. Taking a group of pups to the humane society where they may lose their lives isn't a wonderful experience at all.

Argument: Even though she's a mutt, my dog is so attractive and delightful that we think she should have a chance to have some great puppies.

Counterargument: There is no guarantee that mongrel pups will resemble their mother, since there is no clearly defined set of genes to be carried on. One family who let their German shepherd-collie cross have a litter by the local Irish wolfhound, hoping for a litter of tall, swift sheep herders, ended up with a motley collection of unattractive, aggressive giants whose primary interest in sheep was running them out of the country. As George Bernard Shaw once said to a beautiful woman who suggested that they have a child: "But Madam, what if the child had *my* looks and *your* brains!"

Argument: OK, I'd be willing to neuter my dog, but it's so expensive.

Counterargument: Yes, it is expensive, because surgery of any sort involves the expertise of a veterinarian and the expense of anesthesia, special equipment and drugs, and a recovery period under medical supervision. But there are spay and neuter clinics in many parts of the country (check your local shelter for information) that charge only nominal fees, and there are birth-control drugs being developed for use in animals, some of which are beginning to reach the market. Consider too that the cost of spaying a bitch (virtually the same operation as a hysterectomy in a woman) is usually far less than the cost of keeping the dog in a boarding kennel for three weeks twice a year—the usual route taken by owners who must keep their dog confined and separated from all the local males gathered around the back door. And who can calculate the cost, in emotional terms, that one risks paying every time an unneutered male dog takes off over highway and byway to fight off competitors for the affections of his lady love?

Argument: I can see how castrating a male dog, which can impregnate many females, would be an effective way to control the dog population, but I just can't bring myself to do that to my own dog.

Counterargument: A macho attitude is really out of date, and living vicariously through your dog isn't that much fun. Consider the risks that you are allowing your dog to take—getting hit by a car, injured by another dog, or being slapped with a paternity suit. In Virginia, a Chihuahua owner successfully sued the owner of a dog that had "raped" his little beast, and it may be only a matter of time before canine paternity suits will become as expensive as the human variety!

MATTERS of the flesh are for many very painful and frequently impossible to discuss face to face. Recognizing this, Dr. Dunsworthy Doggerel, the world-renowned mutt psychiatrist, has been generous enough to share with us a few of the thousands of queries he receives each week in the hopes that some of you out there will find guidance, comfort, and inner peace.

Dear Dr. Doggerel:

I don't need no shrink, man, but the old biddy that I live with says if I don't shape up, I'm out. The problem is that I get, well, you know, turned on by pillows. Man, when I see a pillow, it just blows my mind. Now I don't see nothing wrong with that, but the old lady, boy, does she get steamed!

Johnny O.

Dear Johnny:

Your problem could be caused by one of several things. It is not uncommon when there are females in heat in the neighborhood for dogs to acquire habits such as the one you describe. It is also not unusual for dogs who are confined to become sexually frustrated and try to have intercourse with inanimate objects. If the latter is your problem, I would suggest that you get out and get more exercise. If the situation becomes intolerable to your owner, she may consider giving you female hormones or having you altered. I suggest, Johnny, that you try your hardest to walk by those pillows without looking back.

Dear Dr. Doggerel:

I am a most magnificent specimen born into a long line of distinguished mongrels from the Main Line of Pennsylvania. Unfortunately, my mama and papa fell upon hard times when I was but a pup, and I was placed for adoption. I was taken in by pleasant people who are terribly kind but certainly not of the genteel caliber, shall we say, to which I was accustomed. The problem is this: my adoptive parents have some most peculiar and frightfully embarrassing notions about what they feel my behavior should be. Moreover, they are of the opinion that since I do not care to "mingle" with the slovenly male curs who frequent the neighborhood, something is dreadfully wrong with me. They have even gone so far as to invite a vulgar hound into the yard and encourage him to "cosy up" to me, if you know what I mean. They say that everyone needs a release and that they do not want me to be a "frustrated old girl." I say that I am above all that and that I do not need or desire any dalliances in my life. Since this is such a point of contention in our daily lives, the matter has been discussed and we agree to abide by your advice. You must know how abashed I am at having to write this letter, so please, may I have your reply in a plain brown envelope.

Sincerely,
Penelope Martin-
Hurst Suchowski

Even Your Best Friends Won't Tell You

My dear Penelope:

You can relax. Because you do not feel the need to engage in sexual intimacies with members of the opposite sex does not mean you are abnormal. Many dogs live very happily without ever having had this experience.

Dear Dr. Doggerel:

To get right to the point, as it were, last week when my owner had the ladies over for bridge, Mrs. Welch, a chronic overbidder, was petting me and I got an erection. It caused a mild furor at the time, but, wow, when the girls left, did my owner ever let me have it. She told me I was crass, vulgar, abnormal, the scourge of the animal kingdom, and that if it ever happened again, I'd be O-U-T, out. I didn't mean to have that happen—it just did—and I can't be sure the problem won't pop up again. Am I really abnormal? What can I do? I don't want to lose my home.

Sincerely,
Dickie

Dear Dickie:

No, you're not abnormal. Your owner must realize that there's more to life than bridge and that now and again one cannot control bodily sensations. Should the situation recur, to avoid further embarrassment, why not leave the room for a few moments until you have pulled yourself together? Under the circumstances, I would suggest you try to keep a stiff upper lip and leave it at that.

Dear Dr. Doggerel:

Me and the girls have been talking about it and, just out of curiosity you understand, we want to know if us female dogs can have "the big O." We anxiously await your reply.

Sincerely,
Virginia

Dear Virginia:

Yes, Virginia, there is a Santa Claus. Orgasm in the female dog does not generally occur during copulation, however, but during foreplay. Before sexual maturity, it is a common practice for littermates to become sexually aroused by oral and bodily contact. Frequently, they will ride each other, with no differentiation between sexes. After sexual maturity, the male will sometimes allow the female to ride him, resulting in orgasm for the female. During the heat cycle of a female, she will frequently become so aroused that she will ride other female dogs to satisfy herself. This is quite normal at this time and nothing to blush at.

The Facts of Life

Dear Doc:

I'm a handsome son of a gun, and the women, well, they just adore me. The breadwinner around this pad says I drive him nuts because I'm so nervous and excitable, but jeez, he keeps me fenced in and I got places to go and dogs to see. I keep telling him if he'd let me loose so I can get at some of them cute little spaniels I'd be a new dog and cool as a cucumber. All I need is a little action. He says no dice. Help!

Joey

Dear Joey:

Sorry, fella, but I must concur with your owner. A little taste of honey in this case would probably result in your wanting the whole hive. A few nights on the prowl might calm you down temporarily, but chances are you would become a full-time roamer. Take it from me, this is not the kind of life you want for yourself. Appreciate the fact that you have a soft bed and three meals a day. Many are much less fortunate.

Paul Duckworth

THE NUMBER of dogs subjected to euthanasia each year is staggering; some 13.5 million animals are put to sleep by humane societies and shelters in the United States, and no one knows how many more are left to scavenge the streets. The world doesn't need more puppies. Sometimes, however, even in the best of families, your female dog winds up in "a family way." The reason for the information passed on here is not to encourage breeding but to arm you with sound advice should your pet announce that she's pregnant.

When's It Likely to Happen?

The heat period of your bitch is likely to occur any time after about six months of age and will recur approximately once every six months thereafter, lasting for three weeks, give or take a few days. There are tests that calculate fairly accurately at what point the bitch is most likely to conceive, but take no chances: keep your dog confined for the full three weeks.

The beginning of the heat (estrous) cycle is called the proestrus and is identified by a white or yellowish discharge, which then turns bloody, and by vaginal swelling. It is quite possible that the discharge will be so slight as to go unnoticed and you won't know that your dog is in heat. A surefire warning signal, however, is the presence of a legion of male dogs hanging around the front door.

In a Family Way

How to Tell If It Has

Clearly, the most direct way of knowing if your pet is pregnant is if she tells you outright. Whether or not this happens will depend on the manner in which the subject of sex has been handled up until now. If you have been elusive about it, chances are that she will be too embarrassed to say anything. Also, if the mating itself was not a matter of true love, as is so often the case, the whole thing may be just too painful to discuss. So, short of a direct confrontation, here's what to look for:

- Behavioral changes. Most often the bitch will be quieter and more loving; a nervous bitch, however, may become more aggressive.
- Increase in appetite.
- Increase in body weight.
- Abdominal enlargement, normally observed about the fifth week of pregnancy.
- Enlargement and reddening of the teats. This will occur about the fifth week; at about the seventh week, the breasts will begin to fill with milk and become noticeably larger; several days before whelping, they will secrete a watery solution.

If none of these signs has been observed and you still have a sneaking suspicion that your dog is pregnant, take her to the vet. After about the fourth week of pregnancy, he will probably be able to determine by palpation if any fetuses are in the uterus. In some cases where even this is not possible, an X ray can be taken, but it will not show a puppy until about the seventh week.

So She's Pregnant, Now What?

Like humans, dogs should be treated with an extra dose of TLC and sound medical care during pregnancy. There really isn't too much to concern yourself about, but there are a few things you can do to help assure your pet of a healthy litter.

Parasites   The minute you suspect your dog is pregnant, have her checked for worms. If the test is positive, talk to the vet about worming her. *Don't do it yourself.* Worming during pregnancy can be toxic to the puppies, and your veterinarian will know which types of medicine can be used safely. Have her checked for skin parasites at the same time.

Vaccination   If you do nothing else, be sure your dog is up to date on her DHL (distemper, hepatitis, leptospirosis) inoculation. If she is not, she should have a booster shot. A protected mother will pass on temporary immunity to her pups in her colostrum (first milk) just after they are born. Without this, the puppies will be enormously susceptible to these infections, which are at worst fatal and at best leave the puppy debilitated in one way or another for life.

Nutrition   Since the diet of the bitch corresponds directly to the nutrients obtained by her puppies, prenatal nutrition should be complete and balanced. Protein is most important, so see to it that her normal diet is supplemented with meat, either raw or canned dog-food meat, and other high-protein food, such as liver, milk, and eggs (cooked). A vitamin supplement—there are special ones for bitches during gestation—is also important and should be continued throughout the pregnancy. During the first month, feed your dog with quality in mind, not quantity. A fat brood bitch can have enormous problems at whelping time. (On page 104 you'll find a recipe for your gravid gourmet.)

After the first month, increase her food intake by about a quarter (the increase being in protein), and break it up into two or three feedings a day. Add a calcium supplement at this point.

Exercise   During this time allow your dog to have as much exercise as she desires, but watch to see that she does not strenuously tax herself or indulge in antics that might result in a fall. Long car trips are not recommended, as bumps may cause premature labor pains. It's not a good idea to let her roam; she's better off around the house where you can keep an eye on her.

False Starts

It is not unusual for a dog to have all of the symptoms of pregnancy—heftier appetite, mammary gland enlargement, abdominal swelling—and not be pregnant. Some bitches will even become excitable at "delivery time" and experience labor pains. Often, they will make nests for their "puppies," which may be toys, socks, or other objects. This is called false pregnancy and is caused by a growth on the ovary.

If you suspect a false pregnancy, see the veterinarian. He can treat your dog with hormones and make her life a lot more pleasant. It is also wise to reduce her diet, particularly her fluid intake, as the more fluid she consumes the more milk she will produce. Make sure she gets plenty of exercise, and don't expose her to other dogs, particularly nursing mothers with young puppies. The maternal instinct is sometimes so strong during false pregnancy that the dog will try to steal puppies from other bitches.

As soon as the vet recommends it, have her spayed. It is not wise to attempt this when the condition prevails, as her reproductive organs are enlarged and the hemorrhaging will be more profuse than it normally is, adding a greater element of risk to the surgical procedure.

Sometimes a fetus dies within several days or weeks after mating. The bitch may show all the signs of pregnancy right up until the bitter end, then pass the due date and produce no offspring. This is a phantom pregnancy and is different from false pregnancy in that the bitch has actually been mated. Whelping does not occur because of the death of the fetus and its subsequent absorption by the body of the bitch.

One other false start that might be encountered is abortion, caused by injuries, severe illness, or shock. Brucellosis, or infectious abortion, has, for the most part, been limited to large beagle kennels; it's not likely that you will encounter it with your mutt.

Take your dog to a cat house

Keeping the Wolves Away from the Door

TWICE A year, owners of unspayed bitches suffer the tortures of the damned unless they live in an area where male dogs do not, such as the North Pole or the middle of the Sahara (and money could be bet on some male dogs to find a female in heat even that far away). Owners of male dogs suffer, too; their dogs disappear, sometimes for days at a time, returning home exhausted, hungry, and suffering cuts and bruises from fights, if they return at all. (Dognappers often do their dirty work by bringing a truck containing a female in heat into a neighborhood and simply rounding up all the males, not even resorting to the use of nets.) Although the species *Canis familiaris* is hardly in danger of extinction, the drive to preserve the species by reproduction is extremely strong, and nothing short of spaying the female can prevent the male from trying his best to keep the line going.

Again, it is recommended that females be spayed and males be castrated. If for some reason that can't be done, however, here are some alternate suggestions:

Muzzle your dog

Rearguard

Introduce your dog to a sheep

Jim Maeda

NATURE has provided animals with strong instincts and the ability to produce young with relatively few complications, and although dogs are domesticated, they retain many of these instincts so that the normal, healthy bitch should be able to give birth to (or whelp) her pups with little or no help from humans. Nevertheless, there are several ways in which the owner can insure as trouble-free a delivery as possible, and as a conscientious person, an alert eye should be kept on the animal just in case something goes wrong.

A few days before the puppies are expected to arrive, select a delivery room, some area familiar to the animal but out of the usual stream of household activity. Get a box or basket large enough to hold the mother in an outstretched position. The sides must be high enough to keep the newborn pups inside. Line the bottom with a heavy layer of newspaper. Make sure the dog knows where the box is, and when she seems to be about to whelp, put her in the box. It is a good idea in cool weather to see that a source of heat is nearby (a radiator or electric heater).

Shortly before whelping, usually three or four days, the bitch may show nesting behavior, and a day before the event, she will show other signs: refusal of food, lowered body temperature (although this will increase just before actual whelping), restless pacing, panting, and other nervous behavior. During the last few hours, there may be some discharge from the vagina, and about an hour (or less) before the puppies start to appear—preceded by the emergence of a bubble—the bitch will go into labor, which involves straining and intermittent contractions with accompanying pain. Once the bubble has burst and labor has begun in earnest, puppies should begin to appear. Usually pups are born headfirst, abdomen down, but breech-birth delivery (hind feet first) is not abnormal. Although the first puppy should emerge within an hour of the onset of labor, the second and subsequent puppies may take much longer in coming, sometimes several hours.

If the first puppy takes longer than an hour to arrive after labor has started, call the vet, for something is wrong. And if subsequent puppies take longer than four hours, call the vet then. Other trouble signs include: the appearance of a dark-green discharge before (not after) the first puppy; the appearance of two bubbles instead of one and no puppy within a half hour (there may be two of them caught in the birth canal); the appearance of half a puppy while the rest remains in the mother; the mother seems inert or attempts to urinate or has particular difficulty in experiencing labor.

If the bitch has had a litter of pups before and a Caesarean section (removal of the pups directly from the uterus by surgery) was performed, she will need one again, so be sure to alert your veterinarian to the fact and the probable whelping date.

If the birth has gone without incident, but the mother fails to lick her pups clean or to remove the placental material, you must do these tasks for her. Gently pull the sac away from the puppy's body and remove fluid from his mouth with a clean piece of cotton. Rub the pup with a towel to stimulate his blood circulation and breathing. Cut the umbilical cord about an inch from the pup's body with sterilized scissors (you can dip them in alcohol) and tie the end of the cord with a bit of string to prevent

Making Mutts

The Facts of Life

bleeding. Then give the puppy back to his mother so that he can start nursing, which should be within an hour or so after birth.

At some point following the delivery, the female may produce a vaginal discharge, dark in color and perhaps gradually becoming deep red. This is normal; but if the discharge becomes heavy, bright red, and continues for more than ten days, call the vet.

Once you are certain that all the puppies have been born and that all of them are clean, breathing well, and nursing, you can relax and go out and buy some cigars. Don't smoke them around the puppies, though, and don't show off the new litter to your friends until they are at least a day old and then only if the mother is comfortable and friendly. Even the most amiable and low-strung of mutt mothers can become rather defensive about her babies in the presence of strangers, children, and other animals. It is always a good idea to keep other dogs away from the nursing mother and puppies, no matter how well they get along under normal conditions.

The vet is one visitor worth inviting in any case, since the bitch should be checked out to see that all is in order. If the vet wants you to visit the office or clinic, bring the pups along (in a box lined with soft material such as toweling) to keep the mother calm; the doctor may also want to take a look at them.

DOG AND TWO PUPPIES
Morris Hirshfield
Brooklyn, New York
1944
Oil
26″ × 19½″
Mr. and Mrs. Harold Ladas

C aesar once, seeing some wealthy strangers at Rome, carrying up and down with them in their arms and bosoms young puppy-dogs and monkeys, embracing them and making much of them, took occasion not unnaturally to ask whether the women in their country were not used to bear children.

Plutarch

STILL LIFE WITH PUPPIES
Paul Gauguin
1888
Museum of Modern Art
Mrs. Simon Guggenheim Fund
New York

NURSERY detail for a litter of puppies is no picnic. They're absolutely helpless and depend totally upon their mother—and you—to see to their needs, which are not insignificant. In most cases, the mother will do the lion's share of the work, but there are times when you're going to have to pitch in.

As soon as your pet has finished whelping and all the puppies have had their first meal, the area should be cleaned up. First, briefly separate the mother from her pups and gently clean her off. While she is being taken care of, place the puppies in a small cardboard box or other warm place where there's no danger of falling and replace the soiled papers in the whelping box. Look the puppies over, and if you plan to keep track of their weights, now is the time to weigh them. Using a scale that measures ounces, cover the cold metal surface of the scale with a towel to protect the puppy and weigh him; remember to subtract the weight of the towel from the total weight recorded. Make note of any runts and check for any deformities or birth injuries. If there's some doubt in your mind about a particular puppy, have the vet check him over.

Once everything is in order, put the puppies back in the whelping box and let the mother take over. From this point on, do not handle them any more than you must. Bitches tend to be very protective and sometimes aggressive. Any unnecessary handling of puppies is likely to cause the mother to be extremely nervous, a condition that is not good for her or the health of her puppies.

Nursery Detail

Nursing

More often than not, the mother will see to it that her puppies are nursing properly, but check regularly for the first couple of days to make sure this is the case. If you see that a puppy is having trouble, help him along by putting him to a nipple and squirting some of the milk in his mouth. If the puppy continues to be a weak nurser, you're going to have to give him supplementary feedings with a specially prepared formula (see *Hand-Rearing Pups* below). Also, take note of whether or not the puppies are using all of the breasts. If they are not, place them on the breasts that appear unusually full to prevent infections or abscesses from occurring. If the litter is small, rotate the puppies so that all of the breasts get some use during the course of a day.

Weaning

At three weeks of age, the puppies should be ready to begin learning how to take food on their own. Start them on either a good commercial formula, such as Borden's Esbilac, or a formula you can make yourself (see *Hand-Rearing Pups* below). Dip your finger (a clean one) into the formula and allow the puppy to suck on it. Once he gets the idea, place him in front of a shallow saucer or tin of formula and give him a go on his own. He may make an awful mess, but he probably won't have much trouble figuring out what's expected of him. Check the consistency of the pup's stools for the first couple of days after introducing the formula; if they are looser than normal, eliminate the Karo syrup from the mixture. (Both the homemade formula and Esbilac can be made up in batches and stored in the refrigerator. Just be sure you warm either formula before giving it to the pups.)

The puppies should continue to nurse freely during this time, with the formula being introduced twice a day. As a treat, beef or chicken broth can be given once a day. After they have the hang of lapping from a dish, start adding Pablum to the formula, working it into a gruel.

At four weeks of age, the puppies are ready for you to gradually start adding meat to the formula mixture. It can be either fresh meat that has been chopped or ground or one of the all-meat canned foods. Dry dog food can also be used, but allow it to soften in the mixture during the early stages of weaning. A dietary vitamin supplement should be added, which can be purchased in powdered form at your local pet shop, though a liquid human baby vitamin supplement will do the same job. If the puppies are likely to be large as adults, a calcium additive is also a must. From now until about three months of age, the puppies should receive four meals a day: the formula-plus-Pablum mixture in the morning; the formula-plus-meat mixture at noon and again late in the afternoon; and warm evaporated milk or broth at bedtime. The mixtures should become increasingly thicker until they approach a reasonable fac-simile of what the dog will be fed as an adult (see The Mutt Who Came to Dinner, page 000).

Hand-Rearing Pups

It may be necessary for you to hand-rear your pups for a variety of reasons: the whelping of more puppies than the mother can handle, the rejection by the mother of one or more pups, the presence of pups who are either too weak or too small to contend with their littermates for the available milk, or the death of the bitch.

Newborns should have a warm environment, and a cardboard box can easily be set up to house them comfortably. Place a heating pad in the box, with half of it covering the bottom and the other half placed against a side. This will give the puppies the opportunity to be near the heat if they want to be or to crawl to a cooler area of the box where there is no heating pad if they get too warm. Cover the pad with some waterproof material, being sure that it is tightly attached so that the puppy can't get between it and the pad, and turn it on low heat. On top of the pad, place some clean, soft toweling or diapers, changing them when necessary. If you are dealing with more than one puppy, compartmentalize the box so that each pup has his own section. This will enable you to check the condition of each pup's stool easily and will prevent them from sucking each other's tails, ears, and genitals, which could be damaging.

For feeding, you will need some squeeze nursing bottles, a supply of anti-colic nipples (generally with three holes), and a scale. As for formula, you can use Borden's excellent substitute for bitch's milk—Esbilac—a carefully balanced blend of pro-teins, fats, carbohydrates, vitamins, and minerals, specifically designed to meet the nutritional requirements of puppies. Or, you can make your own formula:

1 can evaporated milk	1 egg yolk
1 can boiled water	1 tablespoon Karo syrup (light or dark)

The puppies should be fed at least three times a day at eight-hour intervals. Some puppies will seem especially hungry and will require a fourth feeding, but for the first two or three days, it is best to underfeed all of the puppies and then bring them up to the full feeding on the fourth or fifth day.

As for the amount that you should feed, a somewhat inaccurate method is to give the puppy just enough so that his abdomen is slightly enlarged after feeding. Borden recommends the following schedule:

Week	Formula per pound of body weight per day (ounces)
1	2—2⅓
2	2⅓
3	2⅔—3
4	3⅓

At about three weeks you can start weaning the puppies as you would if they had nursed normally from the bitch.

To feed a pup, place him on his stomach with a towel in front of him. Open the pup's mouth with your finger and work the nipple in, placing it on top of the pup's tongue. If the puppy is too weak to nurse this way, hold him on his back and pull on the bottle to encourage vigorous sucking, but don't allow him to nurse too rapidly. In either case, be sure the bottle is positioned so that the puppy is not taking in too much air. Not unlike human babies, puppies are susceptible to colic. To check the nipple, hold the bottle upside down; the milk should ooze out slowly. If it does not, enlarge the holes with a needle that has been held over a flame for several moments. Be sure to burp the puppy after each feeding as you would a baby, holding him upright against your shoulder and patting or stroking his back.

Regular increases in weight and a normal (firm and yellowish) bowel movement three to five times a day indicate that the puppies are being adequately fed. You may help this along by gently rubbing the puppies' anal and abdominal areas with a cotton swab moistened with warm water after each feeding. Keep this up until the puppy seems to be able to function on his own.

It is most important that you act immediately at the first sign of trouble with a puppy. Keep your vet's number by the phone and call him if:

Calling Dr. Kildare

1. A puppy has acute diarrhea.
2. A puppy cries incessantly.
3. The bitch seems to be ignoring a puppy.
4. A puppy stops nursing.
5. A puppy appears limp or weak.
6. A puppy is dehydrated (lift the skin: if it doesn't bounce back into place, the body is being depleted of fluids).
7. A puppy appears extremely bloated.
8. A puppy's gums are whitish and not pink or reddish-pink.

9. A puppy's skin has a bluish tint or unexplainable marks or lesions of any sort.
   As a matter of routine, have the puppies' stools checked for worms at about three weeks of age and then again several weeks later. If the test is positive, have the puppies treated, as parasites at this age can cause problems for the litter and in some cases death. Also, check to see when your veterinarian wants to begin inoculations.

Mary Bloom

A PUPPY'S emotional needs are just as important as his physical needs. Unattended puppies often grow into unwanted dogs, since a lot of people simply aren't equipped to deal with a neurotic pet. To assure your puppies of happy, *permanent* homes some time should be taken to give them the emotional foundation they're going to need once the umbilical cord has been severed.

At birth a puppy's brain is not fully developed. That part of it that controls temperature regulation and body metabolism has not yet matured, which is why it is so important for the mother and pups to be in a warm, draft-free place. It is incumbent upon you to make sure that the bitch does not ignore any of her puppies in this respect. If you do notice that one is being ignored, remove him immediately from the litter and treat him as though he were an orphan (see *Hand-Rearing Puppies,* p. 234).

During the first three-week period, you may not see any great activity in the litter. The puppies' eyes are just beginning to open, and they will be crawling all around their box, but their ears and noses are not yet in peak operating condition. They do not have voluntary control and are totally reliant on their mother for their excretory functions. She will lick their genital area to stimulate the excretion of urine and feces. Again, if you notice that she is delinquent in her duty with one of the puppies, remove him and take over the job yourself.

At about twenty-one days, a puppy's senses and nervous system begin to go into full gear. You'll see them begin to establish a pecking order among themselves; the bullies will start to show their true colors, the submissive ones may roll over and whine, and, in general, there will be pandemonium during waking hours—kicking, chewing, pouncing, snapping, and even occasional growling and snarling. It is very important during this fourth week that you do not separate à puppy from his mother or littermates. This is his first real crack at socialization, and he needs the security of his mother and the input that he is receiving from his brothers and sisters.

By the twenty-eighth day of life, a puppy is ready to start facing the outside world a bit. This is a very impressionable time in a pup's life; treat him kindly and gently. You are the model for his response to people in general. Give each puppy some individual time every day during this period to play with him and love him. Let him know that he is important all by himself and not just in the context of a litter.

At the end of seven weeks, a puppy is ready to begin learning simple commands. Again, this should be done gently, with encouragement and praise, not punishment or restraint. This is an excellent time for a puppy to go to a new owner, because he is now capable of forming a deep attachment to individuals.

Don't think that your puppies are going to socialize themselves. Studies and experience have proven differently. A puppy who is not given the love and attention so critical during infancy is likely to wind up as just another statistic in an animal shelter's files.

The Social- ization of a Puppy

237

FINDING A home where your pups can live in the manner to which they have become accustomed can sometimes be a problem. There is just no way that you will know, until after the fact, that a puppy has found a good place to live, but the sooner and more positively you attack the situation, the better your chances are of good placement. Don't wait until the puppies are four or five months old, thus putting yourself in the position of having to "get rid" of them. Start looking for prospective owners early in the game.

Begin with relatives and good friends whose life-styles and temperaments you are familiar with. As soon as the litter is born, call around and let people know about it. Invite some likely prospects over for dinner when the puppies are old enough to be played with and cuddled. The best advertisement for your litter is the litter itself, and many a puppy has found a fine home with people who swore they would never have a dog. If, however, none of these people is interested in a puppy for themselves, ask them to check among their friends.

Advertising, of course, is the next step. Ask your vet if you can post a sign in his office. Take a picture of the litter and include it on the notice. Your local supermarket, drugstore, and hardware store might also have a spot to display your poster. If money is no object, advertise in the local paper. Or, call your child's teacher at school and ask for permission to pass out a flyer to his classmates. The possibilities for spreading the word are endless.

If it's at all possible, don't give the puppies to a humane society. First of all, they have more animals than they can deal with already. Most shelters are constantly on the brink of financial disaster, and it's an expensive proposition for them to take care of your puppies while trying to find homes for them. Secondly, although it is true that a puppy is easier to place than a full-grown dog, it is nevertheless quite possible that the shelter will not be able to place your puppy and instead will put him to sleep.

Once your advertising campaign is under way, put together all of the information that a new owner will need: the date of birth, the diet you have used, the inoculations the puppy has received and when he's due for more, the name of your vet, and whether or not the puppy has been wormed. Also, note any mannerisms or quirks you have noticed about the puppy.

And, charge a nominal fee for your puppies. People tend to value more what they pay for, and asking $5 or $10 a puppy will not be enough to deter a sale and at the same time will help to defray your costs in advertising and feeding the litter. If you have children, they will enjoy the selling process and the bank account that accrues.

Sit down and chat with the prospective owners. Let them know about the puppy's sleeping and eating habits; they should be aware of the possibility of being rudely awakened at 3 A.M. Give them a small supply of food to hold them until they're able to stock up themselves. If the puppy has taken a particular liking to some toy or object, send it along to help ease the transition.

New owners may want the dog on a trial basis—to have a chance for a veterinary checkup and to see if the puppy blends in with their family and routine.

Is There a Prospective Owner in the House?

ADORATION OF THE MAGI
Mabuse
Circa 1503
Oil
National Gallery
London

This is fair and should be agreed to. After all, if they're not happy with the puppy, better have it returned to you than taken to a shelter. But set a time limit for the trial period—a week should be sufficient.

In general, prepare and educate the new owners as thoroughly as you can for the responsibility they are about to undertake; don't leave room for surprises they may not be able to cope with. And once you have found homes for all the puppies, have their mother spayed!

Blackie THE DOG FROM THE COAL MINES

NOBODY knows for sure where Blackie was born or how old she is. She just wandered unannounced into the life of a little girl, Heather Thompson, one cold November day in Prestonburg, Kentucky, a strip-mining town.

Heather and her mother live in Pound Ridge, New York, a small village about an hour outside of New York City. One weekend last fall, they made the trip to Prestonburg to visit their friend Kate, a legal-aid lawyer. While the three were out walking, Blackie bounded down the road and joined them. For Heather and Blackie it was love at first sight, and the little girl decided on the spot that Blackie was going back to New York

with her. But, since it wasn't clear whether or not Blackie already had a home, the dog stayed behind with Kate, who promised to find out if the dog was, in fact, a stray.

The trip back to New York was a nightmare—Heather cried all the way home and for several days after that. A month later, though, her dream came true. Kate unexpectedly arrived at the Thompsons' house, with Blackie in tow.

Blackie had no trouble at all adjusting to her new life-style—with one notable exception. She refuses to eat from a dish—only out of a garbage can—and then, only when nobody is around.

MADAME CHARPENTIER AND HER CHILDREN
Auguste Renoir
1878
Metropolitan Museum of Art
New York

7.
A
Guide to
Careers

THIS guide is designed for you—the ambitious mutt—the dog who's not satisfied with his lot in life and yens to have a purpose. There is no longer any reason for you to feel ungratified, for you not to get that promotion because you're a mutt, for you to suffer employment discrimination, or for you not to receive equal pay for equal work.

      If life is passing you by, if that old fire is dying out, if you're getting callouses on your legs lying around, if you don't feel truly appreciated, wake up! Raise your sights and your consciousness. Success is within your reach, but you've got to go after it.

A Guide to Careers

... Oh, naturally, I'd rather be on the legit. My dream is to play Flush in the Barretts. They could easily write her up as a white Pomeranian. Of course my [owner] isn't quite right for Elizabeth Barrett, but one can't please everybody. And between ourselves, you know, at times I do find her a bit of a drag. However, fidelity and service, those are my watchwords. But it's so difficult to get a footing. And then there's Shakespeare. It's a pity that he never wrote a really good part for a bitch. There was Launcelot Gobbo's dog but that's very small beer. I don't know how long we're staying here; Korda is thinking of us for his next historical epic, and we're just waiting to hear. . . . That last picture . . . all those retakes . . . Hollywood is so exhausting."

G. B. Stern, "The Ugly Dachshund"

WANTED: Star. Shapely, shaggy dog (preferably mongrel) with effervescent personality. Intelligence a must. Reply Box TC3284.

You don't have to be a purebred or a transvestite like Lassie ("she" was **Star** actually five male collies) to get into show biz. Benji starred in a movie and made about $10,000, and *Old Yeller* had a mutt in the title role as well. Broadway plays have had their famous mongrels too, the most recently successful of which is Sandy, whose featured role in *Annie* came after an unsuccessful career as a stray.

But these jobs are one in a million, and there's no surefire way of breaking into the business short of sleeping with the casting director's poodle. One area with more potential for the average dog (and one that out-of-work actors have also found profitable) is acting in commercials for television. Because the "average dog" isn't identifiable as a particular breed, and because advertising agencies try to appeal to the widest possible audience in pushing their products, this field is wide open to mutts. In fact, Doug Gruber of the All-Tame Animal Agency in New York City, a firm that specializes in providing animals for modeling and acting jobs, claims that mutts have always been in far greater demand than purebred dogs. (Mr. Gruber, who made his start as an agent by getting animals for the Captain Kangaroo television program, admits that he uses purebreds occasionally, but only if they pass for mutts.)

As for qualifications, it helps to be scruffy and not to be black (black dogs photograph badly); if you're shaggy and adaptable, this may be the job for you.

Appearance, however, is not the whole story, according to Mr. Gruber, who looks for a good steady temperament, a certain amount of intelligence, and a working knowledge of the canine ABC's (come, sit, and stay). Because an actor is required to work under confusing and often uncomfortable conditions, the mutt who can do his job without hesitating or becoming distracted is far superior to one who is high-strung and untrained, no matter how cute he is. So if you're really interested, enroll yourself in an obedience course; the experience you'll get working with other dogs around you will be invaluable. For dog-food commercials, it helps if you are capable of eating anything at any time and can look adoringly at people you've never laid eyes on before (especially Lorne Green), and so much the better if you can read, or at least tell the difference between some brand name and the letter X.

245

Besides good looks and intelligence, a pushy owner who will put together a portfolio of flattering photographs of you, complete with a list of credits (acting roles in high school, etc.), is useful. They should be sent to Doug Gruber at All-Tame, 37 West 57th Street, New York, N.Y. 10036. He'll ask you to come in for an interview or audition, or if you live far away from the Big Apple, he'll recommend an agent somewhat closer to home. California is a golden land of opportunity for the canine thespian (though most advertising agencies are still in the East), and if you live there you might try hanging around one of the big studios and striking a cute pose before the producer strikes you.

Acting in movies hasn't always been a picnic. There was a day when animals were often abused or even killed for the sake of art (well, money). Happily, there are some people who care a great deal about the humane treatment of animals in films, and there are now laws forbidding animal abuse for the purposes of so-called entertainment. The Hollywood branch of the American Humane Association has been particularly active in this area, and representatives are always on hand when animals are being filmed in order to supervise their conditions and treatment and deal appropriately with any violations. And there are many actresses and actors who care a great deal about the welfare of animals. Doris Day (who owns a mutt from the pound), Mary Tyler Moore, and Gretchen Wyler (who recently got the Screen Actors Guild to forbid any actor to work in a scene where an animal was being tortured or killed) are good people to get to know.

CROOK, THE AMAZING DOG
Larry Zingale
U.S.
1977
Oil on canvas
11″ × 14″
Joel and Kate Kopp
America Hurrah Antiques
N.Y.C.

All-Tame Agency

Jack

THE MUTT WHO PULLED MR. BREAKSTONE'S LEG

THE Clio Award is given annually to the best commercial of the year, and in 1977 the award went to the ad for Breakstone's Cottage Cheese (produced by the Gomes Loew agency), a series of three spots featuring the trials of Mr. Sam Breakstone in his search for the perfect cottage cheese. Sam was not assisted in his endeavor by a small black and white dog named Jack, who pulled his pant's leg and raced away with his straw hat, but the advertising agency behind the commercial certainly was, for Jack helped them make this one of the most entertaining ads on television.

Actually, Jack is not a mischievous dog at all but a cool professional who can work for ten or twelve hours in the studio without turning a hair. He is, according to his agent, Doug Gruber, a super-smart dog capable of performing nearly anything that is asked of him. Jack is handled by his owner, who lives on Long Island, and has recently starred in a CBS special, "The Prince of Central Park," in which he played the role of a stray who befriends two orphan children on their own in the park.

If the truth were known, Jack is not only mischievous; he's not even really a mutt, admits his agent, but a smooth-coated fox terrier who is lucky enough to be a mediocre specimen of the breed. By being too large, oddly formed, and interestingly spotted, Jack managed to evade the show ring and break into show business as a mutt. We have, however, heard a rumor that Jack, a clever dog, did have one naughty moment when he attempted to chew up his pedigree so that no one would ever know.

Sandy

by Bill Berloni

Of all the performers in *Annie,* which one is the *only* one to get taxi fare to and from the theatre, a private dressing room on a private floor, complete insurance coverage from the producers, and an ovation from the audience even for mistakes? Sandy, that's who. It's not because he is unusually smart, or handsome, or strong-minded. Sandy is lovable—the only word to describe his appeal.

It all started two summers ago at the Goodspeed Opera House in East Haddam, Connecticut. I was working there as an actor/technical assistant when plans were launched for a new show called *Annie.* The producer, Michael Price, was worried about the role of Sandy. Michael said there wasn't too much that the dog had to do. The most important thing was finding a dog that looked right for the part—of medium size, sandy color, and no distinguishable breed. They could not afford a professional dog trainer; if anyone on the staff knew anything about dog training, they'd like him to volunteer. No one qualified but me. I grew up on a farm near East Haddam, had always loved dogs, and I knew the area. I suggested checking the local pounds for a homeless dog.

The auditions began. After looking at about three hundred dogs, I found my way to the Connecticut Humane Society in Newington, where one dog in particular caught my eye. He was the only one who was not jumping up and down and making noise. I asked if I could see him, petted him a few times, and

he took to me. I decided this dog had the makings of a star.

I needed to have the dog approved before I adopted him, but both the producer and director were out of town, and the attendant said the dog was scheduled to be put to sleep the next morning. I had to make the decision myself. The following morning I arrived at the Humane Society at 8:00 A.M., and I saved this orphaned dog. The vet told me he was probably a mix between an airdale and an Irish wolfhound, and his age was approximately eighteen months. It turned out that everyone at Goodspeed, including the director and producer, shared my reaction. This was the Sandy we had been looking for.

My task was not only to train Sandy but, far more important, to restore his faith in humans. I began by taking him to the shop with me every day to get him acquainted with the crew. Then I brought him to rehearsals to get used to the actors and kept him in the wings with me after each performance so that he could hear the audience and their applause and the orchestra. When the audience had gone I'd train him onstage. I used hand signals and verbal commands for his tricks, and I rewarded him with affection and occasional dog biscuits. The next step was getting him accustomed to the girl who played Annie.

We were to open at Goodspeed for seven weeks. Two weeks before the opening Sandy was hit by a truck and his back legs were dislocated. But Sandy was clearly a trooper and recovered in time for opening

night to share in the good reviews. Even when the original Annie was replaced with Andrea McArdle, it turned out that we didn't need to worry. Andrea and Sandy got along well from the start—as though they had been destined to be a team.

Mike Nichols saw the show and liked it so much that he made plans to produce it on Broadway. He wanted to keep the same cast, including Sandy. In fact, he felt Sandy did well enough to merit a larger part. The writer added two more scenes for him.

Sandy started rehearsing his new scenes in the fall and was ready for the opening of *Annie* at the Kennedy Center in Washington without any problems. We were a great success and the cast was asked to do a special performance at the White House.

In Washington, it was decided that Sandy needed an understudy and I found Arf, who is a cross between a collie and a golden re-

triever, in the New York dog pound. He has learned Sandy's role.

Sandy and *Annie* were a smash hit in New York. One of the show's greatest assets, Sandy has made guest appearances on national and local television and has been featured in interviews with the *New York Times,* the *New York Post,* UPI, and AP. He has rubbed elbows with Bob Hope, Ethel Merman, Liv Ullmann, Tony Randall, Jean Stapleton, and a host of other important people.

As to Sandy's future? More appearances and even greater fame. He is to be the subject of a biography slated for publication by Simon & Schuster in May 1978. The authors are Allison Thomas, of *Benji,* and myself. After all this, if you ask Sandy what he thinks of his new career, he will probably pick up his head, tilt it, yawn, and fall back to sleep. Success has not spoiled Sandy.

EARL EYMAN'S DOG ACT
Earl Eyman
Oklahoma
1935
Wood
W., 14″
Joel and Kate Kopp,
America Hurrah Antiques
N.Y.C.

Mutts Star in Hollywood

A large number of film stars own dogs, which is not surprising, but a large number of them own mutts, which is. Dorothy Maguire has four of them, but many more stars are also mutt owners—Eddie Albert, whose puli-poodle mix is named Socrates; Lorne Greene owns Ginger, who is half cocker and half Manchester terrier; Cloris Leachman, whose Bobby is a schnauzer-basset cross; Hugh O'Brian, who owns a half collie-half Chihuahua named Panda; and Rudy Vallee, who found his greyhound-German shepherd mix, Mony, wandering up his driveway. Several stars have cockapoos—Fred Astaire, George Hamilton, Gene Kelly, and Mrs. Ronald Reagan—but a goodly number own just plain mutts. Desi Arnaz, Jr., owns a thorough mixture named Sophie; Sally Kellerman's spotted mutt is dubbed Roosevelt; Robert Reed has Mr. Stubbs, while Susan Strasberg tends Sunshine, a combination of collie and a good deal more than that. Doris Day and Janet Gaynor got their mutts, Biggest and Missy, from the pound, and Efrem Zimbalist, Jr., managed to find his two mutts—Hobo, a large white dog, and Clarence, a small white one—wandering lost along the freeway.

WANTED: Lifeguard. Muscular, athletic type in peak physical condition. Must tan well and have a way with women. Reply Box LR3330.

Lifeguard   Those of you who prefer warmer weather and summer sports have an equally varied group of useful activities available to you—if you can meet the physical requirements. If you enjoy swimming in cold water for long periods of time, have webbed front paws, a powerful chest, and a good hair coat, lifesaving may be your niche. A good sense of direction is also indicated. To learn more about this vocation, we suggest you contact the Newfoundland Club of America, which has set up a program in water work to insure the survival of the genetic traits of that breed. Students are being trained to carry life preservers, to tow boats along the shore, to retrieve objects from the lake bottom, to haul lines and simulated victims to shore, and to withstand the considerable stress of cold and exhaustion. If that sounds tough, it is, but if you have a life-saving instinct and guts, you might be interested in learning about it.

Even if they laugh and call you Skinny on the beach, if you are dedicated enough, you can still get your licks in as a lifeguard. A docile and well-mannered mutt named Ki dropped his gentle demeanor one day at the beach when he saw a woman he didn't know carrying her child down to the water. Apparently assuming that she was planning to throw the baby into the waves, Ki raced to the scene and barked and danced about her ankles until she set the child down on the sand. Convinced he had saved the child's life, Ki then relaxed and trotted back to his blanket, although he kept a close watch on the woman for the rest of the afternoon.

There are yet other options for dogs that can't resist the lure of the sea—being a fishing dog, for instance. A number of years ago, a Mr. Dunham, from Nantucket, employed a dog in fishing for porgies. His method of catching large schools of fish was to take his boat and dog out some distance from shore. When he sighted a school, he would maneuver his boat around and then throw a stone overboard to get the fish swimming toward shore. Enter the dog, who would jump in behind the school and, swimming in tandem with the boat, chase them onto the beach, Western-roundup style.

If fishing is unappealing, how about crewing? Not only can you claim some usefulness in rescue work, but you can be helpful in other ways. One mutt, Spooky, used to accompany his master on rafting trips down rivers in Alaska, barking at dangerous obstacles and generally keeping things afloat. And when the skipper got a large sailboat to live on, Spooky took over the guard dog activities and managed to prevent a few attempts at pirating.

Boating dogs whose swimming ability may not yet have reached the Spitz level (Mark, that is) may wish to relieve their owners' anxieties by wearing a life jacket. It comes in white or blue and is manufactured by Texas Water Crafters Co. (Wichita Falls, Texas).

WANTED: Sled dog. Must be in peak physical condition. Guts absolutely essential. Dogs with cold feet need not apply. Reply Box BR5262.

Sled Dog   If your interests run to sports—especially winter sports—you might find a good job pulling a sled. And, if you're suffering from the delusion that sled pullers are always huskies or Malamutes, stop. According to Purina, which sponsors a Dog Chow/Keystone Classic in Colorado each winter, some of the top sled dogs in the country are mutts. The work isn't easy, and you can't just go into it cold turkey. You've got to have a good thick hair coat, your muscles must be well conditioned and your bones strong, and you must work well with others and take direction without hesitating. A powerful sense of determination won't hurt, either.

Once you've worked yourself up through the minor leagues with a good team, you can try out for the big time. In February, just north of Denver, the Dog Chow/Keystone Classic offers a number of special events in which you may be able to shine. Seven-dog teams must pull sleds for 9.4 miles over ice-covered lakes and hills packed with two feet of snow. Five-dog teams work over 7.4 miles, and three-doggers cover 3.1 miles. And that's just the first day. The second day involves

the same run over the same course, and the results of the two-day heats events are then combined and the winning team chosen. If you're not much for long-distance running, you can apply for the weight-pulling contest, in which you must drag a 350-pound sled laden with concrete blocks for twenty feet in ninety seconds or less. Weights are added to the sled, and the load may get up to 500 pounds if more than one canine Arnold Schwarzenegger enters the contest.

If you enjoy the snow but are more interested in exploring than in pulling things, you might think about missing-persons investigation around ski resorts. In addition to a good thick hair coat and a tolerance for cold, you will also need the ability to walk on top of the snow (no, not water—that's something else altogether) and a very alert set of senses—hearing, smelling, and that sixth sense often attributed to the dearly remembered brandy-keg-carrying mountain dogs. No one knows exactly what it is—ESP or a powerful sense of direction—that enables a dog to find a person in the snow, even buried under several feet of it, but it has been demonstrated that a dog capable of finding a living being will pass by someone who has died. Perhaps it is some subtle sign of warmth or a tremor in the ground that leads the dog to the rescue; whatever it is, if you think this job sounds appealing, a highly sensitive nature is important.

Guide Dog

WANTED: Guide dog. Keen eyesight and good ears a must. Ability to relate well to humans and act under duress. Strong sense of responsibility essential. Reply Box PR4562.

Seeing-eye dogs are traditionally German shepherds, but the training associations have seen the light and are now using a few mixed breeds as guides for the sightless. To apply, you must be relatively large as well as intelligent, alert, and businesslike. Spayed females are preferred. Even if you meet these requirements, it's not easy to get into the program, since the Seeing Eye association usually breeds its own dogs, placing them as puppies in families (most of them members of local 4-H Clubs) where they are taught to adapt to household living, to community activities (traffic, shopping-center hustle and bustle, etc.), and to basic rules of obedience. So your chances are slim unless your mother belongs to a member of the Seeing Eye staff or to a 4-H Club member. For further information, write: Seeing Eye, Inc., Morristown, N.J. 07960.

A similar job—one that has been developed with mutts in mind—is that of acting as a guide for deaf people. The program of training dogs to guide people with hearing loss was begun by the Minnesota Society for the Prevention of Cruelty, but in 1976, in view of the enormous demand for such dogs, the American Humane Association took over the task of developing the program on an international basis. Because there are no particular standards in terms of breed or size, dogs from shelters are being trained for the job, many of them mutts, and many of them slated for euthanasia. The first part of the training program involves basic obedience, and then special sound-keying training takes place, at which point the students are evaluated. If they pass, they are then placed at no cost with a deaf person, in cooperation with the National Association for the Deaf. If the dog doesn't seem particularly suited to the "auditory awareness" part of the job, they are placed as companions with other types of handicapped people.

The work is not as difficult as guiding the blind. All dogs are equipped with sensitive hearing, but you must have a certain amount of training to respond to a specific sound—doorbell, telephone, alarm clock, siren, automobile motor, bicycle horn, crying children, intruders, etc.—and then to let your master know where it's coming from. As with seeing-eye dogs, the training is done by someone who simulates a handicapped person, and the basic method is the reward system, with a good deal of Pavlov thrown in. If you want to practice at home, have your owner sit in a chair with a supply of tidbits on hand; when the bell rings, run to him for a treat. Eventually, you will associate the sound of the bell with the goodie (which may be simply a pat or a word of praise every so often), and before long you'll run to him the minute you hear the bell. As you progress, you'll be able to respond slightly differently to each sound.

Although the program is still in its infancy, regional training centers that can handle a large number of dogs are being developed throughout the country. So if you're hanging around home or a shelter worrying about the future, write to the American Humane Association, 5351 S. Roslyn Street, Englewood, Colo. 80110.

An American Humane Association hearing dog with Joel Peters, a trainer, and Agnes McGrath, chief trainer

Hope

A Guide to Careers

WANTED: Therapist. Stable temperament
and a high tolerance for unstable
temperaments required. Reply Box
FU7654.

Being a therapist is certainly nothing new for dogs. We've been doing that **Therapist**
since long before Freud was a gleam in his father's eye—licking our owners when
they need to feel loved, letting them pet us when they need to give love, being right
there when they need a pal, offering them a shoulder to cry on, even letting them take
out their aggressions on us.

Finally, we've been recognized at the professional level. According to Boris
Levinson, the author of *Pets and Human Development,* the use of animals by
psychologists in their work has been quite successful. He questioned over 300
psychotherapists in New York State and found that of those who used pets, most
preferred dogs to other animals and felt that canines were especially valuable with
children. It seems that since we can be touched, unlike most therapists, alienated
people think we are more trustworthy.

Jobs are available in institutions, either with individuals or groups. Dogs who
like working with kids can apply to child-care centers, orphanages, schools for
exceptional and retarded children, and even reform schools, where homesickness,
insomnia, fear of the dark, fear of strangers, and alienation can be helped by a friendly
wag of the tail. Old people in nursing homes can be helped too, by providing comfort,
affection, exercise, amusement, and a chance to keep them from withdrawing
altogether once they are separated from their families and friends. For some people,
Dr. Levinson says, a pet may "very well be the only remaining link with reality,
tentative and tenuous at times perhaps, but a great improvement over the absence of
any such links."

Dogs can also act as therapists in prisons. Rags, a mongrel who showed up
one day in 1929 at Sing Sing prison, managed to keep the general morale high even
through the Great Depression. Like most of us, she was highly sensitive to moods and
would spend time with lonely convicts, distracting them and making them part of the
group. She once saved a man from suicide by threatening to bark every time he got
out of his bunk until he gave up on the idea.

So, mutts of the world, do your stuff. Get in there and stroke—help those
humans communicate, get it all together, stop playing games, find some space, shape
up their acts, and straighten out their heads. They sure need to.

WANTED: Stray. Reliable street dog
needed for declining neighborhood.
Experience desirable but not necessary.
Long workweek. References. Write Box
QB2879.

Stray Let me tell ya, bein' a stray ain't a bowl of cherries, but then what is. One thing though, all ya need to qualify is that ya ain't got no home.

I ain't been a stray all my life . . . nah . . . I lived in a pretty classy place when I was a kid . . . a big house, a lotta land, good chow, and a warm bed. And Miss Abernathy—she's the old doll what owned the place—well, she liked me lots. We used to go for walks together in the woods an' when she had folks over she'd always introduce me—real formal like—an' tell 'em what a great dog I was an' how smart I was 'cause I'd get the paper for her every mornin'. But then she died an' her nephew an' his family moved in. They had a coupla real fancy dogs an' they didn't think I fit in, so the next thing ya knows, I'm on my way out. I heard old ''Mr. Snooty'' talkin' ta the gardener an' tellin' him to take me to the animal shelter, so I split . . . an' fast.

I've had some mighty close calls since, too. The dog warden ain't no dummy, an' he's got some good catchin' equipment—he's got the biggest net ya ever seen—but he ain't catched me yet, an' he ain't goin' to. Ya know what happens to those poor suckers he picks up? I do! I've talked ta some of 'em that's got loose. They keep ya around the shelter for four or five days an' then if nobody comes to pick ya up or adopt ya, it's all over . . . they snuff ya right out . . . plant ya! Well, I ain't ready for that yet!

This month I've been livin' over in a vacant house on Delancey Street. It's not a bad place ta hang yer hat except for the rats. The darn rats . . . ya let one of 'em in an' before ya knows it they take over the whole neighborhood. It's not that I don't like rats, ya understand . . . some of my best friends is rats . . . but, jeez, ya don't wanna live with 'em!

But, gettin' back to my present digs, they're better than the porch I was livin' under last month. It leaked like crazy, an' everytime it rained, I got soaked. One week it rained all week, an' I'll betcha I didn't get more than two hours' sleep a night. But this place is OK. Somebody left a couch there, so sleepin' is pretty good. An' there's a butcher shop on the corner, so the grits have been pretty tasty, too. The butcher's a regular Joe an' gives me a lotta scraps an' stuff. It's either feast or famine in this racket . . . there's been times when I ain't had nothin' to eat fer days . . . an' that's a real drag.

There's some nice people around here, too. There's this one guy who sits on the bench out front all day . . . sometimes he even sleeps there. Well, he talks to me and pets me a lot. He's always got a bottle of somethin' in a brown paper bag, and every once in a while he'll give me some in a cup. Man, that stuff really burns goin' down, but it sure makes ya feel good!

There's a coupla kids around here that I could live without though . . . always pokin' at ya and pullin' yer tail . . . an' one of 'em throwed a rock at me an' laid me up fer a coupla days . . . I still got a little limp. There's one real nice kid, though. He wants to take me home in the worst way, but his old lady says no dice . . . she's got enough problems feedin' the mouths she's got around there already. He comes an' sees me a lot, though, an' once we even went over ta the park an' played ball.

I dunno where my next stop is. You can't usually count on stayin' in any one place fer more than a coupla months at a clip. Somethin' always happens . . . the warden gets a line on ya . . . or somebody gets ticked off 'cause they catch ya in their garbage can. Some guy even shot at me once. Do ya believe that? I'm gonna hate to leave this place in a way . . . but what the heck . . . nothin' lasts forever.

261

Kristen Sternberg

Paul Duckworth

WANTED: Pet. Attractive human desires
pet willing to love, honor, and obey.
Lifelong commitment for right dog. Good
fringes. Write Box XE2376.

Pet The trick to being a successful pet is to line yourself up with the right owner. Don't make the mistake of being overly impressed with things that, in the long run, don't really matter too much—a big house, an expensive car, live-in help. What is important is the personality of the person you adopt. Look for someone with a stable temperament and a kind and gentle nature. Most important, look for someone who's willing to put up with your own particular idiosyncracies.

Although it sometimes helps—and there are some people who will insist on it—it's not necessarily true that you have to be good-looking. To the contrary, in some cases the more doggy you look, the more appealing people are going to think you are. If, however, you're not beautiful enough to be considered chic or ugly enough to be considered cute, you're going to have to learn to use what you have to your best advantage. For example, if you have big brown eyes, express yourself with them. If you see somebody you think you'd like to live with, let a big tear roll out of one eye and down your nose. This routine is irresistible to humans and guaranteed to work. Always, but always, wag your tail, and when you think you've almost got them hooked, lick their hand. That clinches the deal every time.

Once having wangled your way into someone's heart and house, and assuming you've been somewhat discerning about your choice of owner, there's really very little that's going to be expected of you except for some basic social amenities. First off, whatever you do, don't use the inside of the house as a toilet facility. People don't react well to that, and it starts things off on the wrong foot. Secondly, assume that when your owner says no, he means it. You won't get too many *no's* if you use good common sense. For example, don't chew up the furniture or shoes or wearing apparel of any sort. That will get you in trouble no matter whom you belong to. On the other hand, there are some marginal areas—sleeping on the couch, snoozing on beds, sitting on laps, eating at the table. All these things are worth trying once to see what kind of reaction you get. Some people are quite willing to put up with them and some aren't. If they are, so much the better; if they're not, it isn't the end of the world.

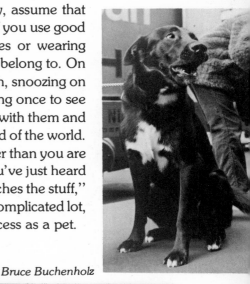

Lastly, it is imperative always to let people think they are smarter than you are and never to put them in a compromising position. For instance, if you've just heard your owner tell her maiden aunt that the man of the house "never touches the stuff," don't drag an empty beer can out from under the bed. Humans are a complicated lot, and that's a fact of life you're going to have to accept to achieve success as a pet.

Bruce Buchenholz

A mutt in Hornbeak, Texas, has found an unusual career in the local post office, licking postage stamps. His owner is a mail carrier, and Rex apparently helps him out occasionally by licking the stamps off a hundred roll, for which he receives a candy bar as salary.

8.
Moving
On

MY DOG AND ME
J.R. Adkins
U.S.
1965
Oil on board
24″ × 28″
Elias Getz

*I*t is a queer difference between this kind of thing [having a dog] and getting married, that married people love each other most at first . . . and it fades by use and custom, but with dogs you love them most at last. They are meaningless to begin with, and if I bought a bitch puppy tomorrow she would not replace Brownie for a long time to come. . . . The whole and single unnaturalness of the position is that dogs and men have incompatible longevities. Everything else is perfectly natural, and I would not have it altered in any respect. I regret nothing about Brownie, except the bitter difference of age.

T. H. White, *author of* The Once and Future King, *writing in a letter to a friend on the death of his beloved dog*

The Aging Mutt

FEW PEOPLE are prepared for the inevitable and relatively rapid onset of aging in their pets. Dogs live longer than many animals—often as long as fifteen or more years—but for most of us, who think of our animals as members of the family, fifteen years is a very short time.

It is not too soon to prepare yourself for the geriatric condition of your own mutt, even though he still seems young at heart, not so much to anticipate his death but to help prolong his life by careful and conscientious care. Aging dogs have certain requirements in terms of food, exercise, and medical attention, and every mutt owner should be ready to fulfill these requirements as soon as the signs of old age start showing up in a gray muzzle or a less-than-spry attitude toward an energetic game of fetch.

Food Every dog requires a completely balanced diet, regardless of age, but the older dog doesn't need nearly as many calories as a normal mature dog. You can simply reduce the amount by about 20 percent (in calories) or you can switch to a food lower in fat and protein. The aging dog will quickly turn extra calories into fat, and an overweight dog is far more prone to disorders than a thin one. Obesity can put an excessive strain on the heart, make the dog more prone to accidents, and increase his chances of developing respiratory disorders. Changes in diet may be necessary also if the dog's teeth are beginning to fall out. Instead of feeding him dry food, switch over gradually to a soft-moist food or moisten the dry food with warm water before serving. If the dog is having trouble digesting his food, a vitamin-mineral supplement may be recommended by your veterinarian, who may also prescribe a special diet if he thinks the dog's condition demands it because of cardiac or kidney disease. If a change is indicated, don't expect the dog to adapt to it overnight. Change the diet gradually, keeping up your regular feeding times and other routines. Dogs don't take well to changes in time, place, or even serving bowls. (Thus, that old expression "You can't teach an old dog new tricks.") Also, make doubly sure that water is available at all times; because old dogs often need extra water to keep their kidneys in working order, the water bowl may need filling more often. Report any sudden weight gain or loss to your vet immediately.

Exercise As in humans, a certain amount of exercise is far healthier even in old age than none at all. Make sure your mutt gets a chance to stretch his legs on a daily basis, even if he has difficulty getting up and down. Many arthritic dogs will show fewer signs of pain as they begin to move around, whereas if they are allowed to sleep all day, it will become increasingly difficult for them to move at all. Nevertheless, excessive exercise can increase the dog's problems, so be sensible about walking—not running—your aging friend. The vet may be able to prescribe drugs to control pain, but you can help prevent trouble by seeing that the dog is kept in a warm, dry environment. Nail trimming regularly may help him in moving around if he appears to have difficulty keeping his footing.

Grooming   Old dogs need to be groomed and bathed as frequently as younger ones, but special care should be taken to give the animal an occasional close examination. Teeth are usually the first place where trouble can be found, since tartar accumulation (which is likely if the dog is getting a soft diet) can cause periodontal disease if the tartar is not removed periodically. You can help prevent this by giving your dog a daily brushing with a toothbrush. Use one of the special canine toothpastes or mix one part of baking soda to one part of salt and scrub with a soft brush. Do not use your own toothpaste, since it may cause digestive upset. If the dog's teeth seem to become yellow and crusty in spite of your efforts, and his breath begins to smell bad, take him to the vet for tooth scaling before infection sets in.

Check the dog's ears, as you have been doing all along, for signs of ear mites and other ailments, but also keep alert to signs of deafness. There may be nothing that you or the vet can do about this, but it's good to know if your dog does have hearing problems, since you might otherwise be upset with him for not answering your calls. Blindness is also a condition that occasionally accompanies old age; although there may be no cure or treatment, you can make the dog's life a good deal easier by confining him to a familiar room and postponing your plans for rearranging the furniture.

Some dogs lose hair as they age, although they rarely become bald or wrinkled the way humans do; regular brushing is important. Graying is common in dogs, as are conditions such as skin cancer and other types of tumors. Unusual bumps or swellings should be checked out by the veterinarian as soon as you notice them.

Medical Attention   The vet will be more important now, since the aging dog will be more likely to suffer ailments than a younger one. His metabolic rate will have slowed down by perhaps as much as 20 percent, while his heart and kidneys will be reduced in their capacity to function. Take your dog to the vet for a checkup twice a year, and more often if anything seems amiss.

Daily Routines   As your dog ages, it will become more and more apparent that even the simplest matters become insurmountable obstacles. Take the stairs, for instance. It may become impossible for an old dog to make his way up to the bedroom to sleep as he has done all his life. If you can't carry him, don't force him to try. If he won't be consoled by his nice, familiar bed downstairs, you can attempt to get him upstairs by using a shopping-cart arrangement, or you can be terribly patient and let him take the extra minutes to make the trip on his own.

It is best not to become anxious and overindulgent with the dog, since he will be sensitive to any changes—not only in his daily routines of feeding, exercise, sleeping, and so on, but also to your moods. Even a dog that has occasional fits of grumpiness because of arthritic pain or impatience at his inability to run around needs your affection—and perhaps more than he once did. But don't let that extra affection take the form of food treats or all-day naps on the pillow. Avoid leaving him for long periods of time, since he will not easily adjust to life in a kennel or the hospital. If he is at the vet's for more than a day, ask if you can visit him as often as possible. In other words, try to keep his life as routine as you can, given the circumstances. Trying to teach him new tricks at this age will only cause him stress.

Inscription on a monument
at Newstead Abbey

Near this spot
Are deposited the remains of one
Who possessed beauty without vanity,
Strength without insolence,
Courage without ferocity,
And all the virtues of man without his vices.

This praise, which would be unmeaning flattery
If inscribed over human ashes,
Is but a just tribute to the memory of
Boatswain, a dog.

Lord Byron

The dog, in our everyday lives, not only is a mirror of our
own nature, but can also be the embodiment of
humanity's highest qualities —acceptance, forgiveness,
loyalty, truthfulness and openness, devotion and
unquestioning, unconditional love. This is why many
prefer the company of animals, especially dogs, to
people. Man had no hand in endowing the dog with such
traits, although domestication and socialization help
ensure his dog will display such behavior toward him.
Anyone seeing a family of wolves, the dog's "pure"
cousin uncontaminated by human interference, will see
the same traits. The lesson of nature is simple: Although
the dog is man's best friend, could it be that man will
someday be man's best friend also? Perhaps being a
dog's best friend is a start in the right direction.

Michael Fox, Between Animal and Man

269

THE LOSS of a pet provokes diverse emotions: grief, outrage, relief, sorrow, guilt, depression. Methods of handling the situation are also diverse. Some people remain inconsolable, while others distract themselves by immediately getting another pet. Some will bring home a dog exactly like the first, even giving it the same name; some will find an entirely different animal. Some will spend lavish amounts of money on burials and cemetery plots, while others will let the veterinarian dispose of the animal with no ceremony at all. Many parents will consider the dog's death a valuable experience for their children, and others will go to extreme lengths to spare a child's feelings.

Some types of dogs will live longer than others, but the average canine life-span is twelve to fourteen years, which doesn't take into account the possibility of accident, illness, or disappearance. A dog with a built-in problem—arthritis, heart defect, etc.—may decline slowly, preparing the owner for his death well ahead of time, but some dogs die quite suddenly without obvious warning.

In many cases, as with a terminally ill dog, one that has suffered injuries from which it is unlikely to recover, or one that is suffering great pain caused by progressive ailments, the owner must make the decision of when the dog's life should end. This is extremely difficult, and the point of no return is not easy for a layman to judge. Your veterinarian is in a position to help at this time; he has a detachment from the animal and a medical background that enables him to better assess your dog's degree of suffering and the likelihood of recovery. Euthanasia, or putting to sleep, is quick and painless, usually involving an injection of an overdose of anesthesia. It allows an animal to die with dignity, an alternative to living out a life of suffering.

When death occurs, there is no reason to think that one will feel any differently with a four-legged being than with a two-legged one. Death is upsetting, often devastating, and those left behind need a time to grieve. If there are children in the house, it is likely that the loss of a pet will be their first encounter with death, and it would be helpful to encourage them to sort out what they are feeling. Talk about what the pet meant: what pleasure he brought to your lives, what problems he created. A funeral or a memorial service might also be helpful. It is important to not simply dispose of the corpse, but to ritualize the event for the child so that he can have his grieving time.

The practical consideration of how to dispose of the corpse must also be dealt with. If you have no particular preferences, your veterinarian can handle this for you. In some areas, the local humane shelter will also do it. In both cases, there is generally a fee involved. Your alternatives are cremation and burial. Some veterinarians have crematoriums and some do not; the same applies to animal shelters. If your veterinarian does not have his own, he will have access to one or know where the nearest facility is. Again, there is a fee involved for this service.

Pet cemeteries—more than 420 of them in the country—are available for people who live in the city or in areas that have restrictions about burying animals and feel strongly about burying their pets. These can, however, be very expensive, and

Breaking Up Is Hard To Do

costs will depend on the size of the animal and the options (casket, perpetual maintenance, special care, headstone, etc.) that you select.

Burial is an easy matter if you live in the country or in a suburb that has no restrictions (your town or county clerk can give you that information). Care must be taken that the animal be buried deep enough so that it cannot be dug up by other animals. Home burial is a lovely way for a child to say good-bye to his pet.

A common reaction to the loss of a pet is to take a new one into our lives. This is a wonderful means to soften the blow of the death of your old one, but a new dog can never *replace* your dog any more than one person can replace another. We are all, humans and pets alike, a unique combination of psychological and physiological characteristics, and that combination cannot be duplicated. We don't think in terms of replacing husbands or wives or mothers or fathers or children. New people may come into our lives filling the same roles, but they don't replace the first and a pet is no different.

Welcome your new pet with an open mind. Given a chance to be himself, your new pal will pay you back with the qualities that make owning a pet so gratifying—unqualified loyalty, understanding, love, trust, and forgiveness. Where else can you get so much for so little?

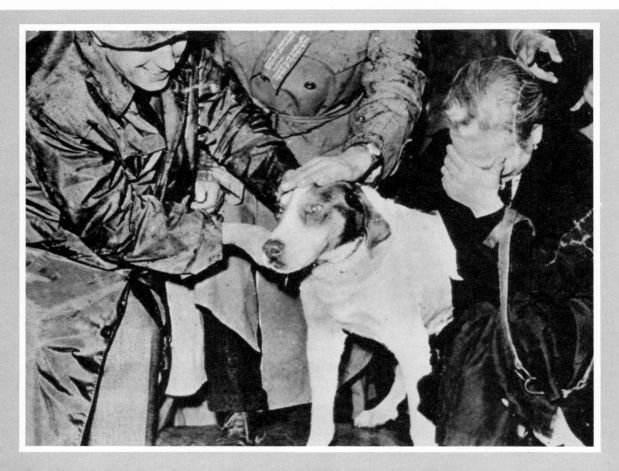

The Faithfulness of Fido

A MOVING story of the love and loyalty shown by a dog comes from Italy. The dog, who has the appropriate name of *Fido,* was only a puppy when he was saved from a flooded river at Luco di Mugello, near Florence, by Carlo Soriani in 1942. After his rescue *Fido* followed his master everywhere, and when Carlo got on to the bus every day to go to work in a factory at nearby Borgo San Lorenzo, *Fido* waited at the bus stop all day until his master returned in the evening. One sad day in 1944 Carlo did not come home, he had been killed in an air raid on the factory. But *Fido* still believes that his master will return to him, and for the thirteen years since Carlo's death he has waited for him each day at the bus stop. Nowadays he waits there all night too, and sleeps under the parked bus. On November 10 the people of Luco di Mugello paid tribute to *Fido* during a ceremony at which Signor Giuseppe Graziani, the Mayor of Borgo San Lorenzo, attached a gold medal for loyalty to *Fido's* collar.

News story, November 23, 1957

*H*ow old is your dog?
A 1-year-old dog = a 15-year-old person
A 2-year-old dog = a 24-year-old person
A 3-year-old dog = a 28-year-old person
A 4-year-old dog = a 32-year-old person.
Beyond four years, every dog year is equal to five human years.

*T*he old mutt was a bag of skin and bones. He didn't see very well. He didn't hear very well. He didn't eat very well. He'd been very close to us for many years, but as he gradually withdrew he acquired a kind of independence that was somehow primeval and majestic.

He didn't object to us, not even to our handling. He was just passive and detached. He paced constantly in a steady long-distance trot from one end of the house to the other. Day after day. When his pacing brought him to a corner he just stood there until someone backed him out. It wasn't so much that he couldn't see. He just couldn't go backward; his drive was onward. And when spoken to it wasn't so much that he couldn't hear; he was listening to a different voice. It was calling him.

A monotonous, rhythmical, pulsating dance of death, an inexorably beating pavane to the call of the unknown. He had left the pack and was off into the forest, mile after mile after mile.

He had a life of love and a death of great majesty.

Yet there are secret moments when I still hear his voice.

Bruce Buchenholz

WINGED DOG
Steven Polaha
Reading, Pennsylvania
20th century
Wood, polychromed
L., 21½"
Geoffrey Holder

GREEN-EYED DOG
Steven Polaha
Reading, Pennsylvania
20th century
Wood, polychromed
L., 17¾"
Geoffrey Holder

*The oldest dog on record died at age 26. In human terms,
this would be about 142 years old.*

Of dogs living past the age of 17, 59.6 percent are mutts.

Moving On

Treve

by Muriel Booss

Treve was part husky, part fox terrier, and part cannonball. We all felt that if only his precise ancestry were known and could be reproduced, the result would be a strain unequaled for strength, nerve, and vitality.

Walking Treve was an exercise in awareness, it being necessary to sight other dogs at least two blocks ahead in order to quickly change route and avoid a horrendous confrontation. No one was ever able to teach Treve not to display his lavish affection for visitors by hurling himself at them in an ecstasy of warmth—whether old friends, strangers, or intruders.

Treve once challenged an ice-cream truck, causing its driver to veer into a ditch and causing himself to sustain multiple injuries (from which he fortunately recovered). At age fourteen, after two more encounters, Treve would still bark at the sound of the ice-cream vendor's bell, ready to do battle once again.

But what we remember most about Treve are his large and gentle brown eyes, beautiful and affectionate, reflecting the wonderful nature that enslaved us all.

275

Heaven goes by favour. If it went by merit, you would stay
out and your dog would go in.

Mark Twain

Scrapbook

Kenya
Part German shepherd. A mutt with motherly instincts. Takes care of a young Pekingese purebred at the Gray family home, Brooklyn, New York.

Tara
Resembles pedigree Lab; descended from generations of mutts. Once a stray, taken to pound after biting a mailman. Found huddled and trembling in a small cage by Robert Sklar of Brooklyn. Personality now transformed.

Mitzie
Blend of Pomeranian and Eskimo. From Carteret, New Jersey. Has her own place at Lenore Case's kitchen table.

Pirate Jenny
From Atlanta, Georgia. Acquired from an Irish woman on the Mississippi River levee overlooking Audubon Park, New Orleans. Member of the McGuire family.

Heidi
Mainly dachshund. Plays with Satan, the cat. Resides with the Lisicki family in New Jersey.

Raffles
Part Great Dane. Owners: Barbara Hahn and son, John, New Jersey.

Cleopatra, a.k.a. Cleo, and Toots
Shepherd, collie, Lab, spitz blend. Pampered by Ghisoni and Pauley families, Bronx, New York. Responds to "Cleo, you want to be pretty?" Enjoys baths, hairstyling, and manicures.

Brandy
Part collie, part shepherd. Found at seven weeks at a Bide-A-Wee animal shelter by the Hecht family. Now comfortably ensconced on Long Island.

Butch
From Bide-A-Wee in New York City. Weimaraner and Lab mix. Adopted by the Pierce family in Mount Vernon.

Gretchen Penelope
Mixture of German shepherd and Sheltie. Likes to pose. Member of the Sansone family of Floral Park, Long Island.

Deenie
A Bronx, New York, mutt who crosses the street alone and hides bones in the bathroom of the Ortner home.

Max
Dalmatian and terrier mix. Taste for alcohol. Home: Lois Berkowitz, Bronx, New York.

Puzzle
Named for puzzle design on back. Picked out by Ruth Krebs and family at a Westchester County, New York, pound.

Muff
A golden retriever cross. Friend of Timber. Also lives in Jefferson with Barbara Palmer.

Blondie
Color of Lab; size, shape, disposition of beagle. Discovered by Ada Kerman in New York City's Riverside Park in 1974 in poor physical condition.

Dog from ASPCA, New York. Waiting to be adopted.

Daisy
Westchester County, New York. Tumbled out of third-floor window as a young dog. She was saved from being put to sleep and adopted by the vet who mended her.

A Mistake
Half Lab, half St. Bernard. Sold for five dollars by former Bridgehampton owner to delighted family of four.

Maggie
Apprehended at four months wandering on the Long Island Expressway. Now stays close to home with John and Jane Fater on Long Island.

Vanilla
Owned by James DiMaggio, New York.

Bingo
A boat-loving mutt from City Island, New York.

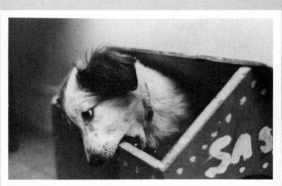

Sasha
Owned by the Charles West family, New York.

Goliath
Part collie, part shepherd. Treated as a son by the Dobrins of Mount Kisco, New York.

Scootch
Helps Parnell Havenor run an auction gallery in Bedford, New York.

A litter of mutts by Calico of The Weston/Mathewson house.

Barger
Cockapoo. Pershing family in Yardley, Pennsylvania.

Calico and Cassady
Lives with Ed Weston and Maureen Mathewson, both of New Rochelle New York. Calico was offered to Ed as a "fare" exchange for a cab ride six years ago. Daughter Cassady is Maureen's dog.

Timber
Explores the woods around Jefferson, New York, home of Barbara Palmer.

Waiting to be adopted.

Index

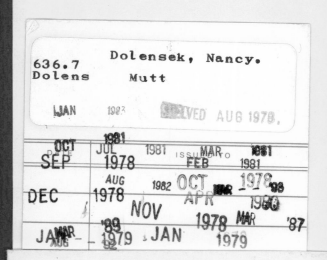